'the Great Little College'

'the Great Little College'

Corpuscles on
CORPUS CHRISTI COLLEGE
Oxford, 1945–2017

STEPHEN HICKEY

Third Millennium
Publishing

First published in Great Britain in 2017 by
Third Millennium Publishing, an imprint of
PROFILE BOOKS LTD
3 Holford Yard
Bevin Way
London WC1X 9HD
www.profilebooks.com

1 3 5 7 9 10 8 6 4 2

Typeset in Sabon by MacGuru Ltd
Printed and bound in Great Britain by
Clays, Bungay, Suffolk

ISBN 978 1 78125 822 4
eISBN 978 1 90899 071 6

FSC
www.fsc.org
MIX
Paper from
responsible sources
FSC® C018072

CONTENTS

PREFACE AND ACKNOWLEDGEMENTS

This account is based on the work of many Corpuscles, who generously contributed recollections of their time at the College and devoted time and effort to supporting the research, writing and publication process.

I am particularly grateful to former President Richard Carwardine, who launched the initiative and encouraged Corpuscles to contribute their recollections; to many others at Corpus – including Skye Montgomery, Julian Reid, Brendan Shepherd, Sara Watson and others – who provided vital support and advice; and to Clare Grist Taylor and colleagues at Profile Books for their support throughout the process.

I want to thank Thomas Charles-Edwards and Julian Reid for early sight of their forthcoming history of the College; and Andrew Purkis and Sir Brian Harrison, who provided invaluable encouragement, suggestions and advice. It was a pleasure to be discussing history with them again, almost 50 years after first doing so at Corpus!

Above all I want to record huge thanks to all those who took the trouble to write in with new and original recollections of their time at Corpus. Although not uncritical, their affection for Corpus, and its impact on their lives, shone through – confirming how formative student years are and how much it matters to capture and reflect on them. The wealth of the material meant that only a fraction can be included in this volume, but the full accounts have been lodged in the College Archive, where they will form an invaluable record and resource for future historians.

A word on conventions. Students' matriculation dates are shown with each citation. Where names have changed, they are shown at the first citation as 'John Smith (né Jones)' but thereafter as 'John Smith'.

Extracts from the new contributors (listed in the Appendix) have no endnote reference: other sources, including quotations from published sources, are referenced. I have made only minor stylistic corrections or amendments.

Deciding what to include or omit proved enormously difficult. Any errors or misjudgements are mine alone.

Stephen Hickey
(né Hickinbotham, 1967)
London, October 2016

FOREWORD

One of the privileges of being President of the Corpus undergraduate community is the perspective it affords me. I have the opportunity to engage with all aspects of College life. Every day I am in dialogue with other students and with staff on a host of issues, going from meeting the College President one minute to a brand-new fresher the next. This makes it all the more fascinating to discover through this volume the experiences of previous generations of Corpus students – in some ways so different but in others so similar to me and my fellow students today.

In a planning meeting for Freshers' Week, I was speaking with a recent graduate of Corpus, now a Fellow here. He told me about his first Gaudy, where he met a student from the 1970s, who told him in turn about *their* first Gaudy, where they had met yet another former Corpus student, this time from the 1930s. All remarked upon how, despite the years, they felt the College's atmosphere had remained, in its essence, recognizable and unchanged. They all shared the same sense of community, of belonging to Corpus, despite being members of our college in very different eras. What a wonderful way to think of my generation as but the most recent link in a line stretching back 500 years to the foundation of the College.

But I believe Corpus also stands for the future, for new thinking and enthusiasm to tackle new challenges. Our alumni have included innovators, philosophers, politicians, authors and activists. As a student body we continue to question, argue and challenge, not least through active involvement in a range of university campaigns. We're known as a progressive college, looking beyond the Oxford bubble, and willing to change and develop. As this book reminds us, Corpus only accepted its first female students in the 1970s. But when I was elected, I was proud to be the fifth female JCR President in a row – an unrivalled record among Oxford colleges.

I applied to Corpus because – amid my fear that Oxford would be austere and intimidating – it stood out for its small stature, friendly student body and above all its welcoming atmosphere (as well as the eccentrically beautiful gardens!). Being such a small community makes it intense at times, but helps nurture a real sense of pride in each other, and remarkable mutual support amongst my fellow students. I have made some of my closest friends in my two years here. And Corpus's culture is not confined to the student body: it includes the dons and the staff – the scouts, porters and all the others who make Corpus run, year in, year out. Speaking personally, it's safe to say that my time as JCR President would have been far more difficult, were it not for their wonderful help and advice.

It is clear from these reminiscences that students across the generations have felt there is something very special about Corpus. But they also give me a real sense of hope for the future. Corpus has shown itself to be caring, progressive, creative and more in these past 500 years: how exciting to wonder what we might see in the next 500!

Jemimah Taylor (2014)
JCR President
October 2016

INTRODUCTION

Student days, for those lucky enough to go to university, are a formative experience. They are a time of exploration and development – intellectually, socially, physically – and leave a lifelong imprint, personally and professionally. Not everyone enjoys it – for some, it can be a confusing and unhappy time. But the impact, for better or worse, is almost always considerable.

Understanding students' experiences is therefore important. This volume looks at one particular example: students at Corpus Christi College, Oxford since 1945. Oxford is unlike most other universities, particularly in its system of colleges: self-governing communities combining academic, residential and social functions which elsewhere are normally separate. And Corpus is unusual, even within Oxford. As the smallest college, it has a character and ethos which distinguish it from its neighbours. Known as 'small and friendly', but with a formidable academic reputation, it became known in the 1950s as 'the Great Little College' – a slogan derived from a contemporary cigarette advertisement.

Using their own words, this book aims to give a student's-eye view of Corpus – how they arrived, what life there was like, and what it meant to them later. The main source has been contributions received from over 150 former students and others – listed in the Appendix – following an invitation to submit their recollections. The book also draws from published accounts in the books, College journals and other sources listed in the Bibliography. These include *Corpuscles*,[1] an invaluable set of recollections edited by Sir Brian Harrison in 1994 – though unlike that earlier volume, which was arranged chronologically, the present book is structured around themes.

Inevitably, despite the impressive number of contributors, they are a self-selected sample who may or may not be 'representative' – if such a category exists – of their peers. And as one would expect of independently minded Corpuscles, their views and attitudes sometimes differed. The aim is to let their voices speak for themselves, reflecting the diversity of those passing through the College.

Did Corpus change fundamentally in this period? It more than doubled in size, from 140 students in 1950 to 343 in 2015. Its appearance altered. The gravel Quad was paved, and soot removed from the sandstone walls. The gardens luxuriated with unusual plantings and admixtures. Jeans replaced flannels, and gowns became limited to special occasions. Vacations ceased to be quiet interludes as conferences grew and tourists flocked in ever-growing numbers. Heating and plumbing were transformed. Computers and mobile phones – nonexistent for much of the period – became ubiquitous. The number and proportion of postgraduate and international students increased. 'Climbing in' and 'sconcing' disappeared, and even language changed – 'undergraduates' or 'junior members' became 'students'. Most striking – after some 460 years as an all-male community – was the arrival of women. Less visible was the gradual tightening of the financial climate: by 2015 previously generous student grants had largely been replaced by loans.

But did these developments change the basic experience of young students? Had the excitement and challenges of living and developing in Corpus altered fundamentally? Would those from one generation recognize the lives led by another?

We get a flavour from some who described their day. **Brian Sedgemore** (1958) highlighted the shared social dimension: 'in the afternoons it was down to the playing fields of England whilst in the evenings it was philosophical discussions over dinner in Hall and thence to The Bear Inn'. For **Eliza Pakenham** (1986) there was 'so much talk about love, agony, and music, sex. We were herd animals, eager always to be in the buzz of company. One night the President threw up his window to complain about our giddy catcalls outside his pink residence. I can remember no punishment, only suddenly feeling young and foolish.' **Rachel Richards** (1993) recalled the meals and conversations: 'I spot my group of friends in the crowded lunchtime Hall. Not a particularly difficult task as the daily seating patterns vary little – as if drawn along invisible Corpus songlines, tribes are called to the same sacred spots every day ... I delight in the conversations – often endless ones – more varied, didactic, erudite or just plain silly than I've ever encountered before.'

All shared a sense of living collectively, as part of a close, intimate community. As we will see, not everyone was happy as a 'herd animal'. But for all its members the Corpus community was the starting point, and often the defining element, of their Oxford experience and identity.

But first, why were they at Corpus at all?

Arrival: Corpus entrance, 1958. *Courtesy of Douglas Long (1958)*

1

'A PIN IN A LIST': COMING TO CORPUS

A procedure strongly resembling scrutiny of the Racing Times *with a hovering pin.*

Bill Gunn

None of my parents or grandparents were university-educated so I followed the guidance of my teachers.

Simon Preston

Corpus is not amongst the most famous Oxford colleges. Balliol, Magdalen, Christ Church and others are far better known. Why then did students choose or end up at Corpus? Was it random chance? Or was it something special about the place and its reputation?

Access

The application process for Oxford changed significantly in these decades. Until 1962 there were different examinations for commoners and scholars. Heads of house personally managed the admission process, particularly for commoners. As Corpus Fellow **Christopher Taylor** recalled:

At that period the role of Tutor for Admissions was performed by the

President; President Hardie took it seriously, taking the view (with which I now have more sympathy than I did then) that the diversity of the College community benefited from the presence of a number of undergraduates whose primary interests were other than academic ('good commoners' as they were called). Since Hardie was himself a keen golfer, it was no accident that many of the good commoners were extremely good golfers. The best way to summarize their performance as philosophy students is to say that, however low their handicaps were, their competence in the subject was usually lower.

Philip Hamilton-Grierson (1953) thought Hardie favoured 'southern Scots with a Classics or legal background who also played golf', and **Brian Sedgemore** (1958) recalled that Hardie 'allowed the Senior Tutors to appoint the scholars while he himself "scoured the country" seeking out brilliant golfers, rugby and hockey players and other sportsmen of distinction to come up as commoners'.

Corpus in the post-war years welcomed applications from the families of alumni: 'We have seldom found it very difficult to find places for sons of Corpus men; their merits have commonly matched our sentiments.'[1] **Peter Waterfield** (1946) served in the wartime navy: 'It was my uncle-guardian who "had a few words" with Sir Richard Livingstone [President, 1933–50] which resulted, in the casually privileged manner of those times, in my being called for interview on my next home leave. It was scarcely more than a friendly chat, as I remember, but it led to my acceptance to the College when the Navy released me.' **Antony Walker** (1947) followed the family tradition:

My father, R. P. S. Walker, was taught by Jesuits at Stonyhurst. So I was taught by Jesuits at Stonyhurst. My father read Greats at Corpus. Ever the conformist, I read Greats at Corpus. My father was taught by Richard Livingstone. I had the good fortune to have Sir Richard Livingstone as President when I arrived at Corpus. I had first met Sir Richard in 1946 when my father took me on a visit to the College. My abiding memory is of walking with them in Christ Church Meadow and listening to them revelling in Max Beerbohm's *Zuleika Dobson*.

Oliver Clauson (1948) 'always suspected that I only got to Corpus by family connection. Richard Livingstone was tutor to both my father and my Uncle Miles and was President when my brother Bryan was up.' According to **Christopher Watson** (1957):

> I was predestined to apply to go to Corpus. My father had read Greats there, and was an enthusiastic Corpuscle, and his good friend Michael Zvegintsov, who had taken me under his scientific wing, always assured me that my election to a scholarship was the result of his advocacy of my cause with President Hardie: as he explained to me, 'in this world, it is not what you know but who you know that counts'!

Nicholas Roskill (1952) – whose grandfather and cousin were also Corpuscles – found 'a strong family presence in the College which was a relatively close community. I recall that many undergraduates, especially Old Rugbeians among them, had fathers who had been at the College.' **David Mark Jackson** (1959) encountered another Corpus dynasty: 'My fellow medical undergraduate was Nick Cornes, elder brother of Colin, John and Andrew who followed him to the College. They were sons of Jerry Cornes, who won a silver medal running the mile at the 1932 Olympic Games – a fine Corpus gene pool, indeed.'

By the 1960s this world was changing. Ironically, it was a University committee chaired by Hardie which led to the 1962 merger of the entrance exams, ending the old division between would-be scholars and commoners and placing greater emphasis on academic criteria. Admissions tutors increasingly displaced heads of house in managing the process, though at Corpus it was only in 1986 that the role was created, with Jennifer Hornsby – the first woman Fellow – in the post. By this time, non-academic considerations were taboo. **Christopher Taylor** recalled one interview:

> it was clear after a very few minutes that the candidate was so hopeless that further academic discussion was pointless. Purely to spin out time to a decent length I said something on the lines of 'What made you think of applying to Corpus?', adding

(unfortunately) 'Was your father here?' A few days later, after the rejection letter had gone out, the President received a furious letter from the boy's father, complaining that his son had been turned down because he did not have a family connection with the College, and adding that he had not served his country in the war to be treated like this. After that I made a point of never mentioning the candidate's family background or possible prior connection with the College.

Some family links continued. **Ben Whitby** (1986) recalled: 'When my school (Queen's Park High, a former city grammar turned comprehensive in Chester) told me I should consider Oxbridge, I always thought of applying to Corpus because my father, Peter Whitby (1953–7), had gone there. I had no expectation of preferential treatment; there just seemed no reason to go anywhere else.' **Nick Hassall** (1989) applied to Corpus mainly for the places it offered in his subject, but also because his grandfather, father and uncle 'had all been at Corpus and I liked the idea of attempting to continue a nascent family tradition'. But such connections no longer gave any assurance of a place. Fellows **Jennifer Hornsby** and **Stephen Harrison** were clear that although they welcomed applications from Old Members' children, they would give them no 'special favours'.[2]

Indeed, the problem for applicants was increasingly the difficulty of getting into Oxford at all. In the 1960s the men's colleges generally had around two applicants for each place. By the late 1980s, across the University, the number had risen to three; but by 2014 it was nearly six, with even higher numbers in some subjects. Academic distinction had become essential: in 2013 98 per cent of Oxford undergraduates had three As or better at A level.

Against this background, the University and colleges had to wrestle with the challenge of balancing academic achievement with social equity – usually measured by the proportion of students from state schools. In the post-war years this had risen, reaching 57 per cent in 1965–6; but in the 1970s the position was reversed, following the disappearance of most grammar and direct grant schools – some into the independent sector but most becoming comprehensives. By the late 1980s well over half of Oxford students were from independent schools. There were complex factors behind the statistics, but concern to equalize opportunities led to further changes to the entrance system in 1987, following another University review chaired by a Corpus President, Kenneth Dover. But the problems persisted. In 1996 the entrance exam was abolished but by the 2010s sole reliance on predicted A levels and interviews was also proving inadequate, and exams and tests were reappearing.[3] Corpus too wrestled with the problem of access. Of the 1950 entry, 17 were from independent schools, 19 from grammar or direct grant schools, and 4 from elsewhere (including a couple from abroad). Although the grammar schools could do well for their pupils, they were based on a narrow selection at age 11, in effect excluding most from any chance of university (though some 11+ failures did reach Corpus through the independent school route). The ratios remained broadly constant until the 1970s. By 1980, however, well over half (35) were from independent schools, with 19 from state schools and 7 from elsewhere.

The College took several initiatives to address the challenge. One was to admit mature students, particularly from Ruskin College. **Anthony Gould** (1973), a former farm worker, described himself and his friend John Bamford (1973), a miner, as part of 'Andrew Glyn's "experiment" to get more mature relatively ordinary working people into Oxford':

> People have often asked me why as a trade union activist aged 30 I consented to be further educated at CCC. It has to be remembered that these were turbulent social and economic times in the mid-1970s and that I was keen to be able to analyse it all. Further to this, Andrew Glyn presented a comprehensive critique of government policy and it therefore was in part the reputation of the PPE tutors. But in addition I had been working for some years in industry and I felt that a period of study before I settled down to work again would not be a bad idea although of course it was a great luxury to be enabled to do this.

Kenneth Pearson (1974) also came via Ruskin:

> It was only after completing a number of years working in the
> printing industry wherein I had become active in the trades union
> movement, and travelling extensively around Canada during the
> 1960s, that the urge to add to my understanding of academic
> things was rekindled. I was accepted as a Corpus undergraduate
> after obtaining a Special Diploma in Social Studies at City of West-
> minster College London, and then spending two years at Ruskin
> College. Although in Oxford, Ruskin wasn't part of the University,
> but it had a close relationship with it. While at Ruskin, I had a
> positive attitude towards the University which was not shared by
> all Ruskin students. It was my time there that made me believe that
> to attempt to gain admittance to the University would be worth-
> while. Nothing ventured, nothing gained.

Martin Deahl (1975) felt he had been saved from a life of menial
jobs by exceptional schoolteachers and positive discrimination by
Corpus:

> I failed the 11+ and attended a local secondary modern school in
> Hounslow, West London. Although the school became a compre-
> hensive during my time this had little impact on standards. Mine
> was the last year in which pupils could leave at 15 ... most did.
> There was no sixth form as such, merely a handful of pupils
> resitting CSEs (there were no O levels). Discipline was harsh and
> the relationship with teachers was largely one of fear. No pupil
> had ever attended a university.

He was unusually fortunate that two teachers took him under
their wing, helped him learn to study – and one asked whether he
had considered applying to Oxbridge to study medicine. 'Neither of
these had crossed my mind – my school was (literally) at the end of
the runway at Heathrow and every boy's ambition was to be a pilot!
Nevertheless, the teacher's suggestion took root and I came to heed
his advice.' Aged 15, he wrote to Corpus: 'At the time this felt like an

entirely natural thing to do and it certainly hadn't occurred to me I was being precocious. The President invited me to meet him, clearly intrigued with my background, thanked me for my interest, encouraged me to apply one or two years hence.'

Getting in, however, remained difficult. After rejecting him on the basis of his expected A level results, Corpus invited him to try the entrance exam. 'I replied to the College that there must have been an administrative error and that taking the exam was out of the question: neither I nor my teachers knew anything about it, I had not prepared and felt it would be a pointless waste of time. I received a further letter from the College urging me to have a go ... "if only for exam practice".' He took it and was summoned for interview:

> I was told I couldn't possibly be considered for a place to read Medicine because of the high calibre of the applicants (many post-A level with up to six grade As in the bag). I was asked what my best subject was. 'Physics', I replied. That triggered an evening with the then physics tutor Dr Hill and one of the most important pieces of advice ever given to me. 'How's your maths?' he said. 'Not very good', I replied. 'Well, I wouldn't be doing you any favours if I offered you a place to read Physics. In my experience the best undergraduate physicists have done little school physics but have studied and have talent for pure mathematics, the best graduate students studied maths as undergraduates, and the best professional physicists are mostly mathematicians by background.' I was heartbroken (with hindsight I should have been very grateful).
>
> I left the College feeling dejected and wondering what to do next. My other UCCA [Universities Central Council on Admissions] choices, London teaching hospitals, had rejected me outright (such was the currency of a Grade 1 CSE and the myth put about by the school that this was accepted as an O level equivalent). I even applied to join the Royal Navy (my father had been a seafarer and I thought if I couldn't study medicine this would at least please him). Imagine then, my utter surprise and joy, when, in the last post before Christmas came a letter and the offer of a

place to read Biochemistry – conditional on achieving two Grade Es at A level! Quite the most wonderful Christmas present ever!

I subsequently learned that I had been rejected for a conditional A level offer as my interviewers knew I was never going to get the necessary A Grades at A level (they were right and I got an A and two Bs). They had made their minds up early on that they wanted to give me a place but realized the entrance exam was the only way I could achieve this.

I consider myself the beneficiary of the greatest act of positive discrimination I have ever encountered ...

In terms of upward mobility I think it is worth reflecting that with today's national curriculum, my two visionary teachers could never have done what they did and I would have spent my working life pushing trolleys around Heathrow airport (the fate of many in my year).

Despite such initiatives, the question of access was becoming more acute. The appointment of **Jennifer Hornsby** as the first Tutor for Admissions was said to symbolize 'the College's concern to increase its proportion of women members. As the list of Freshers reveals, we continue to open our doors to able young people from every type of school and all parts of the world.'[4] She thought it 'debatable' whether enough was being done to attract state school candidates:

But it is certain that we are trying. And luckily, with the Students' Union's (OUSU's) help, we can direct our efforts. OUSU's Target Schools Scheme is focused on those state-maintained schools which have no tradition of sending their pupils to Oxford. OUSU communicates with these schools, and offers them help and advice in finding out more about Oxford and admission to Oxford. Corpus contributes financially to the administration of the scheme, and we have a programme in College for Corpus students to participate in it. This means that each year volunteers go back to their old schools and/or other schools in their Local Education Authority area during the vacations. We think that there is no better way to attract state school pupils than to have them hear former state school pupils speak about their experience of Oxford.[5]

Initiatives included undergraduate 'Welcoming Committees', letters to schools and a revamp of the College Prospectus after a comparison revealed 'to our surprise that Pembroke and St Hugh's are demi-paradises'.[6] **Paul Elbourne** (1989) found the application process fair:

> My family is solidly working class, and has been for as far back as I know about. I was the first person in my extended family to go to university at all, let alone to Oxford. My family, although uniformly supportive, were and are entirely uncomprehending about almost everything that I have done since age 18 – everything in the educational and professional spheres, at least. But in my interviews at Corpus I felt no hint of any kind of social evaluation. There were, needless to say, no secret handshakes, allusions to the rules of polo, or attempts to get me to eat a kumquat with a knife and fork. The interviews were challenging but concentrated entirely on academic matters.

Nevertheless, access remained a continuing source of controversy and concern. **Peter Lampl** (1966), campaigner and founder of the Sutton Trust, spoke to the JCR in 1999 about 'plans to make Oxford more accessible to sixth-formers from less prosperous backgrounds'. According to the JCR President, this 'tied in well with the success of the University Access Scheme, which is designed to develop accessibility to Oxford for deprived inner-city state schools with gifted youngsters. A number of Corpus undergraduates are heavily involved in this scheme, whose latest enterprise is a shadowing scheme, which entailed sixth-formers visiting Oxford for a short time and "shadowing" the lifestyle of individual students.'[7] In 2016 **Brendan Shepherd**, Corpus 'Outreach Officer' – a role dating from the 2000s – highlighted the College's work with schools 'in our regional link areas of Derbyshire and Greater Manchester', observing that 'Corpus is attractive because of its welcoming atmosphere, its lack of pretension, its strong sense of community and its attention to pastoral care'. These initiatives had some effect. By 2016 half the Corpus new entrants were from state schools – an improvement, but still low in comparison with the population as a whole. President **Richard Carwardine** accepted that, despite its efforts, 'Oxford has continued to struggle to attract undergraduate applicants from ethnic minorities and disadvantaged areas' and the issue remained far from resolved.[8]

Why Corpus?

Against this changing background, why did would-be students choose Corpus? Some, as we have seen, followed family tradition. For others, including **Roger Horsfield** (1952), the choice was virtually random: 'In 1952 Dover Grammar School had no mechanism for encouraging or helping pupils into applying and gaining places in Oxford or Cambridge, or as far as I know, anywhere else. My mother, however, was a determined lady and holding the application form she stabbed at it with a pin in order to select a college.' It landed on Brasenose, who eventually offered a place. However, he decided to try for a scholarship: 'Again my mother had recourse to the pin and, avoiding all the colleges which had closed scholarships for one category or another such as "being the sons of ex-clergymen of India", I found myself putting Corpus Christi as the leading college on my list.'

For **Peter Dawson** (1955) the decision also came down to chance: 'At school I was late for a meeting at which pupils could choose for which Oxford or Cambridge colleges they would like to enter. Because I was late I had no choice and could only apply to enter Corpus Christi College at Oxford. It's the most impressive advantage of being late of which I know!' As we have seen, **Martin Deahl** (1975) had no university background:

> Why Oxford? Well, when I was four my mum took me to watch the Boat Race. Standing on Putney Bridge the crowd were all terribly partisan. The rosette seller only had dark blue rosettes left and so my affinity for Oxford was cast. Why Corpus? The College had appeared on *Blue Peter* – tortoise racing, and I thought anyone doing such a thing couldn't be that stuffy or bad!'

Others initially tried elsewhere. **George Richardson** (1947) 'applied for Balliol for a scholarship. But Balliol wouldn't give me a scholarship and passed my papers on to Corpus and Corpus did give me one. I needed the scholarship for the money largely. After the war it was a fairly generous provision.' For **Rhod Thomas** (1961), 'it was by chance that I went up to Corpus'. Although accepted by Christ Church he decided to stay on 'to try for a scholarship and to captain the Radley XV. Christ Church said I would have to compete for a place the following year. As a result, I decided to see if another college might be interested. This led to an interview at Corpus and a place for 1961. The small size of the College appealed to me and that was the main reason I chose Corpus.' **Bill Gunn** (1965) described coming to Corpus as 'more to do with serendipity than any concerted plan':

I had applied, and failed to win, a history scholarship to Christ Church, the choice of college being based simply on imperious advice from a master at my prep school (recently graduated from Christ Church) that any other destination was simply beneath consideration. This perception remained unchallenged when some years later the time came to discuss the options with my housemaster, a procedure strongly resembling scrutiny of the *Racing Times* with a hovering pin. Our relationship, already unsettled, plumbed new depths when unwittingly I placed his own college, Magdalen, at the bottom of my admissions wish-list, having earlier blithely vouchsafed, when discussing careers, that 'if all else fails, I could always fall back on teaching'.

He was rejected by Christ Church but offered a place at Corpus for the following year. 'I could try again for the Christ Church scholarship, or take the bird in the hand. Unhesitatingly, I accepted the place that CCC had offered. It was an easy decision to make and, as things transpired, one of the happiest of my life.'

Paul Vaight (1963) also applied elsewhere:

Being a working-class lad and knowing nothing of universities or admissions processes, I had been selected by my headmaster to

apply to St Catherine's. The interviews are now a blur – para-
doxically the only detail I do remember is a question that I could
not answer about what happens to paramagnetic materials when
you cool them down. However, Robert [Gasser, Corpus Fellow in
Chemistry] was evidently also present at my interviews and hence
my place. Being the first generation in my family to go to university, I still feel very grateful to Corpus for by chance giving me an
opportunity which I really enjoyed; in no way did I regard university as a right or entitlement.

The South African postgraduate **Peter Colenbrander** (1974) aimed
for Peterhouse, Cambridge, but had to submit a combined Oxbridge
application:

I am not even sure Corpus was on my list. When the letter from
Corpus arrived offering me a place, I recall contacting the head of the
English department at Natal University, a former Rhodes Scholar,
for guidance. He had copies of the latest Norrington Table results
[comparing colleges' exam performance], and encouraged me to
accept the offer, which I then did. So, to the question of why I chose
Corpus, the short answer is – it chose me (for better or for worse).

Teachers' advice was often decisive. **Geoff Goodall** (1950), whose
family had no university tradition, recalled:

Schools in the 1940s did not have such posts as 'careers and universities' advisers, but I did have the good fortune to be guided by the
headmaster himself, Mr E. H. Goddard. Ned Goddard had studied
Greats at Corpus during the First World War and had remained
a friend and admirer of Sir Richard Livingstone. As I approached
my Higher School certificate exams, the head urged me to aim for
university, to aim for Oxford, and more specifically, to aim for his
beloved Corpus.

There were many similar examples. **David Jory** (1959) 'applied to
Corpus in 1957 because my sixth-form teacher advised me to'. **Peter**

Stafford (1960) 'applied to Corpus as my headmaster at Birkenhead school, Kenneth Robinson, was a Corpuscle and he seemed happy for me to apply!' According to **Simon Squires** (1962), 'one of my schoolmasters, Brian Ponsford, who had been up at Corpus himself, told me I should try the College for which he felt great affection – and which was known to be strong in the field of Classics. I do not think I can claim to have done any serious research otherwise, but my affection in due course equalled his own.'

The example of a former pupil from the school could be important. **Andrew Thornhill** (1962) initially followed his school's tradition of applying to St John's, Cambridge. However, 'with the appalling priggishness of a 17-year-old I announced that I did not want the offered place as it did not seem the interviews were scholarly enough'. He applied instead to Corpus, following Gerald Toomer, who had been an undergraduate and was now a Fellow. **Jim Waterhouse** (1963)

> chose Corpus Christi because a pupil from my school had started there the previous year and was full of praise for the College. Those were the days when one did not check potential universities or colleges, and the Web did not exist; moreover, nobody else from my family or relatives had been to university and the school's advice on careers was rudimentary, to say the least. The result of all this was that my choice was slightly arbitrary – though I have never regretted it in any way.

Some schools had a tradition of nominating pupils for Corpus. Porth County, in the Rhondda, sent 24 students in the 1960s and 1970s.[9] **Ken Reynolds** (1966), at Humphry Davy Grammar School in Penzance, found it sent a boy a year to Corpus: 'knowing nothing about universities or the new admissions system then known as UCCA, but having a vague idea that a degree might be a reasonable option after A levels, I was more than happy to be nominated by my teachers as the Corpus candidate for my year'. **Simon Preston** (1982), from another non-university family, 'chose Corpus because it was one of a few colleges that had recently admitted Bedford Grammar School boys (the school was single sex then) and I liked its description in the prospectus'. **Sean O'Grady** (1981) also followed his school's tradition:

> Why Corpus? Because my school, a state grammar, told me to apply there. I'd never heard of it before. I followed in a long line of more or less distinguished scholars, some with a cap 'S'. About ten years before I arrived our ambitious (for his pupils) economics master, George Stanlake, spent some time in Oxford on a scheme I can't remember much about. From that 'outreach', to borrow the modern word, emerged a steady stream of PPE wannabes from Wyggeston Grammar in Leicester. Some were outstanding, none were duff, so the College, I guess, took to trusting the school as a trustworthy source of talent. So I was standing on the shoulders of others. (After the grammar school was abolished the flow stopped. No further comment required, I think.)

Sometimes, as **Bill Morris** (1964) recalled, the teacher's recommendation seemed arbitrary:

> We were gathered before Bob Stanier, the headmaster, at Magdalen College School to start the Oxbridge entry process. Mr Stanier ran his finger down the list in the folder in front of him and declared solemnly, 'You, Morris, will go to Corpus.' Mr Stanier then was my college matchmaker and I am eternally grateful to him. Then I was just a nervous *ingénu*; I had little idea what to expect from this betrothal to my new college. Although Oxford born and bred, the University seemed a world away from the working-class end of the Cowley Road where I had grown up as the son of a carpenter and small building contractor. The geography of Oxford was so divided between Town and Gown that I didn't even know where Corpus was.

Theodore Saunders (1975) discovered his 'choice' in a school notice, which simply read,

> The following boys are applying for places at the following colleges

… Saunders to apply for the organ scholarship at Corpus Christi College, Oxford.' I did pluck up the courage to ask Mr Batten why I was applying for Corpus, and he said, 'We think that you will benefit from being in a small college, and you don't want to waste your time having to train small boys how to sing – you should aim for a first.'

David Wilton (1981) described his choice as

rather random and based entirely on the recommendation of my headteacher, himself a Corpuscle. It was of course a great recommendation but it was based on second-hand and out-of-date information with little if any discerning analysis on my part. I do remember being rather surprised when I got there to discover that Corpus was known for its high academic standards! The admission process itself seemed highly competitive and rather Darwinian and the College was rather more rigorous in its selection of me than vice versa.

Jacquie Kelly (1984) visited Oxford and Cambridge – and was attracted by both *Brideshead Revisited* and *Chariots of Fire*. But a teacher was again the decisive influence:

I first heard about Val Cunningham [Corpus Fellow in English Literature] from my A level English teacher, Miss Downes, who had been at St Hugh's in the 1970s and was taught by him for one of her Finals papers. Although she painted a rather weird and scary portrait of him, there was something intriguing about the impression he had made on her. So intriguing in fact that two years later I found myself sitting opposite him and Susan Hitch talking about why I wanted to study English at Corpus. I wish I could remember what we talked about at that interview, because I'm still not sure I have a solid answer to that question, apart from it felt like a good thing to do.

According to **Rachel Collier** (née **Tarnoy**, 1987):

My reasons for choosing Corpus were pretty flimsy. After six years at a girls' boarding school I was reluctant to spend another four in an all-female environment, so I was not going to follow the safe route recommended by my teachers, who were directing me towards Somerville or St Hilda's. I had mentioned Corpus in passing to our idolized new history teacher, a recent graduate of Somerville: 'Corpus is lovely,' she gushed. That was enough for me – not much more than a pin in a list, really.

Although serendipity, school tradition and advice from teachers were important, some made more deliberate choices. Since **Bill Morton** (1949) 'came from a very small Suffolk grammar school with few Oxford links, I chose the smallest college with a good academic reputation'. For **Martin Williams** (1959) its reputation in Classics was decisive:

> My ambition had been to go to Oxford University for as long as I can remember, but to begin with I had no knowledge of or link with any particular college. Corpus was the only college I applied to in the first round of exams in December 1958, as that had the best reputation for my subject, Classics, and I was lucky enough to be accepted.

Robert Lee (1964) was attracted by its 'enviable reputation as a small but friendly College with an excellent academic reputation', and **Jonathan Dancy** (1965) by its reputation for Classics and its size: 'when I was told that it was a very small College, that was enough for me'. Applications were supposed to list the order of college preference:

> But I knew that I wanted to go to Corpus, so I took a risk and filled in only the first three slots, thus: CCC1, CCC2, CCC3. I never knew whether this ploy stood me in good stead, but I got an Exhibition, which was certainly all I deserved, and I was in. But I still remember Robin Nisbet quizzing me in my interview about the details of Horace's life and my attempt to explain to him that these things were irrelevant to the appreciation of his poems. Oh dear.

Penelope Curtis (1979) visited under a Scottish scheme for schools with no Oxford tradition: 'I had never been to Oxford before and chose Corpus simply because it was the smallest college.' In later years more information became available, through prospectuses and the Web. Nicola Feather (née Jarman, 1981) based her choice on the Alternative Prospectus, written by students: 'What lured me was the whimsical, humorous tone of Corpus's entry, and what had clinched it was mention of a college tortoise and summer tortoise race. It all betokened a relaxed absence of academic earnestness, a suggestion that Corpuscles didn't need to strive for excellence. Having striven for years, albeit covertly, I knew that Corpus was where I wanted to end up.' Danielle Sanderson (née Myers, 1982) 'chose Corpus because of its reputation as a "small, friendly" college, and I wasn't disappointed'. Martin Campbell (1992) chose Corpus 'on the grounds of it being small and friendly and not sporty'. For Debbie Welch (1994) there were practical attractions:

> The overwhelming one was full accommodation for all years; I liked the 'small college' feel too – those put it on the shortlist. However, there was one slightly more random one. My school was convinced (totally wrongly) that the way to get in at Oxford was to make sure the admissions tutor knew you. So they took anyone interested up to the three-day open days and told us to write to three colleges and ask to be shown round. Being fairly obedient, and also believing them, I did so. Two of the colleges wrote back nicely giving details of their open days. However, Corpus's Admissions Tutor (Peter Hore, I think) agreed to meet me and show me round. I remember ending up chatting to the gardener for some time with him. But that's probably the reason why Corpus went from my shortlist to number 1!

Accommodation was also important for Catherine Hasler (1997):

> I had chosen Corpus Christi, I am sorry to say, for the most prosaic reason that it provided its students with accommodation for all three years of their studies. What else had I to go on? I had

found Queen's, where I attended an open day, cold and forbidding. Perhaps it hadn't helped to see it in the holidays, when the buildings looked empty and closed. I liked the glamour of Christ Church and Magdalen but was far from having the audacity to apply there. So I made a practical decision, with one eye on achievability, selecting what I hoped would be a motherly college that would be the closest thing to a home from home. Corpus Christi, as we all know, is the smallest undergraduate college, just 220 students when I attended in the late 1990s. The size didn't worry me. Two hundred and twenty people sounded like more than enough to build a wild social life.

Ewen McMillan (1999), a maths postgraduate, was unsure how to choose a college:

In the end I decided to list the attributes that I thought I would like: the college should qualify as medieval (probably my romantic side!), it should be small (allow for a more convivial and relaxed social environment – my hunch was right there!) and it should have a respectable ratio of mathematicians in the SCR. Corpus was the intersection of these requirements and on that basis I made my choice.

For **Ana Aliverti** (2007), another postgraduate, academic considerations were decisive: 'I chose Corpus Christi as my first choice. The main reason was because of the academic strengths of the College in my area – Prof. Lucia Zedner was the Law Fellow and with whom I wanted to study.'

Interviews

After the decision to apply, what stuck in the minds of most students were the interviews. Although **Peter Waterfield** (1946), interviewed during wartime leave, found it 'scarcely more than a friendly chat', **Oliver Clauson** (1948) described his as 'daunting'. **Derek Costain** (1948) 'revelled' in his:

The interviewing Panel was chaired skilfully by, I think, Frank Lepper the Dean. The ultimate interview was with the President, Sir Richard Livingstone, who was sitting by the fire in his room at the corner of the Quadrangle. He came across as a kind, impressive figure. He asked me for my views on the educational system in Britain. Anyway a few days later Corpus wrote accepting me for 1948 to 1951. I was ecstatic. The three days at Oxford had made a vivid impression on me. It was evident that Corpus was eminent and well respected in the academic world. I felt privileged and proud (and somewhat surprised) to be accepted by this small, compact, high-powered College.

Andrew Thornhill (1962) found his interview with the famously shy President Hardie particularly memorable:

No one had prepared me for the President. I think it was the first time I had even heard that deliberate, cautious Edinburgh accent. He said very little and looked at one quizzically as if in intense study (which he probably was). At the end of the interview, he asked: 'Have you got any questions, Mr Thornhill?' Thinking that it would seem good to ask an intelligent question, I did my best. Perhaps the question had some depth because the reaction was complete silence. The silence persisted for two or so minutes. It was broken by my asking a second question in the possible belief that there had been some deficiency in the first one. Again, a silence. After my third question – this was at least six minutes after the end of the first – Hardie slowly and deliberately replied: 'I think the answer to your first question, Mr Thornhill, might be as follows ...' It took another five minutes before the interview ended.

James Shelby Tucker (1955) thought his interview with Hardie took 'treble the time needed for a normally spoken exchange'. After initial interviews with the 'terrifying trio' of Robin Nisbet, Frank Lepper and Gerald Toomer, **Paul Quarrie** (1962) faced 'an even more disconcerting experience, the interview with the President, Frank Hardie, a man of few words and profound silences in front of whom a burbler like me felt a complete ass'. **Ken Reynolds** (1966), however, had prepared by reading reports by previous applicants from his school:

> My predecessors described President Hardie as an undoubtedly outstanding scholar but a shy, diffident person, who seemed ill at ease in interviews and struggled to maintain a flow of questions. I therefore felt completely relaxed when I later found myself in his large, sombre Presidential office, and I didn't mind at all the soothing silences punctuated by our somewhat awkward, stilted conversation. In fact, I thought, this Oxford interview business is a piece of cake! Then, all of a sudden, as I was talking about my regular visits to Paris and Lyons and the joys of immersion in contemporary spoken French, a disembodied voice asked 'Which English city would you say shares certain characteristics with Lyons?'
>
> Being totally unaware that there was anyone else in the room, I was quite jolted from my complacency. Looking around, I could just make out a figure lying flat out on the settee! That person, the owner of the voice that threw me, turned out to be Michael Brock, who was I believe Vice-President of Corpus at the time. I couldn't answer his question and he explained that he had Manchester in mind – a major city, fairly distant from the capital, with what had once been an important silk industry. My rambling incoherence for the rest of the interview couldn't have mattered too much, as I was offered a place which I gratefully accepted.

Christopher Bridgett (1961) had an ex-Corpuscle teacher who 'suggested that at the Corpus interview with President Hardie I should make sure to ask about the stuffed fish over the fireplace. It did the trick.' It also helped **Bill Morris** (1964):

> I soon found myself in President Hardie's study, grinding out some 15 to 20 minutes of awkward silences until we somehow happened upon the discovery that we shared an interest in fishing. The rest of the interview was spent discussing the specimens mounted in the glass cases along his study wall. After brief interviews with Drs

Gasser and Hill, the College's judgement was complete. An offer letter arrived in the morning post the following day. I was thrilled and my parents, both of whom left school at the age of 14, were thrilled for me, God bless them.

Fishing also proved a useful topic for **Charles Overton** (1970):

The offer of a place at the College followed a nerve-wracking interview with Dr Gasser (Chemistry) during which I sat on a leather sofa which seemed vastly bigger than I was, and a much more comfortable interview with President Hardie. I think success was achieved largely thanks to the stuffed pike hanging on the wall of President Hardie's study, which enabled me to steer the conversation onto the subject of angling!

Interviews with later Presidents were generally less memorable, though as **Richard Fitzalan Howard** (1972) discovered, fishing could still feature: 'I was interviewed by Derek Hall, the rather dry President. Most of the conversation I remember was about fishing (much to the surprise, I discovered afterwards, of Mel Johnson, another candidate, who was listening outside the door).' **Nicola Feather** (1981) recalled the walk from the station – 'a long one, particularly when you are hauling a large case of clothes; what do you wear to interview?' – and the 'worryingly steep staircases' outside President Dover's office:

Apart from Sir Ken's kindly patience (was that reserved for the fourth-term state school candidates that he was championing at the time?), the only detail of that interview that I remember was that the proffered chair had a long, narrow seat. On coming up, we successful ones discussed the choice the candidate faced: did one perch on the front, looking intense and earnest; or slump towards the back, feet off the floor like a five-year-old?

The two days of interviews found her

alternately in a state of dry-mouthed mumbling (especially with the interview I mucked up at Trinity) and total high. I have a vivid memory of talking to current students over dinner in Hall on the first evening, and realizing that, for the first time in my nascent adult life, I could say aloud any word I cared to choose from my natural vocabulary without getting mocked or misunderstood. And, even sweeter, my thoughts were appreciated and returned in kind.

Disconcerting interviews stuck long in the mind. **Peter Buxton** (1978) was interviewed for medicine:

'Did you read about the fish they caught last week that had green blood?' My initial relief that the interview hadn't started with a cry of 'Catch' and a rugby ball hurled at my head was short-lived. Was this a trick question? Was it something I should have revised? I was fairly sure we hadn't covered this at school. Even a boy who only paid scant attention in biology would have remembered something about green blood. Honesty seemed to be the best response, that and an earnest desire to see if the limits of my knowledge would be tested in some other direction.

'Oh well, never mind. Where do you think they found it?' No escape. But instead a ten-minute discussion on why an animal's blood would be green. Starting from first principles, and with gentle guiding prods, the answer came to me. I had discovered something, not been taught it or read about it in a book but actually worked it out. It was a revelation.

Ben Whitby (1986) was interviewed by the History Fellows:

I was very nervous. They asked questions about my essays, my coursework and why I wanted to study history. I remember Brian Harrison being able to summarize my arguments back to me very quickly. There was a discussion about the slate mining in North Wales and industrial action there in the early 20th century, where they tried to argue me out of my viewpoint but I held on. I had no idea how I had performed beyond having managed to keep going.

Rachel Collier (1987) found it was 'the uncomfortable parts' of her interviews she recalled:

> not being able to look John Bramble in the eye ('I'm not over there, you know,' he reminded me as my gaze was drawn for the umpteenth time to an elastic band hooked around a pair of cupboard doors); and suggesting, when asked to define the difference between the Greeks and the Romans, that 'the Greeks were more flowery' [*sic*]. I was only 16 and my immaturity was toe-curling. My youth was, in fact, the issue that saw me called back in to see Ewen Bowie the next day. 'We'd like to offer you a place,' he said, with a benevolent, bearded smile, 'but we wanted to check that you're definitely going to take a year off.' I floated home on cloud nine.

Nick Hassall (1989) was interviewed by Dr Rolls:

> He told me that Sir Keith Thomas, then President, had been very impressed with my entrance papers. Flattered and lured by a false sense of security, the interview went downhill fast from there. I had not given much/any thought to the interviews or why I was interested in reading PPP at all. I had no idea that 'Prof. iterolls', as we later nicknamed him, was a specialist in physiology and neural networks, about which I knew nothing. I was woefully ill-prepared. Asked why I was interested in reading Psychology, I think I muttered something about being fascinated by the cause of dreams and a vague interest in discovering the secrets of hypnosis. Dr Rolls's frown said it all.

Arrival

Having survived the application process, arrival for the first time at Corpus could be disconcerting. Roger Horsfield (1952) found his trunk 'kicked off the back of a lorry outside the Porters' Lodge. The porter later told me that he had seen this happen scores of times. Complaints were useless.' He was allocated a room 'with a beaten-up sofa and electric fire on which I could make toast, a comfortable bed and a chamber pot', and was then summoned with the other new arrivals to be addressed by the Dean, who spoke on the importance of punctuality for tutorials (although 'It might well be that at times the tutor would be late but then he was a tutor and he enjoyed the privileges of his rank'). 'As a welcome to Corpus I felt it all fell somewhat short of the mark. I had imagined that Oxford would be different from Dover Grammar School.' There was then an invitation to meet the President and his wife:

> I there discovered my social inadequacy. A light meal had been prepared for us and in a dish in front of me was a large piece of fruit that I could not recognize. Fortunately someone mentioned the word melon and looking around I noticed that there was a bowl with brown sugar in it. I applied this liberally to my slice of melon. I took a good spoonful and felt that I had blown my head off. I presume it was cinnamon or some spice that I also had never encountered before. I had never seen a melon before and I doubt if many ordinary people who went to ordinary schools or did ordinary jobs had as well.

Don Montague (1954) also felt disoriented:

> I arrived at the Lodge, and was directed to my rooms in the Magpie Lane Annexe, smack opposite Merton Chapel and its bells, where I unpacked my pitifully few things and one or two maths books, and wondered what to do next. Apart from a couple of people from Manchester Grammar School whom I'd known slightly at school I didn't know a soul in Corpus, and I can still feel that slightly empty feeling of loneliness. I must have explored, found out where the JCR and Beer Cellar were, and the pigeonhole for my post, if any, in the Lodge. Someone must have explained to me that a gown was de rigueur at dinner in Hall, so I avoided making a fool of myself in that respect. Did I descend into the Beer Cellar that night? I discovered that draught cider was twopence a pint cheaper than draught beer, and as a result never developed a taste for the latter.

We all had, of course, time marks and constraints: three meals a day in Hall – I couldn't afford to eat anywhere else – morning lectures, afternoons on the river, tutorials. There were so many things to do, so many new people to meet, get to know or avoid. At first I found the JCR rather dark and unwelcoming, too many armchairs seemed to be occupied by second- and third-year men who all knew each other and weren't particularly interested in us newcomers. I think part of my problem was the impression I had, that almost all the undergraduates had been at public (boarding) schools and/or had done national service, and were used to institutional or communal living – which I was not. I was wrong, of course.

David Blackmore (1956) was not yet 18:

I arrived as a very junior junior and I felt it. Those first few weeks were a jumble of the new, the strange and even the frightening. I had never met such articulate people, and mealtimes in Hall were notable for the ferocity of opinion and debate on the Suez question which was raging at the time.

But Corpus was a 'great little college' (to recall a slogan used by College faithful at the time). And in very little time I was active on the hockey field, much to the chagrin of the captain of boats who optimistically and extravagantly thought my single performance in a fixed tub showed promise of rowing prowess! And it wasn't long before I was able to engage in several social communities, chief of which were the chemistry lab, the Chapel and the fellowship of OICCU (the Oxford Inter-Collegiate Christian Union).

'The truth is', thought **Keith Hill** (1962), 'that for the working-class, grammar-school entrant there was never a seamless process of assimilation into the life and style of the College.'[10] **Martin Deahl** (1975) certainly felt 'a fish out of water – I had never met anyone from an independent school before – and it took me several months to settle in'. He had an attic room in Magpie Lane:

To get to the bathroom I had to transit a second year's room on the first floor. He cohabited with his girlfriend and they seemed to spend more time in bed than out; knocking on their door when I needed the loo was excruciatingly embarrassing. That first day I cried for several hours and would have got the first bus home and quit there and then were it not for the impact on my parents, who were very proud and would have been heartbroken.

Fortunately, the initial shock was overcome: 'my peers (and tutors) showed infinite patience, kindness and did everything in their power to make me feel welcome and part of the family'.

Until the 1980s, formal induction was limited. According to **Christopher Patey** (1958), 'freshmen were asked to come up a day before the beginning of term to settle in'. An address by the Dean, hospitality by the President, approaches by club presidents and the Freshers' Fair were the main highlights. **Mary Campbell**, College Nurse from 1975, together with the College Doctor, would address the freshers, 'telling them about me being there for their worries and their aches and pains, particularly mentioning homesickness, to which some not having been at boarding school were prone and thought it a bit babyish to tell about'. Freshers would meet their tutors and be given initial essay topics. **Simon Preston** (1982) met his tutor, Robert Gasser, who 'explained that Oxford offered opportunities for academic study, sport and a full social life, but advised that there was only sufficient time for two of the three. Provided that one of these was academic study, he did not mind which other we chose.'

But sharing rooms and staircases, eating and drinking together, and being recruited to clubs meant that any initial disorientation was quickly followed by socializing. **Eric Sidebottom** (1957) was a medical student from Derbyshire:

> I was anxious about whom and what I should meet at Corpus, and whether my luggage would have arrived. After the short cycle ride from the station, I entered the hallowed premises with trepidation and quickly found that I had been assigned to share a large 'set' in Staircase 12 with an Essex mathematician, David Joyce. Our communal lounge was huge and looked out over Merton Chapel

(it is now the Fellows' Guest Room) and we each had our own bedroom off it. David was tall and appeared to be very much more confident than I. He was, after all, a product of a public school whereas I was a grammar school boy. He also had the advantage that a friend from the same school, Peter Jarvis, had just arrived.

However, when the other medic – Gary Hampson, also from Derbyshire – arrived, he found that 'fate had been extremely kind to us. The four of us quickly forged a strong bond of friendship which remains to this day and has only been broken by Gary's untimely death.'[11]

Freshers were inundated with invitations to join sports and other clubs. **James Griffin** (1955), a Rhodes Scholar, was 'bemused by my first week in College: not a word about tutorials or supervisors, but a stream of visitors from representatives of the Boat Club, the Hockey Club, the Union and so on. It struck me as a strange university where play was more organized than work.'[12] **Christopher Patey** (1958) had a surprising initiation:

A friendly face appeared at my door in the afternoon of that first day suggesting that I might like to go to Merton Chapel at 5pm when the renowned English scholar Professor J. R. R. Tolkien would be giving his valedictory lecture. I just managed to get a seat before Tolkien appeared. He had a mane of white hair and wore a gown that had seen much service. Striding the length of the nave he mounted a rostrum and began to recite Beowulf from memory. I had never heard Old English before but picked up the heroic nature of what was being said. His thrilling recitation lasted several minutes after which his voice sunk and he read from a prepared text which he seemed to want to get through as quickly as possible. He ended with the final words of the poem, his voice again firm and resonant, and left to a standing ovation. I had heard and seen the greatest living philologist and author of *The Hobbit* and *The Lord of the Rings*. Not bad for my first day.

Bill Morris (1964) made friends from the start:

I found Colin Mackay and Garth Watson waiting to greet me. Bags were promptly dumped and immediately we were running off down to the Corpus Stadium. From that moment, on a beautiful autumn afternoon, Colin and Garth became my friends for life. That evening I met David Scott, a scholar and a future JCR President, tipped for a top first but destined for a bottom third, instigator of the famous (some would say infamous) Bump Supper of 1967. David is now my daughter's godfather.

Margaret Harper (née **Craven**, 1979) – one of the first female under-graduates – recalled 'standing in the Porters' Lodge with my bags, waiting for my dad to park the car, on my very first day, when an enormous American woman bounded up to me and said, "You must weigh less than x pounds (I can't remember the figure). Would you like to cox?" I can't remember if I even knew what a cox was but within days I was on the river – they didn't hang around!' Soon after arriving she wrote home:

> There is so much going on that we haven't time to do anything much except drink coffee, go to sherry parties (the orange juice is very nice) and talk among ourselves. Corpus is GENIAL and I find that so am I. Far from clamming up, I seem to have never stopped talking, with the result that I am on speaking terms with loads of lovely men, not to mention the girls!

Some, including **Andrew Purkis** (1967), were alarmed by the apparent brilliance of their peers:

> There was quite a lot of showing off, and some of us were nervous in case we might be overwhelmed by very clever people. I remember an early sherry party for freshers and hearing one very confident man saying loudly: 'Well, everything is relative, of course', and laughing at his own 'clever' comment, and I was quite unnerved and impressed. Later I would realize he was an ass.

Jon Hesk (1987) 'completely freaked when I got here to discover my fellow classicists were "cleverer" than me. The fact that they were all

feeling the same didn't occur to me so I compensated by working ridic-
ulously hard for the first couple of weeks. It was counter-productive.'[13]
David Wilton (1981) felt 'probably as prepared for the experience
as any other student. I benefited from having spent many years at
boarding school so I was used to being away from home. What I was
not prepared for was the shock of suddenly moving from being part
of the academic elite at school to being just an ordinary commoner at
Corpus.' Eliza Pakenham (1986), by contrast, felt relief:

> I had been told what to expect. The old boy from Christ Church had
> summed it up for me. 'Going to Corpus? Ah. Intellectual virgins who
> love Bach.' I protested of course, but felt quietly furious. How did he
> know? And I hadn't even started at the College. But on the first day,
> I discovered it was a lie. The sound of something bad and dangerous
> blared from my new neighbour's room. I joined the throng on the
> bed. The conversation was about football, cars and which beer cellar
> sold the cheapest pint. And definitely no sign of Bach.

Camilla Byk (née Forestier-Walker, 1992) was enthusiastic. 'I loved
my first room, overlooking Merton street, with a big old window. It was
in the old bit of New Building, and had a shared phone for dozens of us
… I went to Freshers' Fair and signed up for everything, there couldn't
have been a keener new Corpuscle.' David Sooby (2003) was also excited:

> I got to Corpus early on my first day, probably just before lunch,
> I was so keen to get involved and meet everyone. The first week
> is more or less a blur. I can recall discovering the bar, the library
> (probably in that order) and many friends. Some of the first people
> I met I'm still good friends with over ten years on.
>
> I recall the evening before matriculation. I came down to the
> Beer Cellar and ran into a fellow first-year. While we didn't really
> know each other well at this point, we knew that we were both
> first-years so struck up a conversation. He informed me it was
> 'the 24-hour matriculation party' and we had to down the newly
> replaced bottle of Jack Daniels between now and the bar closing.
> Many other first years joined us and we did manage to empty the

bottle (even if matriculation was a little hung-over). In the ten years since that chance meeting over a bottle of Jack Daniels, I've spent four of those years living with him (two in Corpus and two after).

Catherine Hasler (1997) had grown up 'on *Morse* and *Brideshead*, and the memories of Captain Charles Ryder sang in my ears as my father drove me halfway down the country, the first of 18 round trips for him, in the autumn of 1997'. There proved to be 'no Sebastians and no murders! There was, rather, a collection of fiercely bright, hard-working souls who were as star-struck as I was to be under the dreaming spires.' She found settling in slow. Nevertheless,

> I did make friends; they were witty and clever and we had fun, laying treasure hunts of clues through obscure corners of the College Library, recovering gently after a late night with tea and cooked breakfast at Queen's Lane Coffee House. And we gossiped too long and muddled our timings and missed our introductory tour of the Law Bodleian (and I'm not sure my education ever quite recovered). I had a sweet and friendly student 'father', a second-year lawyer whose smiling face waiting for me at the Porters' Lodge is my first undergraduate memory.

There was strange new language. Corpus in the 1960s and 1970s had a male, public-school lingo, captured in a 1978 spoof. Beer was 'slotted'; 'fester' was 'what one does in an armchair in the JCR/MCR'; 'hacker' was 'a harmless individual, but not solid'; the sight of an attractive woman ('mega good news totty') evoked the cry 'spotted'.[14] According to **Ben Whitby** (1986), 'with hindsight, if you were used to independent schools/boarding schools and their ways, then Corpus must have been straightforward. If not, there were plenty of strange ways to behave and odd names for everyday things to get used to.' For **James Pennock** (1995), 'confusion is the main thing that freshers remember of their first few weeks at Corpus, if they remember anything at all!' and learning terms like 'noughth week', 'minus one week', 'battels', 'collections' and 'moderations' was 'merely the start of the journey into unravelling the enigma of the University of Oxford'.[15]

But it was not necessarily difficult: **Gail Bartlett** (1996) 'got used to the initially strange vocabulary and Corpus quickly became home'. The JCR played an increasingly active role. According to **David Miliband** (1984), 'many undergraduates have played a large part in the new "Welcoming Committees", designed to help introduce first-years to College life and to give sixth-formers coming up for open days a better idea of what the College is like'.[16] In the 1990s the JCR organized 'a full programme of welcoming and induction for the freshers ... The extent to which arriving in Oxford can be very difficult for individuals who may never have been away from home before is becoming increasingly recognized in the University and it was felt that we could go a long way to making the experience very much more welcoming.' [17] The JCR's 1998 Guide described Freshers' Week as 'an infamous part of University life', and set out a programme designed 'to help you settle in and make friends as quickly as possible.' In the 2000s Freshers' Week led to conflict with the SCR over its length and its claims to facilitate study skills. According to Senior Tutor **John Watts**:

> The entirely laudable desire of the JCR to help the incoming students adjust to their studies strikes me as misconceived. Offering companionship is one thing; so is reminding intimidated freshers that they will manage; and so again is intellectual discussion, in which students learn a great deal from themselves and each other – but these things should come naturally in the normal course of student life: they don't require an extensive 'Freshers' Week', or structured sessions of student-led study skills. To my mind, this favours a 'Freshers' Week' which is as short as possible – enough time to unpack, meet the neighbours, find the libraries and get started – but it is easy to see why there is a difference of opinion on this question.[18]

After the rigours of the application process, arriving at Corpus could be both exciting and daunting: but the new arrivals found themselves rapidly thrown together – often quickly forming new friendships. Significantly, the initial experience was focused primarily on the College, rather than the faculty or the University; and the new arrivals found their lives revolving round its rhythms and its members. They were becoming Corpuscles.

Freshers, 1945. The cohort included students from
the USA, China, India, Ceylon, South Africa and
elsewhere. *Courtesy of Robert Newman (1945)*

2

'A SURE CURE FOR STEREOTYPING':
THE CORPUS COMMUNITY

*'Small and friendly' is the universal moniker given to Corpus,
and I found it to be true.*

Gail Bartlett

Corpus students clearly had some things in common. They were well educated and intelligent. They were predominantly, though not exclusively, white. Until the 1970s they were exclusively male. As we have seen, a disproportionate number came from independent schools (though the ratio changed over time). The very fact of being at Oxford gave them potential advantages in later life. Compared with most of their contemporaries, they could reasonably be seen as part of a privileged elite.

But the Corpus community was never uniform. Students did arrive from very different social backgrounds. There were differences of age, ethnicity, nationality and (eventually) gender. Personalities and motivations varied enormously. Some took work extremely seriously while others preferred to pursue the different opportunities Oxford offered. Academic, political, sporting or cultural interests brought some together while leaving others cold. Corpus, in other words, was never monochrome. But how important were such distinctions? Was

Corpus characterized by fault lines and divisions, or was it a largely harmonious community?

Size

Corpus was the smallest Oxford college. During the Second World War it was tiny – 45 students in 1944 (including 19 from St Peter's Hall who shared the premises for the duration). This was exceptional: by 1950 there were 140 and by 1960 196 (including 22 graduates). But even in 2015, with 343 students (including 94 graduates), Corpus remained the smallest, apart from special cases such as Harris Manchester (mature students only), All Souls and Nuffield (postgraduates only), and the 'Permanent Private Halls' such as Blackfriars and St Stephen's House.

The College's size had a marked impact on its character. **Jim Griffin** (1955), an American Rhodes Scholar, found it 'a very self-contained little community – almost like a small public school in the country. One worked in the College Library, one's tutorials were in College, and one's social life – chat, discussion groups – was largely in College too.'[1] **Christopher Watson** (1957) thought 'being in one of Oxford's smallest colleges was a huge blessing – you got to know everyone by name, you met up with people across the whole academic spectrum, and you had opportunities to take a lead in activities which were less accessible in larger colleges'. **Stephen Linstead** (1959) found it 'small enough for you to know most people by name, but not so small that it was in any way stifling'. For **David Blackmore** (1956),

Corpus was a particularly accepting community. Its small size meant that we were thrown together maybe more than in other colleges. And its mini subject-communities were also small enough that they didn't consume us: I went through three years with only a single contemporary chemist (Michael Bamford), and so I mixed with other scientists as well as classicists, lawyers and so on. I also benefited from the tactic of the room allocation whereby in the first year, we were deliberately placed next to men of other academic persuasions.

In such a small community it was almost impossible to feel isolated. **Simon Bainbridge** (1968), whose first year was 'on the whole a wretchedly unhappy period', wrote that 'I shall always be grateful that I was at a small college; even for a shy man of solitary temperament it was impossible not to make friends'.[2] There were drawbacks. According to **Polly Low** (1993), 'one of the defining features of the place is its flourishing supply of gossip and rumour: small, friendly, and (rarely stated in the prospectus, but always implicit) no place for the secretive'.[3] **Catherine Hasler** (1997) initially found the College 'stifling':

> it was small, close-knit, and it was wary. What I would come to appreciate only much later was that the smaller the student body, the less room there is for different crowds, and nor was it possible to become invisible. After my big, brawling, quick-paced northern comprehensive school, the College felt tight, every dalliance widely known and every argument public knowledge. And I sensed an academic hierarchy which made me doubt my own abilities. But the University is not just a college, and, tentatively, I ventured out and found the people who were my fit.

Generally, however, Corpus students welcomed its size and intimacy. **David Sooby** (2003) echoed earlier generations: 'one of the best things about Corpus was its size. Because it was small, everyone knew everyone and there was mixing across subjects and year groups.'

Social mix

Into this small community came students from many different backgrounds. Unlike its neighbour Christ Church, Corpus did not have a reputation as an aristocratic college. Nevertheless, **Antony Walker** (1947) found himself sharing rooms with Milo Cripps (1947), son of the Duchess of Westminster – 'a charming lady who brought me quantities of butter at a time of severe rationing, together with supplies of cigarettes to be locked away and doled out to Milo at intervals'. **Geoff Goodall** (1950) described his contemporaries as 'a mixed bunch, from grammar school boys to Old Etonians, with a leavening of demobbed ex-servicemen thrown in'.

As we have seen, Corpus always contained a mix of students from state and independent schools – plus a minority from abroad – though the ratio changed as the proportion from state schools declined in the 1970s and 1980s before recovering to around half by 2016. But social and educational background was not the only potential fault-line within Corpus. In the post-war years, and until the end of national service in 1960, one of the differences which most struck new arrivals was between the youngsters straight from school (usually scholars) and the older and more experienced ex-servicemen. According to **Al Alvarez** (1949), who had been rejected by the military on health grounds, 'about half the College were ex-servicemen and many of them had fought in the war. Now they were making up for lost time and didn't want to waste it on frivolity or chit-chat. As a result they had little to say to us callow know-nothings from school and we, in our turn, were shy of them, these blue-jawed toughs who had been places and done things we couldn't even imagine.'[4]

Christopher Patey (1958) thought that 'about a third of my intake had done national service before coming up'. He had served in Cyprus, in 'the campaign led by Colonel Grivas which sought the end of British rule and union with Greece. I suppose I still behaved somewhat like a soldier as I was coming to terms with civilian and academic life. Anyway, I soon acquired the nickname "Major" which stuck fast and which is still common currency among my Corpus contemporaries.' But generally the subject was avoided. **Norman Miners** (1952) thought national service 'was practically never mentioned; it was an episode in our lives best forgotten'. He recalled how one contemporary, posted to a local unit for his annual reserve service, 'occasionally turned up to breakfast on a Sunday morning in battledress before going off for a day's training, but to avoid revealing what rank he had risen to he did not wear his jacket in College'.[5]

Social and class difference was another potential divide. **Roger Horsfield** (1952) felt that 'in personal friendships it was natural for undergraduates to chum up with those of similar backgrounds and interests'. He was from a working-class background: 'The first Christmas concert I attended in Corpus was brilliantly funny but when an enthusiastic choir of public school chaps burst into "the working class can kiss my arse, I've got the foreman's job at last", I did wonder, "What the hell am I doing with this lot?"' Nevertheless, he found Corpus 'a magical experience', and the overriding impression from recollections of this period is of a surprisingly harmonious and inclusive society. **Francis Oakley** (1950) described himself as 'unmistakably (and self-consciously) provincial – in accent, dress and (probably) demeanour – I was the youngest son of Irish immigrant parents who, bright though they undoubtedly were, had finished their own formal schooling at the age of 14'. Nevertheless, he quickly settled in:

> Happily, whether because of its intimacy of scale or its particular mix of students, the Corpus community I encountered as a somewhat diffident 18-year-old was accessible and welcoming. The great public schools were, of course, well represented among my contemporaries, but so, too, were the first-rate grammar schools then to be found in almost every part of the country. There was an interesting group of Marshall and Rhodes Scholars from the United States, Canada and Australia, a handful of students – black as well as white – from Africa, and one or two postgraduate students from the Continent. And, given the College's particular history and tradition, it was also graced with a leavening and invigorating Scots presence. I rather doubt if much (or any) social engineering had gone into all of this but it seemed, nevertheless, to work.

John Harrison (1950) was only 17 when he arrived:

> To my embarrassment, I was the only undergraduate with a child's ration book. Many of my year group were at least three years older than I; some of those in years above were considerably older, with war experience. But though I felt in comparison a 'baby', the scale of the College – I think there were only about

140 undergraduates – made it a very inclusive community. The remorseless need to produce a multitude of sports teams, the College societies, two play productions in my time and the general conviviality of the JCR created a remarkably cohesive and supportive group, to which I owe, I think in retrospect, a relatively easy and painless transition to adulthood. To one coming from a sheltered day-school background, Oxford offered countless new experiences. It was intriguing at first to meet people from public schools, with their relative self-assurance; people who could boast High Court judges as their fathers, men with evident ambitions which seemed attainable, mountaineers who talked of Everest, and – though we were almost entirely white – people who lived abroad.

Philip Hamilton-Grierson (1953) thought his contemporaries comprised

about 60 per cent clever scholars largely from Manchester Grammar, 30 per cent public school commoners in smart tweed jackets who had just completed two years as national service officers and so thought themselves as men of the world ... and 10 per cent from overseas. It was a friendly college. Being small we had to join in.

Ian Wylie (1958) described Corpus as 'a gathering of people of all classes and backgrounds, with a span of intellectual and sporting pursuits, from many races and countries'. For **Bernard Jacobson** (1956), 'one of the things that impressed me most about Corpus was its lack of cliquishness'. **Christopher Patey** (1958) thought 'it was possible, indeed inevitable, that one would know almost everyone in the College. I suppose the intake was roughly 50:50 from private and public sector schools. I don't recall any snobbery or discrimination among us. There were no very rich undergraduates and no members of the Bullingdon.'

Many others found Corpus welcoming and friendly. **Simon Squires** (1962) thought 'relations were genuinely warm, and there was little or no tension between men from grammar schools and those from independent ones (unlike some other colleges). Nor did there seem to be antagonism between an intellectual and a sporting fraternity.' **Tony Coady** (1963), an Australian postgraduate who found 'the rigidity of the class barriers in Britain both unappealing and somewhat comical', felt that 'fortunately, Corpus was less afflicted by the divisive influence of class'. **Kelvin Roberts** (1963), arriving from the Rhondda, discovered 'there were a significant number of undergraduates from Winchester and Eton, schools which I held in awe. Yet to my amazement, Corpus was largely classless.'[6] When **Jim Waterhouse** (1963) arrived, 'I soon met another student who was reading Physiology. This gave us something in common; I then discovered that he had been head boy at Eton, which I thought was far removed from my experience of having been head boy at the local grammar school. I need not have worried. He soon became, and still is, a close friend.'

By the 1960s there were signs of greater challenge. **Paul Vaight** (1963) was from Merseyside:

> Although a reasonably affable person, I think that my background and values distanced me from most of my cohort year. Indeed, my enduring friendships from my six years at Corpus have all been with people from similar grammar school backgrounds as my own. The social class divide was as deep in a small community like Corpus as it was then in society at large.

According to **Robert Lee** (1964):

> Within each year group most students knew who everyone else was, at least at a superficial level, and this was inevitably reinforced by any involvement in College-based activities, whether sporting, cultural or administrative (as distributed by the Junior Common Room). At the same time, there were undoubtedly cliques within each year group which were probably based on shared values, whether as a result of attendance at an elite public school or political and sporting commitments. With few exceptions, however, the links between the different years were

generally weak. Each cohort tended to keep to a large extent to itself.

Malcolm Underwood (1966) thought Corpus 'a small, intimate, community', noting the importance of clubs and 'the strongly bonding activities like rowing'. But there were also 'echoes of the past, in narrowly class-based associations such as the Wasps and Chevrons dining clubs, the chief distinction between which seemed to rest on which rank of public school their members had attended'. **Ken Reynolds** (1966) – 'a rather lost peasant boy newly arrived in Oxford from the far west of Cornwall' – initially felt out of place. And the existence of cliques was confirmed by **Jonathan Dancy** (1965): 'At Corpus I was a member of a close social group which consisted mainly of those people reading Classical Mods with me who had been to private school. I am not proud of this now, and was uneasy about it at the time. But it was so.'

The 1960s and 1970s saw new fault lines, between those who embraced or rejected the emerging culture of radicalism. This was often expressed most obviously in dress, hairstyle and attitudes to sex, and reflected cultural and political attitudes as much as social class. As **Andrew Purkis** (1967) observed:

> side by side at table in the Hall would be someone who looked like George Harrison in flowery clothes, and someone with short back and sides and a sports jacket; people who were all too obviously sexually liberated next to shy and inexperienced nerds. Was this degree of variety new? My own impression was that the 'liberated' feel of youth culture at that time made it seem more oppressive and frustrating to be in an all-male environment. Pride at being in the elite was tempered by some envy and guilt at being detached from the passionate political, social and sexual forces of 'liberation'.

According to **David Archard** (1969), 'there was some hostility in College between the "lefties" and the public school conservatives. The latter were a recognizable social group who spoke an extraordinary dialect, concocted from public school abbreviations, Evelyn Waugh and *Private Eye* colloquialisms: "totty" was a woman, and "What's in the wedges, God[frey]?" a familiar enquiry at JCR teas.[7] **Rob Stepney** (1971) distinguished between

> those whose non-academic interests focused on rowing and rugby, often to the exclusion of politics, and those for whom sport was of little concern. There were students from public schools and those from grammar schools or comprehensives. (Sporting interest was generally correlated with the school divide, but foot-ballers and students from South Wales tended to span the gap.) And there were those who regularly smoked dope (and inhaled) – who made up perhaps a third of the College – and those who did not.

Mel Johnson (1972) distinguished between 'freaks', 'straights' and 'beer heavies':

> The three categories were not entirely exclusive and some indulged in a 'pick and mix' approach. Straights were often even more outlandish than freaks, with their antediluvian clothes and views; heavies simply preferred a different drug to freaks – alcohol instead of dope. All had sexist attitudes to women, the only differences were in the terms employed: totties, chicks or ladies.[8]

Nevertheless, within Corpus tensions were generally moderate and contained. According to **David Archard** (1969), 'the hostility between "lefties" and "righties" never, in my recollection, led to any explicit nastiness ... I also think that the "righties" included few if any unpleasant people, and some, I know, displayed exemplary kindness when a College friend of mine was in personal difficulties.'[9] Harmony was helped by the fact that after the first year he and his circle lived mainly outside the College and kept clear when, for example, the dining clubs were celebrating. Similarly, **Richard Abernethy** (1973), a socialist revolutionary, devoted most of his energy to the 'vibrant Left milieu in and around the University'. Although Corpus was 'a beautiful place to live and work', he felt 'on the margins of College life. My relations with others at Corpus were more pleasant than not, but they were never close, and four decades later I do not remember them well. I had zero interest in sport. I steered clear of the Beer Cellar and The Bear.'

Nor was revolutionary socialism the only pursuit kept apart from College life. **James Dixon** (1966) was active in the University Air Squadron: 'Few at Corpus knew of my involvement, and even those who did know seldom asked many questions about it. Rather more Corpuscles were members of the somewhat larger army Officers' Training Corps, but even that did not seem to jell readily with Corpus traditions.' **Richard Fitzalan Howard** (1972), who spent 'too much time on country pursuits', kept quiet about his interests:

> By my second year I was hunting the Christ Church Beagles three days a week and often had one day a week fox hunting. Such activities, certainly at that time, were politically incorrect and in my cowardly way I would creep out of the College wearing my grand-father's ankle-length motoring coat to hide my hunt uniform. Another distraction which scarcely helped my academic duties was membership of the Bullingdon Club. At least the worst excesses occurred mostly in London as the club was banned from meeting in Oxford.

Most of the time, Corpus remained friendly and harmonious. Small enough to know the other students, it was diverse enough for most to find their niche. But **Nick Witney** (1969), who loved its 'intimacy', recognized another side:

> Intimate, but I suppose insular. Few of us bothered much with university life. We classicists had only to climb a staircase to learn from the best tutors of their generation. I played University rugby, but never felt wholly comfortable in that milieu: it is College friends that I have retained. And, even within Oxford's smallest college, we were unconsciously cliquish; contemporaries who were not sportsmen, classicists or in the Owlets I never got to

know. So I spent a couple of years rubbing shoulders with the New Tolstoy and never shared a word with him. Most of us, I think, were deplorably lacking in curiosity outside our fields of study. Opportunity, I now realize, is wasted on the young.

Gregory Wilsdon (1978) thought Corpus 'introverted' and was concerned about cliques: 'not just dining clubs like the Wasps or the Square Table, but coteries like one centred on the Rugby Club. This did not have a name, but some of us dubbed them the "nastoids" because of their tendency to make the room which they occupied unusable by anybody else.'[10] **Sean O'Grady** (1981) thought Corpus socially divided:

There was a silent system of segregation, self-imposed, entirely voluntary, unspoken, taken for granted. The public school boys and girls tended to stick together, as did the state school products, comprising the few from comprehensives, e.g. on the ILEA scheme (Inner London Education Authority was permitted looser entrance criteria), and the larger grammar school contingent. Academic disciplines overlapped with background and class; thus most of the Classics students went to fee-paying schools; the majority of the PPEists came from state schools. Only sexual desire, and to a lesser degree, sport, was able to break through the class divide, with mixed results. No one seemed to mind, but the more I look back on it the more striking this social apartheid was. No overt snobbery or inverted snobbery. Just a glass wall.

Jacquie Kelly (1984) was also struck by the divide:

The alienation began with a dawning awareness that what seemed a totally new and surreal environment to me was a home-from-home for my fellow students who had come from public schools. It didn't help that I had discovered politics during my year off and found myself unwittingly in the bosom of class supremacy and privilege. I genuinely applied to Oxford because I wanted to see if I was clever enough to get in; I had no idea it was full of rich people from public schools. I was entranced by Sebastian Flyte as a quaint historical stereotype from a pre-war past, but was rather surprised to find real-life people like him in the Oxford of the 1980s.

   In hindsight, I was having a lot of trouble with my class identity. Now I would describe myself as second-generation middle class, but back then I wasn't sure what I was. I growled around Corpus with a scathing chip on my shoulder, eating my breakfast in my room and my dinner in the Beer Cellar, avoiding JCR tea because I wasn't quite sure what it was, avoiding rowing because I didn't understand the jargon, and feeling different to everyone else.

By the end of her first term she felt so 'displaced' that she came close to transferring to London. 'Obviously I had to speak to Val [Cunningham, her tutor] about my decision, and my impression was that he was irritated by it and didn't understand it, but he didn't try to make me change my mind. I am grateful to him for that conversation, because he did somehow leave me with the idea that it might be foolish to turn my back on Oxford, and I changed my mind.'

Corpus was therefore showing greater signs of division. Nevertheless, its 'small and friendly' character still generally prevailed. **Nicola Feather** (1981) wrote positively about its mix:

Though we were a small undergraduate body, we were nonetheless fairly eclectic in our backgrounds. The JCR photo taken in the summer of 1983 shows people from public schools (ancient, major and minor); fee-paying day schools (girls' and boys'); northern and southern grammar schools; comprehensives from all parts of Britain; schools of religious foundation; and a few international students. You could sit next to anyone at any meal and be sure of hearing something new and interesting. In my school, a Church of England comprehensive, there was a clear divide between the sporty and the brainy, but Corpus was a sure cure for stereotyping. I remember chatting with a classicist in my year and being quietly gobsmacked when I found out that he was also a proficient footballer with an interest in French medieval poetry and archaeology.

David Wilton (1981) found the atmosphere 'friendly and relaxed':

> The social mix at Corpus was certainly more representative than anything I had previously experienced, which was not entirely surprising bearing in mind that I arrived there after ten years at two boarding schools in the south of England. It seemed to me that the College had a good mixture of people from different backgrounds and places and studying different subjects. There was a striking mixture of accents and, more interestingly, views. It was all very different from a press article at the time which, in true and enduring *Daily Mail* style, gave the impression that most Oxford undergraduates kept at least one polo pony.

Ben Whitby (1986) shared this sense of Corpus as a 'friendly' community:

> I found it much more diverse than the small city in north-west England where I had grown up. There were foreign students (Chinese, South African, Canadian, Swiss, German, American and Mexican) and people from all over England, Scotland and Wales, although I don't remember any Irish. Oxford felt comparatively cosmopolitan (even if the Londoners moaned about it being small). Whilst there were a lot of undergraduates from independent schools, there were plenty from maintained schools. No one much cared about anyone's social background unless there were points to be scored in undergraduate politics.
>
> The College atmosphere was overwhelmingly friendly, although first impressions tended to stick for a term or two. While a small college, there was enough space in Oxford to stay out of the way of people you did not want to mix with, except in the queue for lunch or dinner! I can't remember any physical fighting, even on the sports pitch, which was different from my school.

Paul Elbourne (1989), from a 'solidly working-class' family, found Corpus 'an egalitarian and welcoming place. I never felt judged by my background. In fact it is only in retrospect that it occurs to me to think about these things at all.' **David Massam** (1989) concurred. He noted the calls to revive traditions such as Formal Hall:

> Perhaps surprisingly, many of the staunchest advocates of this revival were from the state and grammar schools. This illustrated how difficult it had become to distinguish between the College's state- and public-school intake ... For the vast majority, such matters were an irrelevance and I am proud to be wholly unaware of the bulk of my contemporaries' origins.[11]

Brian Swift (1993) was impressed by the mix: 'There were no Etonians in my year. The 1993 intake included a girl from the impoverished Valleys of South Wales, a Trotskyist from Ruskin and several students from comprehensive schools. I found it liberating that a student from Fettes College was best friends with a student from a comprehensive in Yorkshire.' **Debbie Welch** (1994) too 'liked the atmosphere – you generally knew most people fairly quickly'. She knew 'very few people's class, or educational backgrounds, even of my closer friends. There was one lad who was definitely aristocracy, and we used to watch him during Formal Hall to see what we should be doing, but other than that I really don't know.'

There were places and events which helped people to mix and socialize across class and other barriers. As we will see later, Corpus's size meant that almost anyone could – sometimes despite themselves – get involved in sports, theatre or music. JCR tea was often mentioned as a highlight of College life, and College dances, 'sweaty bops' and dinners were important communal events. **Eric Dugdale** (1990) thought facilities like the Plummer – the washing complex in the basement of the Thomas Building – were still bringing people together: 'It is the ideal place to get to know those who have long remained anonymous faces; even the most reticent of Corpuscles warm to its balmy atmosphere, like that of a Victorian washhouse. There the resident astronomer will venture a few words even to the "rugby lout".'[12] For **Camilla**

Byk (1992), meals were the glue: 'The College was small enough not to be cliquey and you could sit with any group at mealtimes. I appreciated this as I spent a lot of time outside College and didn't invest a lot of time trying to get in with a group, so the dining room and bar and JCR were always welcoming.'

Nationality and ethnicity

Corpus had always welcomed international students. According to the *Biographical Register*, between 1941 and 1960 there were students from at least 26 countries – spanning Europe, North and South America, Asia, Africa, and Australasia.[13] Some already had a degree in their home country. At any one time they formed a small minority, though by 1992 around 8 per cent of undergraduates were from non-UK schools, and by 2014 this had risen to around 14 per cent. The proportion amongst postgraduates was significantly higher, reaching between a quarter and a third.[14] Non-whites were an even smaller minority. Traditionally they came mainly from overseas, from their homeland's social and educational elite. **Douglas Long** (1958) recalled meeting 'a very noble-looking young man in our group and was told that he was Constantine Bereng Seeiso, a member of Corpus who would later become paramount chief of Lesotho'. On independence he became King Moshoeshoe II.

For post-war British students, foreigners and non-whites could be a novelty: **Roger Horsfield** (1952) recalled meeting a black African: 'the first conversation I've ever had in my life with someone of a different colour to myself'. He also met an African student with his wife. 'They were sitting on a bench and were weeping. I asked, "What's the matter?" He answered, "We don't want to go home, but we have to. Here I am respected PhD of Oxford University, back home I'm not considered worthy of untying the shoelaces of the most minor colonial official."' **Geoff Goodall** (1950) met Eldred Jones from Sierra Leone – 'a black face when these were very rare in England'. **Eldred Jones** (1950) himself recalled a (white) friend from Southern Africa who 'confessed to me that I was the first black person with whom he had shaken hands and talked on equal terms'.[15]

Jones threw himself into College life, enjoying bowls, drama, choir, sports, cycling to Oxford villages and punting. **Mueen Afzal** (1960), from Pakistan, also enjoyed traditional Oxford life, including 'bird and bottle parties', trips to Lords, socializing in The Bear and bridge parties. As **Ian Wylie** (1958) recalled, in this generation racial anxieties might be handled by being more English than the English:

> I was lucky enough to play in the University Golf Club, and eventually made it into the Divots, its second team, against the Other Place. We had the first black man to play golf at (indeed, above) that level. He cured us of any tendency to belittle his race. Often the team would play matches against great clubs like Wentworth. When he hit the ball into the rough, we would say, 'There you go, African, back to the jungle.' The club members we were playing would be aghast, until he grinned from ear to ear and gave his inimitable response: 'Shut up, white trash.' Everyone would fall about. What an Ambassador (as he became in later life)!

Arriving two decades later, **Farzana Ahmed** (née **Choudhury**, 1979) recalled that even then 'there were no Bangladeshi immigrant students in Oxford – most Bangladeshis had come from overseas and from the middle- or upper-class families'. A diplomat's daughter herself, she had lived in the UK from the age of ten, and chose Corpus knowing of two previous Bangladeshis who had got first-class degrees there. 'My personal experience as a Bangladeshi at Corpus was very good. I never felt any racism or discrimination of any sort from the College authorities.' But by now Britain itself was becoming more diverse and British students from different ethnic backgrounds were arriving, albeit in small numbers. Like Ahmed, **Beverley Patterson** (1979) was one of the first female undergraduates:

> Like most students who had never spent time away from home it was a little frightening but not in a bad way. I recall meeting the biochemists in the year above me and they were friendly and welcoming. I made friends with their friends and some of the girls in my year; I had many friends outside of College (my champagne

and party friends). I had my own sense of style and independent character so I did not want to be like anyone else. I think some of the other students saw me as exotic and stylish. I think they would have been disappointed had they known I hailed from South London and not the Caribbean or Africa.

My life at Oxford was very varied. I was also involved in extracurricular activities arranging social events for the African Society. This led to friendships with some amazingly talented individuals. There were so many wonderful and talented people in my life both in College and outside. My only slight disappointment is that in my early years there were several suitors but mainly undesirable. I had to wait until my fourth year to meet someone suitable. When I look back that was clearly something to do with colour on both sides; at the time you had to be brave to be in a mixed relationship.

David Upshal (1984), however, described his first year as 'a lonely, traumatic time which I wouldn't wish on anyone':[16]

Being black, being from a one-parent family, being working class (or shall we just say poor), I arrived half-fearing I'd find Brideshead and half-hoping for something more progressive. I found elements of both. I did not find the reassurance of 'people like me' that we all of us seek in any new situation. There simply were not 'people like me' at Oxford, or certainly not many. If they existed at all, I did not find them. And for the first term of my first year I was in a condition of daunted withdrawal. Afraid to speak at – or even attend – JCR meetings, which seemed dominated by the opinionated, intolerant dictates of well-bred, self-promoting cliques. Regardless of their political persuasion, the only persistent ideology was that of self-importance. I felt thoroughly alienated. I was also rather subdued by the apparent genius of the people around me, who all seemed to talk as though they were strolling towards a first-class degree with some ease – even if, as time would prove, they actually had no hope of one. In short, I was made anxious by the whole size and scope of the place and full of a sense that it was not for the likes of me. I was well and truly out of it. Come the end of Michaelmas Term I was close to leaving.[17]

Pushpinder Saini (1986), from a close-knit Indian community in Southall, described arriving at Corpus as 'extremely frightening':

I was going from a 90 per-cent black/Asian school and community into an almost 90 per-cent English or 'white' community. For my friends at home my departure was very much a trip into the 'white man's world'. Happily, I found that most of my fellow New Building freshers were just as much at sea as I was, although for obviously different reasons.

My lasting impression of being a fresher is that of being stereotyped by others as being an overseas or foreign student. Stereotyping was common practice in those first days in the New Building: you were a 'public-school type', a 'working-class hero', or one of those 'overseas students'. I very much felt that I fell into none of the prevailing stereotypes; the 'British Asian' stereotype had obviously not taken hold at Oxford, and time and again I found myself answering the following question:

Q. 'So where are you from?'
A. 'London.'
Q. 'No, no, where are you *really* from?'

I am pleased to say that the fact that Corpus was so small and itself a close-knit community provided me with the security and friendship that helped me overcome the feeling of being different and in an alien environment. I soon made extremely good friends, and was able to start to play a part in College life.[18]

Ihsan Malik (1996), a devout Muslim, found that 'obeying the rules of God in Corpus Christi has obviously been difficult, especially with no other Muslims I know of in this college'. Alcohol and drugs, for example, were forbidden: 'so when a College team wins a rowing race, or when students want to celebrate the end of exams, by going to the local pub, because of my beliefs, I have increasingly chosen not to go to such places'.[19] **Sarabjit Singh** (1997) also felt at sea: 'I was a confused teenage boy. I had developed certain expectations of what Corpus, Oxford and the world would and should be like and I was disappointed when those expectations were not fulfilled' – feelings expressed at the time as 'sometimes Corpus is unbearable' and 'I can't help getting the feeling that I don't fit in, that I don't belong'.[20] Fortunately this didn't last: he went on to make 'lifelong friends' and felt his later years 'must have been pretty good because I decided to come back to Corpus shortly after I graduated to teach on a part-time basis'. **Sun Park** (1996), a Canadian postgraduate, found Corpus welcoming:

> Not only does Oxford have a reputation for being a realm of the economic elite, it also has the reputation of being dominated by the white Protestant middle and upper class. This image is just that, an image, and one that lacks a basis in reality. I feel strongly that this is especially true of our college in that Corpus has very much a multicultural face. Granted, much of its multicultural aspect exists due to a high number of overseas students (especially in the MCR), but I don't think this totally accounts for it. I believe that our college is very much a place where cultures are allowed to meet, where experiences are exchanged and where differences are respected. To say otherwise, I believe, for me would be a grave ingratitude for the many British friends that have welcomed me here. I do admit that this is very much a personal experience, but to stay silent on this topic would be perpetuating a myth, in a present-day society which is ever striving to be inclusive. One of the great attractions about Oxford when I was applying here was that the application procedure did not go out of its way to point out racial or ethnic differences. I really felt that I was being judged on my academic merits alone; that, to say the least, was very refreshing.[21]

Initial impressions did not always last and at least some of those who initially felt marginalized came in time to feel full members of the Corpus community. **Sarabjit Singh**'s (1997) 'memories of Corpus now are only fond memories'. **Pushpinder Saini** (1986) became JCR President, observing that 'with an excellent balance of undergraduates from all types of educational, social and ethnic backgrounds Corpus provides a warm and welcoming atmosphere for all'.[22] By the end of his first year **David Upshal** (1984) too felt part of the College. Living in close proximity, pursuing similar interests, even facing similar financial conditions ('few people's parents were wealthy enough to give their children more than the maximum grant we poorer folk received'), he found himself 'bonded by friendships more intimate than any I had known before (nor shall ever know again, I suspect). For there we were, living together, eating together, drinking together, studying together, cinema-going together, soccer-playing/rugby-playing/rowing together, celebrating and commiserating together and, not least, partying together.'[23]

Corpus types

There were other important dimensions of diversity in Corpus – the arrival of women and the growth of postgraduates – which will be discussed in later chapters. But despite the increase in its size over the years, and the range of backgrounds from which it drew its students, Corpus remained a generally tolerant, harmonious community, able to successfully mix people from different backgrounds.

This does not mean it was monochrome. It was possible to stereotype Corpuscles into distinct groups, though the categories, as well as the individuals in them, could overlap and did not straightforwardly mirror educational or social backgrounds. **Sean O'Grady** (1981) thought that, in contrast to some other colleges, 'Hooray Henries' were 'mercifully few' and 'easily outnumbered by "northern Chemists", say, (who didn't need to come from the North, as the stereotype was socially rather than geographically based)'. **Eric Dugdale** (1990) recalled a spoof, but 'remarkably accurate', Hall seating plan in which tables were labelled according to their habitual occupants: 'rowers, biochemists, the God Squad, dark-haired Sloanes, mousey-haired

Sloanes, blonde Sloanes and so on. When this was circulated, it had people self-consciously reshuffling for a few days until they succumbed anew to habit.'[24] **Rebecca Rist** (1995) identified six 'College Types' – though 'no one of us belongs exclusively to any one type – or should I say clique? Most of us swing between one or two groups, and there is certainly a smattering of individualists':

- *the River-Corpuscle*: generally 'a gentlemanly, well-turned-out public schoolboy'.
- *the PC-Corpuscle*: 'kind-hearted, well-meaning, but occasionally bordering on the officious, he/she is committed to doing staggering amounts of good deeds in the realms of welfare activities, charity work, women's issues'.
- *the Beautiful-Corpuscle*: 'never to be caught doing any work', and in summer 'lounging in the garden, nonchalantly playing croquet, sunning himself by the Pelican, and entering into the bizarre mating ritual of trying to attract the female of the species by downing as much Pimm's as possible'.
- *the Christian-Corpuscle*: 'surprisingly active and prevalent at Corpus ... Definitely Low Church'.
- *the Good-Time-Corpuscle*: 'a nocturnal type, to be seen propping up the bar on a Friday night'.
- *the Classicist-Corpuscle*: 'not strictly a type, but a group, this motley crew is to be found in all walks of Corpus life. To be spotted with tedious regularity in Corpus Library'.[25]

Gail Bartlett (1996) recognized, but was unfazed by, the stereotypes. Her friends were 'all sorts of people from all sorts of backgrounds':

'Small and friendly' is the universal moniker given to Corpus, and I found it to be true. Small and friendly was exactly what appealed when I applied, and small and friendly it turned out to be. This was not without its problems. For 'small', read 'gossipy'.

Everyone tended to know everyone else's business, but the gossip was rarely malicious. For 'friendly', read 'cliquey'. There were the classicists, the Corpus Cool, the rowers, rugby players, thespians and politicians, to name but a few. But these were never hard-and-fast stereotypes, more like a massive, complicated Venn diagram of partly shared interests. As the College was so small, it relied on everyone to muck in to fill sports teams, put on a Cuppers production and so on. The place was overwhelmingly tolerant, and I loved it.

Julian Thompson (Christ Church 1995), who switched to Corpus in 1996, contrasted the inclusivity of Corpus with his former college:

> In Corpus I found so much less posturing, and more open friendliness which eased the transition with a warm welcome. Fewer social pressures seemed to give College affairs a rather amateur feel that was a relief from the self-conscious control of Christ Church. I am wary to avoid sententious generalizations, but Corpus does seem to present a less ostentatious and perhaps more uniform front in its undergraduates.
>
> The small college, the Beer Cellar, the well-used JCR etc. unify the members of College to a far greater extent than those of Christ Church, where expressions of popular spirit are almost sneered at. The recent Corpus sporting success provides a tribute to such a small college's spirit, and the last Corpus vs Christ Church rugby match an illustration of the difference between colleges: despite massive numbers and considerable talent, Christ Church could not raise the 15-man team to face Corpus. Corpus is lucky not to have the apathy that its larger neighbour suffers and instead to have people competing enthusiastically at every level.[26]

Despite its growth and the social and other differences to be found within the student body, Corpus does seem to have retained its character as a small, tolerant, friendly community. Staff too thought it special: **George Ross**, Master of Works, thought Corpus 'unusual in that it's such a friendly little place'.[27] **Dave Yeatman**, who joined as

Head Porter from Balliol, thought 'the students were so much friend-
lier. Although the Balliol ones were friendly, the Corpus ones were
something different.'

In the Corpus gardens, 1982. *Courtesy of Farzana Ahmed (1979)*

3

'CONTRARIAN IRREVERENCE': THE CORPUS ENVIRONMENT

The whole place felt like a secret garden.

Nick Witney

It's surprising how many of my memories involve food.

Caroline Knapp

Arriving at Corpus was a physical as well as social experience. The ancient buildings – the Gateway, the Quad, the Pelican, Hall, Library and Chapel – told newcomers they were joining a historic community with a long pedigree. The worn stone at the gate reminded **David Jory** (1959) of 'the multitude of students who had trodden on that step before me over nearly 450 years'. In the Library, he wondered if Erasmus had sat on the same bench ('which looked and felt old enough'), while **Eleanor Bird** (1982) recalled how 'thousands of students over hundreds of years had sat in this very same place, struggled as I struggled, and in the end completed their tasks, as I was sure to do ten minutes before the tutorial'.[1]

The immediate impression was of timelessness – a feeling reinforced by fiction: *Brideshead* remained a defining Oxford image and scenes from *Morse* and *Gaudy Night* were shot in Corpus. **Tony**

Coady (1963) was not the only student to be struck by the College's 'gem-like beauty' and an Oxford 'glowing with the romance of the past'. Nor was this sensation limited to the physical setting: customs such as College 'scouts', eating together in Hall – especially on formal occasions – as well as traditional recreations from punting on the river to 'festering' in the JCR, all reinforced the sense of living in a timeless place, where ghosts from the actual or fictional past might appear at any moment.

But it was not entirely true. Physically, as in other ways, Corpus changed. Summer vacations saw the College echo to building and repair work. The Quad itself looked very different in 2016 compared with the post-war years, and even the worn step at the gate, which Jory found so evocative, had been replaced. For the individual student, present for only a few years, the College might appear timeless. It was when he or she returned, years later, that the changes became more visible.

The setting

The beauty of the College was a constant refrain, remarked by students of every generation. **Al Alvarez** (1949) described 'falling in love with Oxford, with the graceful stone and lush gardens, with all that silence and history. Whatever the teaching was like, the place itself got to you and you learned from its beauty.' He particularly loved the Corpus Library:

> It was a long, high room, with a pitched roof and coconut matting on the floor. The bookshelves were set at right angles to the walls, dividing the space into pews, and each pew was divided down the middle by a high-backed wooden double bench. I worked there every day and, because the benches were hard and the air was frigid, I usually had the place to myself. When I said I liked it there my friends wrote it off as affectation, so I covered up by pretending that I needed the discomfort to stay awake. But really I was besotted by the atmosphere.[2]

Later generations reacted similarly. For **Christopher Patey** (1958), 'what I remember best about Corpus is its setting, with buildings on a human scale – a quiet refuge in which to pursue one's life free from threats or too much direction'. **Andrew Purkis** (1967) thought Corpus a 'beautiful' college:

> I and my friends were forever setting off for walks through the Meadow and down to the river and back along the lovely edge of Merton. The beautiful bells of Merton, and the lovely timbre of old stone, flagstone floors, hammer-beam roof and of course the Pelican itself, became a constant source of quiet enjoyment. I loved the Library, its deep quietness, its ancient volumes, its mellow views over the Fellows' gardens and beyond. I always felt it a privilege to be able to concentrate in this silent, almost holy and timeless atmosphere. I also loved the Corpus garden with its handsome lawn and herbaceous borders and splendid copper beech, the unshowy, satisfying classicism of the Fellows' Building, and the wide views over Christ Church and the Meadow.

Nick Witney (1969) loved the College's 'intimacy':

> it still retained – the last Oxford college to do so – a quadrangle of Thames sand and gravel. You half expected chickens to come scratching out through the doorways. In the corner of the Fellows' garden, where the splendid new auditorium now abuts the city wall, was the gardener's potting shed – and a view down on to a romantically derelict hothouse in an unkempt Christ Church orchard. The whole place felt like a secret garden.

Anita Gilman Sherman (1979) remembered 'emerging from the darkness of the arched passageway under the Fellows' Building into the light of the garden: green washes of colour, the promise of warmth in the air, the haze coming off the river over the Meadow, and Christ Church Cathedral looming out from behind the copper beech'. **Eliza Pakenham** (1986) recalled 'the dark Chapel, the pregnant silence of the Library, the glorious garden with a secret view over Christ Church, a time of lights and shades'. **Ben Whitby** (1986) felt 'like I was living in a National Trust property that was still evolving, not stuck in one period'.

The superficially timeless environment was indeed subject to change. The ancient soot was cleaned from the sandstone buildings. In 1967, after being scaled at a Bump Supper, the Sundial was rebuilt on a stronger base and 'a newly sculpted pelican replaced the damaged one'.[3] In 1971 the look of the Quad changed when the gravel – described by the College as 'quagmire prone' – was replaced with flagstones.[4] Although **Malcolm Underwood** (1966) recognized the problems of the old surface – 'the gravelly slush which it produced in wet weather' – he looked back with affection on its 'ochre tinge' and how it evoked 'a time when roads and squares were also unpaved'. It had formed 'a mute link with a vanished past'.

There were other visible changes, including the creation of a new SCR, offices and extensions to the Library. As we will see below, three new student accommodation blocks were built; and 2009 saw the opening of the MBI Al Jaber Building, providing a large modern space for lectures, concerts and events. **Christina Lee** (2011) felt its contemporary look complemented the older buildings and symbolized the College's 'ability to accommodate tradition alongside modernity'.

One of the more surprising changes was in the gardens, following **David Leake**'s arrival in 1979 as Head Gardener. He rejected the 'City Council' style of gardening whereby 'orange and yellow marigolds are planted together with pink and scarlet begonias in rigid geometric patterns'. Instead of regimentation, weedkillers and fertilizers, he introduced a naturalist look, with plants and flowers juxtaposed to form a 'romantic garden, full of scented pinks and roses, silver-leaved Mediterranean herbs, clematis, day lilies, Madonna lilies, campanulas, and bulbs of every description – black tulips, white narcissi, lilac alliums and sky blue squill'.[5] The result, as Fellow **Peter Cane** observed, was unique:

> After its famous sundial and its infamous association with tortoises, Corpus was, for most of my time as a Fellow, and

remains to this day, perhaps best known to the outside world for its gardens and – I add advisedly – other plantings. In the late 1970s, the Corpus garden could fairly be described as uninspiring. Then, along came David Leake. For the past 30-plus years, David has made a splendid and widely celebrated contribution to the annals of Oxford eccentricity. Compared with the typical 'gardening-by-numbers' style of the classic Oxford garden, David's uniquely creative horticulture brims with surprises, jokes, puns, quirky juxtapositions and sheer humanity. It expresses a sense of contrarian irreverence for traditional academic pomp and stuffiness that only a college as self-confident and unpretentious as Corpus could permit, let alone promote and admire. Emerging from the tiny Fellows' Quad to be presented with the mound, the copper beech and the wide vista of Merton fields, Christ Church Meadow and the Cathedral, embroidered with the ordered chaos of David's imagination, is one of the great experiences of an Oxford summer term.

Accommodation

Some of the biggest changes to students' lives came from improvements to their basic physical amenities. Around the end of the Second World War, coal fires were largely replaced with electric. But, as **John Brown** (1955) discovered on the day he arrived, little else had changed:

There was a knock on the door. It was an old gentleman who asked if he could come in and have a look round, having had the same room when he was an undergraduate in the 1890s. He settled himself on the chaise longue, patted it, looked round and then said: 'Well, they haven't changed the furniture!' Clearly the College did not think it should spend money on fripperies such as new furniture during the first half of the 20th century. There was no plumbing or running water laid on to the staircase in the 1950s, although one's scout did bring hot water in a jug for shaving each morning. But all other facilities were two quads away!

In retrospect, as **Rolf Christophersen** (1939) observed, conditions looked primitive:

> One thing which stands out in my mind, especially whenever I have been in Corpus in recent years, is how spartan the conditions were. In the winters it was not unusual to find the water in the jugs in our washing basin was frozen over. Of course there were no sanitary facilities available in the bedrooms and anything from having a bath or going to the lavatory required crossing the Quad and on to the Plummer. How different it is today.

George Richardson (1947) lived in the Front Quad: 'There were no lavatories of course and every morning a rather wheezy scout hauled up the staircase with some hot water for shaving. This was before electric shavers. You had to pee in a chamber pot, which was carried out across the Quad. There was still rationing so when one went to breakfast one had to take one's own butter.' **Peter Waterfield** (1946) experienced the famously bad winter of 1947, when the water meadows froze, the snow lasted until March, and the College saw burst pipes and restrictions on electricity: 'rationing was as strict or worse than ever; at one point even bread was rationed. The heating in College was rationed, so that unless we could find a place in the Radcliffe, one read or wrote huddled in overcoat and with a hot water bottle at your feet. Sometimes we had no hot water for days.'

According to **Roger Horsfield** (1952), 'the ones who probably found it hardest to adapt were the mature students and the Americans', who 'complained about the medieval plumbing as they described it, and were probably very shocked by having a chamber pot and a scout coming well before breakfast to empty it into a pail'. But **Al Alvarez** (1949) thought the conditions no worse than elsewhere:

> In terms of comfort, life in Oxford after the war was still grim and impoverished. Meat was rationed, the cooking was dreadful, the nearest bathrooms and lavatories were two quads away, and to keep warm you bundled yourself up in sweaters and hurried

from one pathetic electric fire to another, like Polynesians island-hopping across an icy Pacific. Even so, it felt like a holiday after Oundle.[6]

Geoff Goodall (1950) was also unfazed:

Creature comforts in those post-war days were limited but perfectly adequate, in spite of the fact that most basic foods were still severely rationed. Warm water for washing and shaving was brought each morning before breakfast by my splendid scout, Alf, for whom I had great regard. However, hot baths were always available if one went downstairs into the Plummer. There was no central heating, but a two-bar electric fire quickly warmed my study which looked out onto Merton Chapel Tower and in the spring onto hosts of heart-warming daffodils.

Christopher Patey (1958) had only a 'small electric fire' in his room. But 'as I came from a home where central heating was despised as evidence of moral weakness, I was not much worried by the cold'. The Plummer, in the Thomas Building basement, was an abiding memory. **Michael Barnes** (1953) thought it 'one of the centres of College life. The comradeship that went with shaving in adjacent basins in bitterly cold weather or taking steaming hot baths after rowing or playing football was very real'.[7] **Roger Horsfield** (1952) found it an improvement on home:

My greatest luxury was the baths. At home we had a gas geyser which had a habit of exploding when you turned it on, not huge explosions but somewhat disturbing. Also we followed the Lancashire tradition that you do your washing on Mondays and have your bath on Fridays. Now I could luxuriate in gallons upon gallons of lovely hot water. I did this every morning before breakfast. Forgetting the other bathers I would usually sing some of my favourite tunes in a language that I made up but which could have passed for the ancient Basque, assuming of course that you had never heard a Basque singer entertaining the world from his bath.

The College introduced major improvement programmes in the post-war years, replacing coal fires with electric, installing a new College boiler, modernizing the Fellows' Building, repairing roofs, reconstructing Beam Hall and altering the President's Lodging. For students, however, the major change was a programme, launched in 1959, to modernize student rooms, introducing hot and cold running water, wall-mounted electric fires, improved lighting, a bathroom on each staircase and improvements to the scouts' pantries. By the early 1960s, for the first time in the College's history, chamber pots, lugging coal and hot water, and having to cross the Quad to the Plummer – or even, in emergency, pee against the Pelican – had ceased to be part of the routine of daily life.

Bathroom facilities were still shared, albeit normally on a single staircase or corridor, and the cold in winter remained a refrain. **Simon Squires** (1962) experienced another famously bad winter, 'when the Isis froze over and gentlemen were invited to keep their electric fires permanently on without charge in an effort to safeguard the plumbing'. According to **Anita Gilman Sherman** (1979), 'it was cold in the winter, and the only building with central heating was the modern part of the Library'. **Margaret Harper** (1979) wrote home after a thaw: 'Buckets have sprung up everywhere to catch the drips, the ceiling has fallen in on Staircase 4, and in our old room 12.6, the water is streaming through the roof. We've also been subject to intermittent power cuts and water stoppages! One night the temperature dropped to a mere −21°C, so my major worry has been keeping warm!' But as **Ben Whitby** (1986) remarked, 'Corpus had good enough facilities for its time. My first year was in the New Building in a modern room (with a sink). It was warm enough. There was a shared loo and a shared bathroom.' In his final year he had rooms near the Library: 'I thought it was great to have my own living room, with an electric fire. I was still sharing a loo and a bath. For showers, you had to go to the communal ones in the Plummer in Thomas Quad. The washing machines and dryers were there too.'

By the 1990s – driven as much by the burgeoning conference business and security concerns as by student expectations – things improved again, with central heating, locked doors at the foot of staircases, and en-suite facilities. **George Ross**, Master of Works, thought the Thomas Building had been 'a terrible place to live. It was so cold, the water used to run down the walls inside and soak up into the carpets. But since I've centrally heated that, it's a lovely place to live. It's changed completely.'[8] In 1997 the JCR President could report that 'in a great rush of contractors' deadlines, the College completed the refurbishment of the rooms on the main Quad. Suddenly rooms were not merely freshly painted, but centrally heated and equipped with state-of-the-art en-suite bathrooms. Even the JCR President's room/JCR Office, long known as a haven for damp and rodents (not just the committee) had become inhabitable.'[9]

It was not just the quality of accommodation which changed. Faced with growing student numbers and a tightening housing market Corpus had to increase the quantity. For much of the period undergraduates lived at least one year away from the main site, in a College hostel or private digs. The College leased or bought several houses, including Iffley Road, Banbury Road, Wellington Square and Park Town. New student rooms were also created at the main site, including the former attics at the top of the Fellows' Building and in the former President's Lodging after he moved to another building in the 1980s.

But more radical steps were needed and Corpus was to build three entirely new accommodation blocks. The first, in the 1960s, was the modernist New Building in Magpie Lane. It proved somewhat inefficient in practice. Living there in the early 1980s, **Penelope Curtis** (1979) described it as 'only ten years old and already unsung, even though it was designed by significant architects and built to a high standard'. In the 2010s it had to be comprehensively redeveloped, reopening in 2016 as the Jackson and Oldham Buildings.

The decision in the 1980s to build a second new block followed recognition that the accommodation problem was worsening, as student numbers grew and private housing became increasingly scarce and expensive:

In Corpus we currently provide accommodation in College or in College hostels for first- and third-year undergraduates, for those sitting examinations and for most graduates. But most second-year undergraduates and some graduates have to look to the private sector. The College is determined to remedy this situation by building or acquiring the additional 70 rooms or so which are needed.[10]

The result was the Liddell Building in Iffley Road, opened in 1991 (and followed, as we will see later, by a bitter dispute over rents). The year 2013 saw the third new block, the Lampl Building near the Castle: 'Forty-five en-suite rooms, in five-room clusters around a dining-kitchen, provide Corpus with some of the best student accommodation in Oxford, which means we can promise College accommodation to all undergraduates who want it.'[11] Private digs were no longer needed. In 1970 36 of the 175 undergraduates had lived in some form of non-College accommodation, but by 1992 the number had fallen to 11 out of 224, and in 2014 to 11 out of 232.[12]

Physical challenges remained. As **Christina Lee** (2011) discovered, 'when Corpus was established in 1517, it was not designed for wheelchairs', though 'the College did its best to cater and adapt to my needs'. But it was not straightforward:

> Every time I leave or enter College, I would wait by the gate for the porter to open the heavy wooden gates, a scene which I imagine may resemble a cat waiting to be let in the house, if cats had wheels, a pink/orange backpack, wore sunglasses, and occasionally carried loaves of white bread on its lap. Though they didn't know me personally, other Corpus students were generally keen to assist when needed, moving bikes that were blocking the pavement for me to pass.

She was allocated a ground-floor room and her tutors proved highly supportive. Nevertheless, access proved 'the biggest obstacle to my academic studies' and the new MBI building was 'the only building in Corpus which I can fully access'. She relied heavily on the College Library but could only enter on the ground floor, where she was allocated a desk to which the librarian would bring books. 'On days when I lack the energy to leave my room or when I need more books than I can carry, Hannah [Morgan] would even deliver the books to Staircase 12.' Making the historic buildings more adaptable remained a challenge, though by 2015 improvements were planned: the New Library Project included a lift, meaning 'those with mobility problems will be able to move freely between the floors'.[13]

Scouts

Day-to-day life was influenced not just by the physical accommodation. It also involved a feature which surprised some students: the system of 'scouts'. They were formally 'College servants' and the role carried echoes of the days of personal servants. The relationship between student and his or her scout was intimate – in some ways closer than between student and tutor – but clearly hierarchical. At pre-war Aberdeen the staff had addressed **George Richardson** (1947) as 'Richardson': 'but the scouts would never have said that. They would have said "Sir", and still do. But you mustn't think it's snobbish either. It's more complicated – it's an older culture.' As **Al Alvarez** (1949) recalled, 'My scout, who cleaned my rooms and brought me a jug of hot water every morning to shave in, was old enough to be my father, but I called him by his Christian name, he called me "Sir" and both of us accepted that this was how the world was ordered.'[14]

The work itself was traditionally hard – carrying coal and hot water, emptying chamber pots, making up fires, cleaning students' rooms, making their beds and serving at mealtimes. Although less well paid than factory work at Cowley, it carried status and an important degree of independence, within a hierarchical structure. The demarcation of roles was clear. On one occasion, **Tony Coady** (1963) encountered 'an elderly, frail-looking scout carting a load of coal. I offered to help him and was rebuffed with annoyance and some comments addressed to "Sir" that made it plain that he had his role and I had mine and never the twain would meet. It wasn't just an assertion of his independent ability to cope, but shock at my casual flouting of the rules by which his life and destiny had been partly defined.'

It could also be a job for life, with a paternalistic employer who might provide accommodation, and work for the scout's wife, as well as a wage packet. Several worked at Corpus for decades and became renowned College 'characters'. **Roger Horsfield** (1952) recalled Ben Standen:

> His task was to try and keep my rooms civilized and report me for any damage, failing to sleep in my bed, or serious misbehaviour. He told me a good many great yarns and especially about his service in the First World War in the Ox and Bucks Light Infantry. He said that he and his mates had filled with earth the mouths of two or three particularly unpleasant sergeants in the trenches, a matter which I have not seen recorded in any history of the war in Flanders. He was a conservative man and woke me early one morning full of joy to tell me that Stalin had died.

Nicholas Roskill (1952) lived in Magpie Lane, in a College house run by Bob Dickens and his wife:

> Bob was Steward of the College and much respected and loved by all. They were always Bob and Mrs Dickens: indeed I never remember learning her Christian name. Mrs D had a somewhat fearsome reputation and few would have dared argue with her. She served fried eggs to us every single morning. One of my colleagues disliked fried eggs which made him sick but he never plucked up enough courage to speak to Mrs D on the matter. So he stowed, it was said, his fried eggs each day in a drawer in his room. We never heard what was said when the eggs (presumably by then well past their sell-by dates) were discovered by Mrs D at the end of term!

Like many others, **Mueen Afzal** (1960) recalled his scouts with affection:

> The scouts dusted and cleaned the rooms, washed all the crockery and periodically vacuumed the rooms. Godfrey [Price] was

meticulously dressed and a man of few words, while Tom Trinder would invariably have a chat about anything and everything. Ben Standen, who had been my uncle's scout, kept a paternal eye on me, particularly when I moved to Magpie Lane. As a senior scout he wielded much influence in administrative matters. In June 1961, Ed Johnson was asked by the Dean to leave Oxford immediately after a particularly rowdy post-Schools drinking session, which had ended with Ed singing very loudly outside the house of the Chaplain the Revd Baker, who lived in Kybald Twychen, late into the night. Ben went up to Brock, pleaded mitigating circumstances, and managed to get Ed Johnson a short reprieve.

For **Bill Morris** (1964), they were 'such a vivid group of individuals that their idiosyncrasies remain etched on my memory to this day':

Ben Standen in the last of his 40 years of service, with rapidly fading eyesight, once made a bed with somebody still in it and at dinner one's plate was often whisked away with barely a morsel touched.

Their names still echo – Long Tom, Welsh Tom, Phil and Godfrey (the master of the JCR staircase). Stan Plumb in the Lodge was a master of that 'I will have you one day my lad' look (and one day he did, as I climbed into College from the Meadow). Bob Dickens was in charge of the Beer Cellar. He served from a small hatch at the bottom of a spiral staircase leading down from the Buttery. After flinging up the shutter at opening time, the first person to be served was always Bob himself, with a brandy glass thrust several times at the neck of the optic behind him. We used to speculate that Bob's optic operated a bit like the choke on the engine of a Ford Anglia – exactly the right amount of mixture would have to be drawn into his carburettor before he sputtered into life.

Andrew Thornhill (1962) also recalled Standen:

Ben was short and fat with a bulbous red face with a tiny nose. He was very proud to have been described in the *Daily Express* as a 'rosy-cheeked cherub'. He had been gassed in the First World War and as a consequence he wheezed terribly as he came up the stairs to my room, literally falling on the handle and catapulting himself into the room. He would then sit on the bed and talk about life or politics or the College. Little if any cleaning was attempted. His knowledge of the College was excellent.

When he retired, Simon Squires and I were invited by him to the East Oxfordshire Conservative Association to write down his memoirs. We were ushered into the Committee Room (Ben was a past chairman) and off Ben went. Pints of beer came in and were consumed. To our eternal regret we did not take a careful note or recording and our memories somewhat failed us when we had to write the interview up for the *Pelican Record*.

One story which I do recall was that of the Indian prince who had my room. The account went something like this:

'I went up the stairs to see 'im and there they were twittering away in the window.'

'Who were, Ben?'

'His concubines of course, putting up silk curtains and suchlike. So I says to 'im: "You can't have them," I said. "Sir Richard (Livingstone) won't have that." So they had to go.'

'Where did they go, Ben?'

'I dunno. Probably up to North Oxford I expect.'

He too recalled the Magpie Lane house run by Mrs Dickens. The Dean (Dr Jamison) would come round once a week 'and he, Bob and Mrs D would get through a bottle or two of whisky until one or two in the morning'. She was 'not only formidable but very intelligent. When one of her tenants was having problems with ancient history in the pass degree, she got hold of the textbook and asked him questions.' The loyalty of her former students was demonstrated when, after Bob's death, the College decided to give notice in order to rebuild Magpie Lane:

In fact, they made a mistake. The tenancy was in Mrs D's name and she refused to budge. Frank Lepper was dealing with the matter for the College and asked Mrs D whether she was represented. She replied: 'Here is my team' and out came an impressive list, Lord Pearce, Bertie Monroe QC (who founded the Corpus Association), James Holroyd Pearce, Bruce Holroyd Pearce QC, Mark Sheldon (later President of the Law Society) and lastly, Mr Thornhill. These were previous tenants of Magpie Lane. I talked the matter over with Frank and the College kindly bought 55 Lonsdale Road in North Oxford on terms that Mrs D gave priority to Corpuscles. Here she continued to see a stream of old tenants. She was a remarkable woman.

College staff identified strongly with College traditions. When **Stephen Linstead** (1959) proposed the first 'Ladies Night' in Hall, 'I discovered that the scouts were mortally offended at this breach with College traditions and I don't think my relations with them ever fully recovered.' **Michael Minns**, Head Porter from 1982, thought 'gowns should be worn for tutorials and things like that. I'm a great believer in the old traditions' and **John Nowland**, a former Lincoln scout who became Corpus SCR Under-Butler, disapproved of self-catering:

> I think that's wrong, myself. I think students have lost all respect for the Governing Body. You know, they wander in the Hall, they go out of the Hall, they climb on the tables. My idea is that when they came to Oxford, they knew what they'd come for, and if they didn't like it they shouldn't have come, because there was always somebody else ready to take their place.[15]

Some students, including **Thomas Nagel** (1958), an American postgraduate, were uncomfortable: 'I had never before been addressed as "Sir" by anyone, let alone by a middle-aged man, and I never managed to talk to them with unembarrassed natural conviction, but always felt and sounded vaguely apologetic and uncomfortable, which they must have found tiresome.'[16] The system was based on an assumption – increasingly a myth – that the 'young gentlemen' were used to

servants, and on the clear roles each party was expected to play. For
David Jory (1959):

> It took a while to get used to the idea of having a scout to take
> care of our rooms and us – something my working-class back-
> ground had not prepared me for. It turned out that our scout and
> his wife were both alcoholics, though this never interfered with
> his performance of his duties. We marvelled at how he could pull
> himself together when drunk and go and serve in Hall. His wife
> once climbed into bed with one of the Annexe students; he smartly
> got out of bed on the other side and fled. None of us thought to
> mention all this to the College authorities.

Robert Lee (1964) found it 'took some time to adjust to the role
of College servants and ancillary staff, some of whom had quite
a standing amongst the student body', and felt 'there was already
something anachronistic about the traditional College system of
scouts and "bedders" by the early 1960s'. His scout was Godfrey
Price:

> Godfrey, unless I am mistaken, had been cared for by Barnardo's
> as a child, while Mrs Davies, my 'bedder', was already well past
> the statutory retirement age and clearly enjoyed working for the
> College despite the fact that her mobility was sometimes compro-
> mised because she had almost certainly suffered from rickets as
> a young girl. In the 1960s, Corpus, like all other colleges, still
> operated essentially in a paternalistic manner as an employer of
> local labour.

Malcolm Underwood (1966) shared the unease:

> Scouts, it seems to me, were as devoted to the service of the under-
> graduates as in earlier days, but were unprotected (or unencum-
> bered as it sometimes seems) by limitations of health and safety,
> job descriptions and the paraphernalia of modern work. My first-
> year scout in whom I, as a rather lost freshman, found a helpful

kindly friend, would willingly have cleaned my shoes had I left them out each day. There lingered traditions of service which could be bewildering to the undergraduates of the 1960s, emerging from grammar and secondary modern schools in a greater wave than before.

Andrew Purkis (1967) took part in a history project based on interviews with Corpus scouts: 'One of the fascinations was the tensions exposed between traditional college scouts' value system of identifying with Oxford and its students as an elite institution, and the mores and style of late 1960s students affected by the zeitgeist.'[17] Simon Bainbridge (1968) was unequivocal: 'I am ill at ease today on the rare occasions when I encounter domestic staff, and [then] I was very much more so. I thought the system of scouts and bedmakers inappropriate and unnecessary and much of their work could and should have been done by the undergraduates for themselves.'[18] Mel Johnson (1972) felt 'uneasy with the idea of College servants and could never accept their help without feeling guilty. Not that they were insignificant in our lives – they were important, often better known than tutors. Beryl, my cleaner for two years, knew more about the vicissitudes of my love life than my closest friends.'[19] But despite such disquiet, David Stogdale (1969) noted how

> the scouts ensured Corpus ran timelessly on. In the Buttery Phil daily counted out and counted in the Georgian silver tankards from which we drank water in Hall. Long Tom and Welsh Tom cheerfully dished out the pies at lunch to a queue variously attired in kaftans, tweeds and cords or tie-dyed Kashmiri headbands. Sanitary Sid tirelessly tended the washing machines, baths and showers amongst the juddering basement pipework of 'Plummer' while every afternoon in the JCR Godfrey's teas were a dependable still-point in our turning world.

Some scouts still filled the role of College 'characters'. Peter Buxton (1978) described Godfrey Price as 'a scout of such immense age we speculated on whether he was a contemporary of Bishop Fox.

But he smiled benignly on us, he had looked after generations of undergraduates and had seen it all before many times over. For all our teasing, he was as much a part of Corpus as the Sundial or the old oak tables in the Hall, and we loved him.' **Farzana Ahmed** (1979) thought him 'adorable. I loved him and he loved me. During tea at the JCR he always reserved a nice plate of sandwiches and cakes for me and charged me half the price!' **Sean O'Grady** (1981) also recalled the 'delightfully quaint' JCR tea, 'run by the unforgettable Godfrey who, like the Queen Mother, was not as nice as people thought'. **John** and **Alison Vile** (née Hawkins, 1980 and 1981) thought Tom Blake 'a star among scouts', who represented 'a bygone age of the self-educated Oxford scout as he sat in his little pantry on Staircase 2 reading the *Oxford English Dictionary*. He did not view keeping our rooms clean as his top priority, and generally regarded his vacuum cleaner as being available to us should we wish to borrow it.' They too recalled Godfrey and JCR tea: 'Every afternoon, when we should have been more profitably employed, many of us would be lured away by the thought of tea, cakes and sandwiches provided by the ever-genial Godfrey, who managed always to leave you with the impression both that he had forgotten who you were and that he knew something you'd rather he didn't.'[20]

Change was coming, albeit slowly. Scouts had traditionally been male, worked long hours and done everything from waking students with hot water to serving in Hall. Their year reflected the University cycle, with time off for other jobs or activities in vacations. By the 1960s the physical toil had reduced as plumbing and electric fires spread. As the older generation retired, women were recruited, often part-time; and the growth of conferences meant work continued most of the year. **Margaret Scully**, a long-serving scout, thought conferences harder than term time and noted that it was 'nearly all women' who did the work ('I think it is just that the men aren't coming in for these jobs now. I don't think there are any men doing staircases any more'). College staff were also becoming more international: 'We are getting a lot of foreign girls coming now, Korea and all over, an awful lot now. Quite a few I noticed were Polish.'

But scouts, with their semi-paternal – or maternal – role, still loomed large in students' lives. **Margaret Harper** (1979) described Beryl as 'positively motherly'. With many students away from home for the first time, **Julian Roskams** (1981) wondered 'was it College policy, or just coincidence, that scouts had such reassuring names – Ethel, Edna, Beryl – with manners to match?'[21] **Margaret Scully** felt she got 'very, very close' to her students: 'We used to talk to them, used to always talk to them.' She felt one girl was trying to take on too much: 'So I said, "Join something, if you are interested in sport or rowing or whatever, or something else, but don't commit yourself too much. Your work's got to come first." Some found it very hard, especially when they came straight from home at 18 or 19.' For **Simon Preston** (1982) scouts were still 'a treasured part of the College community and held in high regard by undergraduates'. They were also a source of gossip:

I particularly remember Ethel who used to walk into my room six mornings each week at the same time as she knocked, to bring my half-pint of milk. In my case there were no embarrassing incidents but she used to say she had seen sights she had never expected before she started the job, and didn't mind if she caught me in bed with the Princess of Wales. She told me that another scout was less broad-minded and had been known to fetch a ladder to gain access to rooms. Peter Hore, the subsequent Fellow and Tutor in Chemistry, lived in College in his first couple of years of appointment. Ethel knew that he was my tutor and would tell me whether his 'lady friend' had stayed over and about the estate agents' descriptions of houses they had been viewing which she found in his bin. In other words, private information which I did not seek to know but was told by her nonetheless.

Ben Whitby (1986) recalled Joan and Margaret: 'I thought it an incredible luxury to have someone clean my room, and tried to be polite to them. I remember leaving a tip each term (I hope I did). And we knew that there were limits on what level of mess or damage they would accept.' **Nick Hassall** (1989) had 'a wonderful scout, Margaret Minns, wife of the Head Porter. We got on really well and used to enjoy a cup of tea, a cigarette (or several) and a chat in my room most mornings.' She turned a blind eye to his girlfriend. **Brian Swift** (1993) thought the scouts 'excellent. They were patient and kind, always ready for a chat.' **Debbie Welch** (1994)

> always had lovely scouts. My one in the first year was very motherly, which was nice. The one we had down in the Liddell flats was great too; she didn't complain even when we tried making ginger beer and it fell all over the kitchen floor and it was so sticky I think she washed it four times (we'd already washed it at least twice) over the course of the morning. We explained what had happened and she chuckled and said these things happened.

Perhaps surprisingly, scouts had remained an important part of Corpus students' lives. The other members of what **Kenneth Dover** called 'the Third Estate of a college', the staff 'who operate the Lodge, kitchens and offices, tend the gardens and repair or clean the premises', were generally less visible to students, though there were exceptions.[22] 'Sanitary Sid', the maintenance man who looked after the Plummer in the 1960s, was one. As JCR 'Guardian of the Plummer', **Paul Vaight** (1963) had to collaborate with 'that master of the underworld, the elusive and slightly sinister Sanitary Sid. We did not have a close working relationship.' According to **Bill Morris** (1964):

> Sid had a profitable line in reconditioned bicycles. I remember once seeing my own bike being wheeled across the Quad by its new owner, for Sid's early recycling efforts did not always seem to require the consent of the original purchaser. At the Ball of 1966, Sid was in attendance in a professional capacity, dressed in his smartest blue overalls. Unfortunately his role at this event allowed him full access to the stock of wines and spirits and before too long, women in elegant long dresses, found themselves forced to step over Sid's recumbent form, slumped on the floor at the bottom of Staircase 8. Sid was formally dismissed from office the next day, but reinstated 24 hours later, following special pleading

by the JCR (the nearest thing the College had in those days to a Commission on Human Rights, or, in Sid's case, the Committee for Endangered Species).

Other staff were less close to students' day-to-day lives, though JCR officers dealt with relevant office-holders. JCR Social Secretary **Tim Clackson** (1983) thought Norman Beech, the Steward, 'effectively runs the College, and it is amazing the number of wheels he can oil. He once managed to sweet-talk the Dean into giving permission for an outdoor disco in the SCR Quad.'[23] College Gardener David Leake was described by **Nicola Feather** (1981) as 'a man who intrigued us':

> One of his first gardening 'statements' was to plant black-and-white tulips in the borders around the main Quad. His slightly quirky choices of planting, and the fact that he favoured an artistically wild look in the garden, led to the undergraduate rumour that he was growing cannabis in hidden corners. We enjoyed such silly talk, knowing perfectly well that it couldn't be true: Corpus is far too small for hidden corners.

Leake's politics were very different from the older generation such as Ben Standen, who had chaired the East Oxfordshire Conservative Association: Leake was highly critical of Corpus's 'almost feudal' structure.[24] Standing as a Green candidate for the City Council, he lost by just 11 votes 'despite strong support from the Liddell Building'.[25] 'Improbably', as one interviewer put it, he applied to succeed Tim Lankester as Corpus President.[26]

Some students took College jobs themselves. As JCR Domestic Officer, **Greg Wilsdon** (1978) dealt with the Manciple, David Harrison, 'known universally as Harry. A firm believer in innovative combinations such as chips with curry, he brooked no criticism from junior members.' However, 'Harry became a good deal less antagonistic to me when I started working as a Lodge porter. It was as if this admitted me to the staff "club".'[27] Working as a vacation porter enabled **Steve Waters** (1984) to 'trangress/overcome the student–staff divide'.[28] **Ben**

Whitby (1986) found vacation maintenance work 'made plain a lot of the workings of the College, and gave me a sense of the effort keeping the show on the road. Not much money, but not much work either – we were told not to paint the rooms too fast!' **Brian Swift** (1993) also did maintenance, working alongside two former Cowley shop stewards:

> Our relationship was good and I fully understood the 'Town and Gown' mentality. We were so lucky to be there and they felt we did not appreciate it. I think they were right. In term time our friendliness did not change. I lived in Kybald Twychen and had to have a tap changed. When they arrived they strongly accused me of wasting their time. There was no reaction to my working for the College from other students, or none that I knew of.

The porters were more visible to most students. **Debbie Welch** (1994) found them 'always welcoming and helpful, and also ready to have a joke with you, which was nice'. **Rachael Wright** (1996) recalled 'Bob the porter who helped me smuggle my belongings into storage at the end of term, as Northern Ireland wasn't counted as "overseas" for storage but I couldn't bring all my stuff onto the plane'. **David Sooby** (2003) thought the College staff 'brilliant':

> I remember Dave the Head Porter, who was always available for a chat and would often look out for you (more than once he let me use the College car park when my parents visited on the basis that I didn't tell anyone – I'm pretty sure everyone had the same offer). There was Terry in the kitchen, who used to live in the house on the Iffley Road where we had several house parties, but he nearly always let us get away with it as long as we bought him a beer if we saw him in the pub on the way home. Bob the night porter was another College fixture and I spent many evenings chatting to him and testing the limits of my bladder after a night out. He lent me several CDs that I enjoy to this day and his knowledge of the blues in particular was astonishing. The College is and will always be made by the people there, not just the students, but the tutors and the wider staff.

Meals

Shared meals are part of the social glue of many communities. Dinner in Hall, with its rituals of High Table, Latin grace, ancient silver, gowns and 'sconcing', was an expression of the College community and its sense of tradition. As **Robin Clarke** (1955) recalled, 'except for some third-year people, dinner in Hall brought us all together at the end of the day'. The College regarded eating together as so important that in the 1950s 'the total number of those *in statu pupillari* is limited by the number who can be accommodated for lunch or dinner in Hall'.[29]

Until the war breakfast and lunch had been eaten in students' rooms. Now all meals were served in Hall. Despite rationing, 'our reputation for good catering has been maintained, and praise has been earned at a time when to avert complaints is achievement enough ... We now feed our own pigs and grow our own vegetables: at Temple Guiting, not in the College garden.'[30] Although rationing lasted into the 1950s, **Jeremy Hewett** (1953) thought the food 'pretty good':

> Meat appeared occasionally. Brussels sprouts were the mainstay and often appeared more than seven times a week. It was assumed that one of the College holdings was paying its rent in kind. Scouts attended breakfast bearing large urns offering 'Tea or Coffee, sir?' Whichever you requested was poured from the same urn.

According to **Roger Horsfield** (1952), 'the quality of the cuisine from the ex-chief chef of the Savoy was superb. I remember eating whole tureens of roast potatoes. And of course we quenched our thirst with silver tankards going back to the 16th century, left as leaving presents by rich commoners. I never heard of one of these highly valuable items going missing.' **Jim Griffin** (1955), an American, was less impressed: 'Some of my compatriots and I eventually solved the problem of what we took to be a health-threatening deprivation of red meat by dining in College and then going straight to a restaurant for a second meal – the Café de Paris in Alfred Street and The Roebuck in Market Street were favourite refuges.'[31] Not all

Americans were so dismissive: **Douglas Long** (1958) thought Corpus food

> was really quite good and very welcome after having sampled the fare available at that time at various establishments housed above the High Street. I still have one small menu card that lists Potage Garbure, Braised Beef Steak, Carrot Vichy, Chipped Potatoes, and Cheese & Biscuits. I was especially fond of the variety of cheeses served on the different nights of the week along with the trifle. I recall being introduced to Caerphilly and Wensleydale, as well as Stilton and Cheddar.

Growing numbers meant the introduction of two Hall sittings from 1959, one relatively informal. The 1960s saw the Beer Cellar expanded and snack lunches introduced. In 1968, according to the *Pelican Record*, 'we no longer have the monotony of the same food on the same day of the week. Our diet may not be ambrosia and nectar; but if we do not feast like gods, at least we dine like scholars.'[32] Hallowed traditions like High Table and Latin grace continued. **David Mark Jackson** (1959) described the 'quaint custom' of sconcing:

> If a diner committed certain peccadillos, such as talking shop or mentioning a living woman's name, he could be challenged to drink a quart of ale. If he succeeded, the challenger had to follow suit. Then, if he succeeded, the culprit had to drink another sconce – this time, three pints and so on, the loser paying for the beer. The sconces – beautiful silver tankards – were ceremoniously produced from the Buttery. I once arranged a sconce with Jim Celarier, an exuberant American drinker. I managed two sconces, which he followed, and then I departed for the Plummer, which I reached just in time. But Jim said he felt thirsty and ordered another pint.

By the 1970s **David Archard** (1969) and others thought such customs anomalous:

During my time the JCR voted to abolish formal dress and grace at dinner in Hall, and sconcing. The latter had degenerated into occasional (and well-planned) exhibitions of oafish drunkenness which dishonoured any pretensions to virtues of gentlemanly dining, and which merely seriously incommoded the College staff who had to stay behind and clear up.[33]

In 1982 **Margaret Harper** (1979), after dining at Worcester, wrote home of her surprise at encountering 'the uncivilized and ancient custom of sconcing … It all seemed very childish to us. Corpus, being a sensible place, banned the custom some years ago.'

College food attracted growing criticism. For **Robert Lee** (1964), 'despite (or because of) the Manciple's best efforts, the quality of the food served in Hall was seldom inspiring', relying on 'old favourites' accompanied by peas and potatoes. 'The Hall in winter was an inhospitable place to have breakfast, particularly as the fried eggs were often cold and covered in cooking fat. It is not surprising that food parcels from home were eagerly awaited.' **Vincenzo Morelli** (1972), an Italian who otherwise found Corpus 'an extraordinary, truly blissful experience', was unimpressed by 'the awful College food of the time. I seem to remember that the College Cook had spent his previous life serving in the Royal Navy, presumably on submarines, where he must have specialized in cooking stale food!' When **Beverley Patterson** (1979) arrived, 'I thanked God I had observed my mum cooking and shopping. So I knew how to cook and sustain myself.' **Joanna Wagstaffe** (1980) thought she must have been the first vegetarian for many years:

By the end of First Week I knew that the kitchen had someone who was very good at making omelettes. They came to the table freshly made and delicious. By Fifth Week I was tiring of them; by Eighth Week I never wanted to eat another egg, ever.

I went to see the Dean, Valentine Cunningham, to ask whether I could be exempted from the minimum dinner requirement. Without putting it in these words exactly, he implied that if he allowed this for me there would be a flood of disaffected diners beating at his door. Instead, he suggested that I might go and speak to the Chef.

I was lucky to get out alive. Formerly a merchant seaman, Chef had no truck with women and was scornful of any faddy nonsense. I should be grateful for an omelette and a different packet soup, he said, lovingly fingering his meat cleaver.

I was rescued by two lovely friends, acquaintances at the time, who declared themselves to be vegetarian also. Thank you, Harriet and Rod. Soon after that there was a new menu item: quiche. Also eggy, it is true, but a start.

Nicola Feather (1981) was also unimpressed:

We rebelled at being served minced car-tyre under a pastry crust ('Cumberland Pie') whilst plates of real food were making their way to High Table. It was even worse for vegetarians: dinner for them alternated between cardboard pizza (8-inch, tomato and cheese, no toppings) or, for variety's sake, a plain omelette.

Possibly, the advent of women meant that too few people were willing to tolerate these conditions. Briefly, there was a JCR Food Committee who met the Manciple with a view to seeing how things could be improved. My memory is of him snorting at our suggestions.

Happily, things changed in my second year and a cafeteria system meant that we were offered three positive choices rather than 'take it or leave it'. The crowds rolled in, and a delighted, hitherto irascible Manciple, rejoiced at being able to balance the books.

The switch to a cafeteria system proved popular, with queues stretching out of the door. Traditional dinners, with gowns and grace, continued on Sundays, which became more special. But the food itself remained undistinguished. **David Wilton** (1981) described it as 'simple and wholesome', but found it 'a constant challenge to avoid the tempting but unsavoury fare offered by the fast food vans'. **Louise Sykes** (1984) was mandated by the JCR to request a large bowl of salad at lunchtime:

A simple request to the Manciple was simply rebuffed. Other tactics were required. The first, which met with moderate success, was to invite the College Doctor for lunch. He gamely agreed and, perhaps not surprisingly, wholeheartedly supported the suggestion that salad would be an improvement to the diet. The powers that be in the kitchen remained unmoved.

A second, bolder, step was to invite the new President (Keith Thomas) to a standard student cafeteria lunch. He was a model of good manners, not only accepting the invitation but inviting me for sherry beforehand. As we entered the servery I realized I had made a dreadful mistake: the entire staff looked horrified – no one had warned them the President was coming for lunch. I began to wonder if they would ever speak to me again.

After the shock had worn off things happened quickly. A Food Committee was convened, attended by the Manciple, a Fellow who shall remain nameless (but who dealt superbly well with a situation that was threatening to run out of control) and myself. The meeting started in a jolly mood and eventually the Fellow turned to the Manciple to discuss the (by now infamous) bowl of salad. Again the Manciple stated his opposition – no, never. The poor Fellow was apoplectic – 'but you agreed before the meeting!' Whereupon the Manciple smiled, said it must have slipped his mind and yes, he was prepared to provide the salad.

Ben Whitby (1986) thought Corpus food 'of middling quality. It felt like school dinners. Formal dinners were better.' **Andrew Wilson** (1987) put it more strongly: 'The Manciple during my first two years appeared to have a violent antipathy towards students, which made everyone wonder why he worked in a college. To judge from some of the food served in Hall, he had an antipathy towards food as well.' By contrast, food at Formal Hall and special occasions was 'excellent', and in his final year 'the kitchen staff changed and the food improved considerably, before perhaps relapsing somewhat. Or maybe by then we had begun to forget how bad the food had been beforehand.'[34]

Meals continued to reflect their symbolic as well as practical character. **David Massam** (1989) noted a reaction against the loss of formality and tradition:

> it seemed that previous egalitarian-minded junior members had been unable to accept the rituals and privileges of Oxford. For those of us who had never enjoyed such privileges, the lack of them was a major disappointment, and so the new intake who had never known them began to press for their reintroduction … Consequently a gradual revival of formal functions marked my final year: Formal Halls were fully booked weeks in advance and Black Tie made a spontaneous return to the College's special dinners with Mr Bowie's incomparable bagpipes on Burns Night spearheading the resurgence. Recognizing the trend, the SCR subtly reintroduced gowns for the annual dinner to which Corpus treats her undergraduates, and extended a general invitation to begowned graduates to attend High Table.[35]

Brian Swift (1993) thought the food was 'of a high standard'. But expectations continued to change and Manciple **Mike Curran** observed in 2013 that 'these days, special dietary requirements – such as real and imagined allergies, coeliac diets, and the general rise in vegetarianism – are a complication for any kitchen, and menu-planning is much more complicated than it used to be'.[36]

A more fundamental change, however, was that students were increasingly cooking for themselves. **Peter Myerscough** (1954) recalled that in his day

> nearly all domestic activities were done by the scouts and the kitchen staff. You could certainly boil a kettle and make tea or coffee for friends, or even perhaps toast a crumpet in front of an electric heater but, apart from washing up the cups afterwards, that was the limit of any domestic chores you did. There were no cooking or laundry facilities you could use in College. I posted washing home each week, and my mother (bless her) sent it back washed and ironed together with a fruit cake.[37]

David Jory (1959) found even toasting crumpets discouraged:

Each living room had a two-bar electric fire to warm it (mine was not equal to the task) and we would lay the fire on its back in order to toast the crumpets – which is what I was doing when there was a knock on the door (I don't think I ever 'sported the oak') and four men asked if they could come in. I was introduced to them and one was the Bursar. I have no idea of the purpose of the visit but they asked if I was happy with life at Corpus, etc. I was, and said so, and then offered them a toasted crumpet, which was politely refused. After a few minutes of polite chat, they left. As the last one (not the Bursar) reached the door he turned and pointed to the electric fire with the crumpets on it and quietly reminded me that that was not allowed.

'Though cooking in rooms was banned,' **Julian Roskams** (1981) occasionally resorted to Pot Noodles: 'I guessed I'd get away with pouring hot water on dehydrated vegetables.'[38] College hostels often had kitchens. **Ian Britain** (1974) lived in Southmoor Road: 'Many of us – beyond the boundaries of this particular house – ought to be very grateful for the direness of College food in those days. It forced us to discover our own culinary resources.'[39] Former scout **Margaret Scully** recalled that in Banbury Road students 'weren't allowed to have a toaster in your room because all the fire alarms would go off. You couldn't have a toaster and you couldn't have what a lot of the Japanese and Chinese would have, these rice cookers.' But there were kitchens on each floor: 'they cooked for themselves and they each had a cupboard with their name on'.

By the early 1980s – perhaps encouraged by the arrival of women – cooking was becoming more common. **Margaret Harper** (1979) cooked fairly frequently for herself and friends, often using a slow-cooker. But fridges remained rare: 'our milk is off by lunchtime, even if you stick it in a basin of cold water'. **Rachel Richards** (1993) would 'reach out of the window to retrieve the Oddbins carrier bag hanging on the outside of the frame, containing a carton of full-fat milk'. **Ben Whitby** (1986) found 'there were kitchens in the New Building which

I used in my first year'; and by 1998 the Freshers' Guide advised that 'you can cook for yourself in the kitchen facilities' and that 'all the blocks/staircases have a kitchen with at least a sink and a fridge, and most have good cooking facilities'. This did not mean all was plain sailing. **Elizabeth O'Brien** (1990), Warden of the new Liddell Building, recalled being 'shaken by a loud bang from the kitchen':

> Apparently a student had decided to make a banoffee pie which required that two tins of condensed milk should be heated in order to produce the filling. She decided to do this by boiling the tins in a pan of water. What she did not understand was that in using this method she should first pierce a hole in the tins in order to counteract the expansion which would take place upon heating. The result was of course that the tins exploded.

Despite the growth of self-catering, communal meals continued to play a central role in College life. They were still occasions which brought students, particularly those living in College, together – if not every day then still frequently. Indeed, **Caroline Knapp** (2005) was struck by 'how many of my memories involve food':

> The queue for 'Hall' was a great place to meet people in the first week and to catch up with friends, but woe betide anyone who disobeyed the queuing system! Eventually, a kindly soul made a diagram to help out the many confused new Corpuscles. The weekly Formal Hall offered a very reasonably priced three-course meal as well as a great excuse to get dressed up. Subject dinners were among the food highlights of the year, involving a meal in the SCR Dining Room followed by port and chocolates. And then there was welfare tea – held every term during Fifth Week, as an antidote to the dreaded Fifth Week blues. When I joined the MCR a whole new set of food-based opportunities appeared – MCR exchange dinners, High Table dinners, graduate adviser lunches, cheese and wine evenings, welfare brunches ... I think it's safe to say that I was well fed during my time at Corpus!

Technology

Some physical features of College life, such as bikes and punts for transport, remained largely unchanged. Eldred Jones (1950) enjoyed cycling 'on summer afternoons to Blenheim, to tea in Burford, Banbury and villages in the Cotswolds' and 'floating in punts on the river'.[40] Over 30 years later, Eliza Pakenham (1986) 'cycled around in Edwardian petticoats that were soon stained in oil'. But other features, including clothes, changed markedly. College photos show jackets and gowns as standard wear in the 1940s and 1950s. But later generations, as Ben Whitby (1986) recalled, generally dressed more casually: 'I don't remember wearing gowns often and subfusc only for Matriculation, Prelims and Finals. Most of the time it was jeans and T-shirts and jumpers – everybody sending signals to each other as to their social affiliations through what they wore.' Men's hair became longer – and then shorter again.

But one of the most striking changes to daily life, in Corpus as elsewhere, was the appearance of information technology. As Geoff Goodall (1950) recalled, in his day 'personal computers and iPhones were still another 30 years off. One went out of College to a telephone box at Carfax to make a telephone call, but these were infrequent. Most communication was face to face.' Christopher Patey (1958) agreed: 'Looking back it is hard to realize that so much we now take for granted did not exist. There were no mobile phones, social media or Internet. Messengers on bicycles took letters between colleges. Television was in its infancy.' Even cameras were unusual. Mark Sainsbury (1961) was not alone in having no personal photos of his time at Corpus: 'It seems hard to believe now, when photographs are so omnipresent – hard to remember that in those days a camera was a fairly rare object!' Communication was by letter: Margaret Harper (1979) wrote home weekly throughout her time at Corpus.

In the 1960s colour TV appeared in the Beer Cellar, financed from a foray into *University Challenge*. Television – including favourites such as *Top of the Pops* and soaps – became a recognized part of College life. Rachel Richards (1993) recalled how, after lunch, 'a large group go to the upstairs TV room where they'll settle down for their daily dose of Australian soap operas and, if there's time (and for some there always is), *Columbo* and *Bush Tucker Man*, maybe even *Ready, Steady, Cook*.'

Computers came later. When **Pat Heavens** joined the Bursary in 1978, 'there was one photocopier in the College Office but many documents were printed on a Gestetner machine. There was an old accounts machine in the Bursary.' Computers were used for science in the 1970s and by 1980 had arrived in Corpus, initially for administrative purposes:

A Research Machine 380Z microcomputer (which we have got in the habit of calling a 'word-processor' – not quite rightly, I gather) is now installed alongside the xerox photocopier in the little room adjoining the College Office. The Assistant Librarian (compiling and updating lists of missing books) and Fellows and graduate students (writing articles and research papers) are using it avidly. But we can't claim to be pioneering visionaries; Balliol already has two machines, and the secretaries love them.[41]

In 1983 the JCR purchased a machine (though initially it 'languished from damp and solitude' in the basement of the New Building). By the late 1980s 'a suite of computer rooms' was in place – the first in Oxford – supported by a part-time Computing Assistant, Marion Ellis. The machines were used for administrative and academic tasks: 'Many Fellows do their own word-processing, many graduates type their own theses, and the JCR is equally industrious. With the recent connection to the University network, scientists will no doubt find a terminal in College to be useful.'[42] But as **Ben Whitby** (1986) recalled, for day-to-day communications the technology was largely irrelevant:

I used 'pigeon post' between the colleges to communicate with friends in different colleges, and be communicated with by tutors. There were a couple of word processors used for JCR minutes and the *Smallprint* College magazine. There was a JCR telephone which you could use (and be charged for) in the JCR Office (behind the JCR itself). And there was one phone in the New Building, in a stairwell on the ground floor with no privacy. I don't remember using it very much. I just wrote to my parents and agreed pickups at the end of term.

David Henig (1990) recalled essays

cranked out on a second-hand Amstrad word processor, which could then be printed in the computer room thanks to another stand-alone machine. The serious computer types such as Tony Brett were meanwhile mucking around with computer networks and suchlike that I never understood, but shortly would become the Internet and change the world for ever. In those days the main communication method was the phone in the Porters' Lodge along with written notes sent by intercollege mail.

By 1992 one Fellow was 'receiving and sending a daily average of three messages on E-mail', some students were word-processing essays, and at least one used an electronic 'note-book' to take notes in lectures and tutorials.[43] But for **Rachel Richards** (1993) technology remained a mystery:

Checking my pigeonhole is an obsessive compulsion of mine. Save for the New Building payphone with its lengthy post-six o'clock queues and an answering service that is entirely reliant on someone bothering to pick up the ringing phone and, if you're lucky, yell your name up the stairwell, pigeon post is the principal way I have of receiving and sending messages. Apparently a few of my fellow students communicate with their tutors and department, even tutorial partners, via the computers in the College IT suite. I have no idea how this might work – I'm not even sure I'd know where to find the IT suite let alone figure out how to send a message. And to whom would I send one anyway? Most of my friends are as technologically illiterate as I am. So pigeon post it is.

Letter writing was still normal. **Catherine Hasler** (1997) had 'not a

single recollection of writing to my parents – but I did, regularly and
freely, a mix of postcards and letters which went on for years after I
left university. I wonder when and why I stopped.' By the mid-1990s
mobile phones were sufficiently common for the JCR to vote that 'antisocial' users should be 'banned from all public areas of the College'.[44]
Networks were also spreading. In 1997 the MCR 'plunged headlong
into the twentieth century with the installation of an email terminal
in the little room behind the kitchen; members can now keep in touch
with one another far more easily without having to actually speak.
Mothers everywhere are having to come to terms with the fact that
they may never receive an actual letter from their children again.'[45]
New students were told:

> There are seven terminals in the Computer Suite and one in the
> JCR Computer Cupboard, all of which are on the Corpus network,
> which uses Windows '95 and has email and Internet access. You
> will automatically be given a network password, and email is free.
> If you are lucky enough to have your own computer then you are
> encouraged to bring it to College, where it can be connected to the
> College network.[46]

By the early 21st century this already looked dated. The rise of the
Web and ubiquitous technologies – laptops, tablets and smartphones
supporting a rapidly evolving range of functions – made instant
communications and instant access to information on any topic,
anywhere in the world, part of daily life. This was quite different from
the experience of earlier generations. Corpus had grown in a relatively
closed world where knowledge and information resided on paper or in
individuals' heads, and where communication – personal and scholarly
– was face to face or through paper. By its Quincentenary, a new global
communication and information infrastructure had emerged. The full
implications of this revolution were not yet clear, but were likely to
prove profound.

Corpus goes mixed: matriculation, 1979.
Courtesy of Farzana Ahmed (1979)

4

'A MEN'S COLLEGE WITH WOMEN IN IT'? GOING MIXED

Women in the University formed another world.

Charles Thomas

We were Corpuscles, and that was that.

Nicola Feather

The biggest single change at Corpus in this period was the admission of women. The College had been all-male since its foundation, so the decision overturned centuries of tradition. Even in the 1960s it seemed unlikely, indeed almost inconceivable. But, like the fall of the Berlin Wall, it appeared afterwards both inevitable and the natural order.

Post-war Corpus was, in the words of **George Richardson** (1947), 'very single sex'. Women were not in evidence, except for the occasional dance: 'I remember importing a young lady from Cambridge. She came all the way and stayed the night in College and came to the Ball. And went back to Cambridge again. Women were not conspicuous because they weren't there.' Only a minority had girlfriends. 'There was no pressure to become mixed or anything like that. The idea didn't surface.'

Schools and the military were largely segregated, so an all-male institution was familiar and comfortable. Many undergraduates had limited experience of women. **Al Alvarez** (1949) noted how institutional barriers combined with the gaucheness of youth:

> In those days women and men lived in separate colleges and meetings between the sexes were tightly controlled. No women were allowed in Corpus after 6pm and invitations to their colleges were desperately hard to come by. Not that it mattered since the girls mostly came from the same type of segregated, unisex schools as the boys and were equally shy and awkward. I steeled myself to chat to one or two young women I met at lectures and went through the expected motions – sat in a punt on May Day morning listening to the choristers singing on the top of Magdalen Tower or poled up the Cherwell while some studious young lady lay on the cushions and talked about Chaucer – but neither of us knew what to do next and that was as intimate as it ever got. I kept my tiresome virginity until the beginning of my final year, then lost it to a married woman, the wife of one of the older undergraduates who had come up to Oxford after national service.[1]

Geoff Goodall (1950) recalled Dean Frank Lepper addressing the freshers:

> With dry understatement, he wittily explained the curious rules and habits of College life. We all had to be in by midnight, when the main door would be locked and bolted until next morning. All women had to be out of our rooms by 7pm. As one or two students gasped at this, he added as an afterthought that if a gentleman could not obtain what he wanted from a woman before 7pm, he was unlikely to achieve this after 7pm. So there it was. I used to usher my mother, during her Sunday visits, out into Merton St at 7pm and on for a cup of tea in the Cadena Restaurant in the Cornmarket, before seeing her onto her coach back to London.

Nicholas Roskill (1952) noted the absurdities:

There was a prohibition on entertaining ladies in one's room after 7pm. There was never a satisfactory explanation as to why activities permitted before 7pm were disallowed after this time. I was once fined half a crown by the Dean for having a lady friend in my room at 7.15pm. She was indignant and took the view, not unreasonably, that a quarter of an hour of her time was worth much more than 2s. 6d. I may add that she later married: we are still in regular touch and I am a godfather to her son who is now a bishop!

Not surprisingly, **Charles Thomas** (1948) described University women as 'another world':

In Corpus one would join the Owlets because the play-readings gave a chance to meet Nice Girls from Lady Margaret Hall (LMH) or Somerville who were asked to come and read female parts. In general, these girls were so nice that, for a Saturday night out, recourse was had to another group of females: the nurses, who were less refined, reputedly so hard-up that they would do anything for a square meal and an outing to The Trout, and – at the time – available in droves for University males. More than one young man found himself marrying, willy-nilly, into the predecessor of the Health Service.[2]

Although College rules were clear, it was understood that not everyone complied. **Michael Goodman** (1950) recalled his scout 'alleging that a previous occupant had screwed the door to its surround to prevent ingress while he was entertaining a young woman from a local music shop. Doubtless they were discussing the merits of the long-playing gramophone records that were just appearing!' **Roger Horsfield** (1952) was amongst the rule-breakers:

Much time was spent on seeking ways of climbing into the College, by night; the most popular was through the spikes overlooking Merton Street. Some gymnast had managed to bend two of the bars with their ugly sharp points aside to leave a space in which one could, carefully, get one's legs and lower body through and then jump around 10 feet to the ground. Jimmie, my future wife, decided this could cause me a serious injury and being a very practical lady she found an alternative route. There were bars over the window of my room and this could be approached externally along the drive leading to the President's front door. I was fortunately on the bottom floor. So with a penknife she picked her way at the mortar at the base of one of the bars which could then be lifted allowing plenty of space for one simply to climb into my room. Afterwards the bits of mortar could be pushed back into the hole around the bar to conceal the illegal entry. This worked fine and several other undergraduates, one of them a future government minister, who had social reasons for coming back to College late at night, also made use of this route. A year later during an inspection this was discovered, the President was very cross, and I was fined. Like decent chaps the others who had used my illegal entry contributed to the fine, which was not excessive.

Later he fell foul of an ancient College rule on matrimony:

I recall marrying my sweetheart, getting her pregnant, in that order, and coming up to confess to the President that I was married despite the rule of 1516 that no Fellow or scholar of the College should be married. As I was pretty certain that all the dons had actually married their partners I felt the rule had become obsolete. President Hardie, a moral philosopher and serious Scot, announced that, 'while matrimony in itself is not immoral we have to live by the rules upon which the College is founded'. So I lost my scholarship and my long gown and received a grant for the same amount and a short gown in exchange. I then proceeded to have Christopher Evans [the College Chaplain] baptize my baby son Gyllmard in Catherine of Aragon's rose bowl in the College Chapel.

This was unusual. **Jeremy Hewett** (1953) described a contemporary as 'the only person who actually had a girlfriend! Ladies in those days were outnumbered about 7:1 and strictly confined to four colleges [*sic* – there were four women's college up to 1952 and then five with the addition of St Anne's in that year]. Hormonal pressure was intense.' This did not mean the single-sex nature of the College itself was seriously questioned. **Peter Myerscough** (1954) noted 'our relatively ready acceptance of the somewhat monastic side of College life', and thought it might be due to experience of military life. 'It was then inconceivable that, within a relatively short period, women would be admitted as members of the College.'[3]

In this environment some, like **Don Montague** (1954), had to learn new social skills: 'At school I had been a complete, total loner, with no friends whatsoever, hating parties and grumpily unable to talk to the opposite sex. I didn't know which end to start at.' He joined the Corpus Reel Club ('Reelers'), where he met someone from LMH:

> Our relationship ended when she went down at the end of my second year, but through her I had met some very bright LMH women, and developed, with the aid of Bob Dickens, that mythical Corpus scout, my 'sherry round'. Bob supplied me with bottles of Dry Fly sherry at 16s. 4½d. each (RRP = £1), which I packed into my rucksack, and I cycled up to LMH each Sunday morning to sell for 16s. 6d. Not much profit but a lot of fun – we still count two of the buyers amongst our closest friends.

Romance blossomed with another girl met through the 'Reelers', turning his last term into 'a long succession of parties and dances, that and rowing. We had too much fun, and I didn't do nearly enough work.'

Robin Clarke (1955) recalled that lectures allowed 'some much-wished-for contact between sexes, and nurses from the Radcliffe and other hospitals were always in demand'. **Peter Jarvis** (1957) thought the lack of women 'a bit of a shock to those who had come from mixed schools or spent time out of school'. As well as being 'few and far between', female undergraduates 'for the most part appeared to be ferociously dedicated to their studies and equally fiercely guarded at their colleges. Most seemed dowdy and awkwardly immature. The better-endowed ones, such as most of those who gravitated to the Oxford University Dramatic Society (OUDS) or the Experimental Theatre Club (ETC), could act like queen bees and practise being

Zuleika Dobson.' Girlfriends therefore tended to be imported from outside, or be found from the Oxford secretarial and language schools, or the nurses. 'In the summer, punt-parties lasting well into the night led to quite a lot of pairing off on boats and in meadows. But women were always at a premium, and the parties often split between those who hoped to acquire a lady, and those who reckoned they had no chance and decided to get drunk instead.'[4]

David Jory (1959) recalled that competition for places at the women's colleges meant 'they were brighter than students like me'. He went out with a nurse from the Churchill Hospital:

> In those days doctors would prescribe brandy to older patients, some of whom did not want it. So after finishing an essay one night around 2.30am I rode my bicycle up to the Churchill to drink some of the patients' brandy and have a chat with my nurse-girlfriend in one of the outdoor barracks/wards. All was well until Matron arrived on an unexpected tour. The only place to hide was in the toilet, so in I went. It would not do to show obviously male footwear so I climbed on the seat, bent down so my head didn't show above the partition, and stood there holding the two brandy glasses until Matron left. I didn't visit the Churchill again after that.

Mark Sainsbury (1961) recalled 'bird and bottle' parties, though the first was harder to find than the second:

> By the time I knew a girl well enough to invite, I was no longer interested in that kind of party. Women had to be out of the College by 10pm, and as my friend lived in London, and there was no question of money for a hotel, pernocation posed problems. At one period she would stay until the early hours and then slip through the Fellows' garden into Christ Church Meadow, and to my car, where she would gallantly pass the last hours in cold and discomfort.[5]

But life for many – probably most – students seems to have been celibate, even innocent. When **Richard Gott** (1958) heard in his first term of a Corpus student found with a condom, 'it seemed an almost unimaginable event, a shock to tender susceptibilities. Later, my susceptibilities were not so easily harmed. I learnt a lot during three years at Corpus – and not just about history.'[6] Homosexuality – illegal until 1967 – also seems to have been rare. **Tom Hassall** (1962), living in Iffley Road, recalled the 'sensation' when one of the residents was found in bed with a male friend.[7] **Peter Jarvis** (1957) 'had no recollection of homosexuality at Corpus. Perhaps I just didn't notice':

> There was an outrageously camp gay scene elsewhere in the University. The queer club was the Gloucester Arms, where the theatrical set (of which I was a member) camped around and women were made to feel unwelcome – unless actresses, in which case all was forgiven. Corpus seemed curiously innocent. I doubt if my medical friends had more than the vaguest idea of what a homosexual was until they arrived at hospital. Of those who came to Corpus straight from school, regardless of their inclinations, I reckon most arrived virgins and many departed three years later in the same lamentable condition.[8]

According to **David Jory** (1959), homosexuality 'was said to be widespread among the artistic community in St Ives, just outside of which I lived, but I was not part of that community':

> One of the boys at my grammar school had been 'sent away' for preying on little boys, which was what homosexuals were thought to do at that time. There were stories about a significant proportion of Oxford students being homosexual but they were based on gossip. Following some (uninformed) discussion of the topic one evening in The Bear, someone took us to what would now be called a 'gay bar' and was then called a 'queers' pub', somewhere near the railway station. Shortly after we arrived two large middle-aged men standing near us – dressed like workers, not students – embraced and kissed passionately. I remember being shocked and scared and leaving the pub immediately.

Shyness combined with female inaccessibility could mean

frustration and unhappiness. **Paul Vaight** (1963) thought 'a single-sex college precluded easy relationships with half the population'. **Robert Lee** (1964) wondered if 'the perceived need to isolate students from the real world, by limiting their nocturnal mobility or by restricting their interaction with the opposite sex (at least during term time)' helped the College's academic success; even if so, it had costs 'in terms of a wider appreciation of the realities of life at a time of changing social values and behavioural norms'. **Paddy Griffith** (1965) described himself as

> an embarrassingly late social developer, and a large cyst in the middle of my forehead during my first few months at Oxford made me doubly self-conscious. So I associate my years at Corpus more with the excruciatingly painful struggle to grow up and come to terms with myself and with girls than with any of its excellent intellectual or sporting facilities. As an undergraduate I was nevertheless able to sublimate this problem to a considerable extent through intensive academic work combined with a hearty physical association with Phil Hall's Boat Club.[9]

By the late 1960s youth culture was in full swing and sexual aspirations – if not, for many, the reality – were changing. As **Andrew Purkis** (1967) observed, this added to the pressure:

> If the zeitgeist tended to inflame emotional and sexual ambitions even beyond the normal concerns of 18- to 20-year-olds, the all-male college became the more frustrating as a living and learning environment. These forces propelled some of us to participation in opera and plays and other activities outside the College, but the ratio of available men to women was of course highly unfavourable, and for many of us our emotional and sexual maturity had to wait for life after Corpus.

Nick Witney (1969) described the all-male nature of Corpus as 'a source of constant angst except for those able to import girlfriends from home'. **David Archard** (1969) described his personal life as 'not happy':

My diaries record seemingly endless complaints about a miserable existence. Much of this is probably common to all undergraduates. Certainly the tales of frustrated, unconsummated, and unhappy love are familiar enough. I do think that Corpus, like all other Oxford colleges, suffered badly from being single sex. It reinforced the prevalent, and unhealthy, atmosphere of public-school masculinity. At the same time the College maintained the absurd notion that it was the legitimate guardian of our private morals. It is astonishing to recall that in 1969 women were effectively barred from the College – as fellow undergraduates, as guests in the JCR or as girlfriends entertained overnight.[10]

Richard Abernethy (1973) thought that, 'with my personality, I would have found dating difficult anywhere, but being at an all-male college in a predominantly male university certainly did not help. My love life worked out happily much later, but at the time I might have been happier at a fully co-educational university.' Nevertheless, some did find girlfriends. **Chris Patey** (1958) recalled:

Social life in Oxford in those days was somewhat limited. There were only two [*sic*] women's colleges, and years spent in a single-sex boarding school, followed by two years in a single-sex army did not provide much in the way of preparation for encounters with girls. Philip Larkin's inaugural date of 1963 was some way off. But I was very lucky. I met my future wife Carole at an adult education course in the summer vacation of my first year. We were to marry in 1962 and last year we celebrated our golden wedding. She would come to Oxford to join me on Sundays during term and I would meet her train, counting the minutes till it arrived. I still can't pass through Oxford station without getting a lump in my throat as I recall our meetings and our partings.

Ian McNeill (1959) met, and eventually married, the secretary of a Roman Catholic chaplain. **Paul Vaight** (1963) was to marry another student of his Chemistry Fellow, Robert Gasser. **Chris White** (1977) attended a Freshers' Disco at St Hilda's: 'Many of us had been to all-boys' schools and had never met a woman with A levels. This heady experience could lead to many a hasty judgement, repented of by the time Fourth Week had come along. In my case repentance has still to happen, since I married the first woman I danced with.'[11] As a postgraduate, **Michael Baker** (1967) worked in the Bodleian:

> The trick with girls was, discreetly, to elucidate from casual passes of their book-strewn place in the Reading Room what they might be researching or studying, as a cue for opening chat-up remarks. I was notably poor at this technique, making it far too obvious what my ulterior motives were, and so risking being flagged up as a kind of library stalker. On the one occasion when I was successful (she did in fact become my girlfriend until I finally left Oxford in 1972), I couldn't for the life of me work out from the books she ordered every day what she was studying, so heterogeneous was their subject matter. It turned out she was not a research student at all, but a lexicographer working for OUP on the *Oxford Shorter English Dictionary*.

In the post-war years, when segregation was accepted as natural in most spheres, the single-sex policy itself was largely unquestioned. Those who found rules irksome used their energy to find ways round them, rather than challenge their existence. Distinctly misogynistic attitudes were to be found. **James Whitelaw** (1941) was taught French by Dikran Garabedian, an Armenian at Keble: 'He had two hates – Turks and women.' **Geoff Goodall** (1950) described him as 'eccentric, benevolently mischievous and quite brilliant'. His seminars were 'full of wit, erudition and misogynistic barbs, designed to frighten off any women undergraduates bold enough to attend his classes'. When Goodall married, 'he ignored me, as a traitor to my gender'. **Roger Horsfield** (1952) had a tutor (outside Corpus) who 'refused to take "female persons" as his pupils, looked back to times when there were just 1,000 people at the University and grass grew down the centre of the High' – but was 'still my best tutor who set out to actually Teach us'. Less extreme but more widespread were the assumptions which made mentioning a woman's name at dinner an offence under the rules of sconcing, or the description of women as 'totty'. In 1969 the *Pelican Record*, reporting the departure of Kim Taplin from the Library staff, referred to 'her successor as Library "totty"', while the forthcoming marriage of Anne Wood (to Robin Nisbet) meant, 'We have now to report, with consternation, her inevitable and consequential retirement as College Secretary.'[12]

By the 1960s the exclusion of women was being questioned. **David Jory** (1959) recalled 'some talk of the need for [women] to be a "civilizing influence" in the College'. **Martin Williams** (1959) was JCR President:

> [One] hot issue we grappled with concerned the admission of women, not (or course) as fellow undergraduates, which was unimaginable in those days, but as guests in Hall. The JCR was the scene of impassioned debate. One speaker warned in apocalyptical terms against making any concession to women, on the grounds that if they were given an inch, they would take an ell. Other speakers thought this not a convincing argument. After much discussion, the JCR approved a modest compromise proposal, that twice a term, up to eight men could invite one woman guest each for Sunday evening dinner. The next step was to get the SCR's approval. I went to see the Dean, but he wanted a formal proposal in writing. So, following Churchill's precept, I summarized the arguments in the JCR debate and the resulting proposal on a single piece of JCR notepaper. To my surprise, the SCR agreed.
>
> The admission of women into Hall for dinner, for the first time in history, would clearly be a momentous development. So we decided to make an occasion of it. The eight pioneer women, with their hosts, were invited to gather beforehand for sherry in the Middle Common Room. The women all looked distinctly nervous, and the consumption of sherry was even higher than usual. When all was ready, we were given the signal to move down to Hall. It was thronged for the occasion, and High Table too was exceptionally well attended. My guest and I led the way, to be greeted by a veritable barrage of bread rolls as we entered the Hall, and be subjected to intense scrutiny, especially of the guests, by every pair

of eyes. Well fortified by our Spanish courage, we were unflinching under fire, and proceeded to the places reserved for our group at the top end of the central table. After that the intensity of the missile attack subsided, but the scrutiny was maintained throughout the meal, until we retired to the MCR for coffee.

Despite the bread rolls, Martin Williams's guest eventually became his wife. But as noted earlier, not everyone was happy. According to **Arthur Sanderson** (1962), Ben Standen 'was not impressed when the first Ladies' Guest Night took place. We half-dozen who were bold enough to invite the first ever female guests were placed prominently on a central table and served with a certain show of reluctance. "Arr," said Ben, gesturing at the portraits of the Founders, "those old genl'men would fall off the walls if they could see this."'[13]

This change, modest as it was, was followed by questioning of other rules. **Simon Squires** (1962) noted that although there was little 'activism' in Corpus and that 'JCR meetings were really quite parochial', they did include 'petitioning the Dean for some relaxation of women's permitted visiting hours'. **Bill Morris** (1964) recalled 'the JCR debating the vexed issue as to whether women should even be allowed in the Beer Cellar'. By 1966 the JCR could report that 'Despite determined resistance [it] has decided to allow women in the Beer Cellar at lunchtime, though the Hall still remains a safe haven for misogynists'.[14] Two years later, 'women were permitted to enter the Beer Cellar every evening, to the horror of a few who envisaged a female invasion'.[15] But change went only so far. **Julian Weitzenfeld** (1967), an American postgraduate, 'committed a real misstep while showing a female friend round the College, stepping through the door of the JCR. Another member of the MCR, who had been a Corpus undergraduate, tactfully took me aside and murmured that "in case you weren't aware, the JCR had voted down the proposal to allow women in". Apparently members were concerned that if women were present they would have to "watch their language, and such".'

By the late 1960s, as **Andrew Purkis** (1967) recalled, the debate began to move on from visiting hours to co-education itself:

In my third year, there was a passionate (by Corpus standards) debate in the JCR about the unnatural frustrations and distortions inflicted by an all-male environment, and some sort of demand was made of the College Fellows to consider introducing women. We toyed with the idea of a nocturnal 'exchange' of students between Corpus and a women's college as a demonstration to protest against single-sex regimes, but we never did anything about it. But the pressure was undoubtedly building, and those students who tried to defend the all-male ethos as something traditional, comfortable and precious, were in a small minority.

JCR President **Henry Hardy** (1967) thought the Governing Body's arguments against co-education 'so ludicrous that I wondered why they felt able to say such things'.[16] **Rob Stepney** (1971) observed a broad consensus for change:

> The 'overnight guests' question spanned the political–social divide since almost all were at risk – at least in theory – of being sent down if caught. And the severity of the possible punishment seemed iniquitous. There was clearly an element of College staff turning a blind eye to what was going on – to the benefit of all.

The College recognized the need for change. The year 1968 saw

> the introduction in Corpus of a late-key system. Such a system is becoming increasingly common practice in Oxford colleges. It enables those who wish on a particular night to return to College after the closing of the gate to do so by a civilized method, having applied for the loan of a key. A further alteration in Decanal arrangements has been a half-hour extension, to 11.30pm, of the unhappy time when members of the fairer sex have to be expelled.[17]

Ken Reynolds (1966) found enforcement becoming more relaxed:

> I never did manage to come to terms with the bizarre notion, in a university celebrated for its clear thinking, that suppression

of libido somehow contributed to the achievement of academic excellence. We were strictly single sex at Corpus in the supposedly swinging 1960s, and young ladies, however virtuous, had to leave the college by 9pm. Head Porter Stan nobly and indefatigably dedicated his best years to protecting us young gentlemen from the worst excesses of teenage lust by making sure that he knew the female acquaintances of every undergraduate. He daily counted them all in and then counted them all out. When one day a girlfriend of mine failed to pass through the gates at the appropriate time, Stan was instantly on the case.

A visit to my room gave Stan clear evidence of my transgression and I received soon afterwards the inevitable invitation to explain myself to the Dean, Dr Jamison. Following a severely cold shower, I started to worry about the potential consequences. Had I really committed a major sin? Would I be sent down? Was my fledgling academic career about to come to a dismal, premature end?

With considerable trepidation, I knocked on the Dean's door. 'Ah yes,' he said as he invited me in. 'Sherry? Very foolish of you to get caught, you know.' I admitted my guilt and muttered some pathetic apology, before he said, after a second sherry, that he would have to fine me. I braced myself for the scale of my punishment. 'How about half a crown?' I paid up with astonished relief.

Sometimes the rules were ignored altogether. JCR President **Mel Johnson** (1972) sometimes clashed with President Hall. Nevertheless, 'although we were on opposite benches in student politics, he was generous to me personally. When my wife and I were poor, unwed, cohabiting in Corpus and trying to beat off the cold with a two-bar electrical fire, Derek and Susan Hall were considerate and kind to us both; he ignored our flagrant breaking of College rules and invited us to a number of official functions as a couple, providing free meals and a warm fire.'[18] According to **Clive Britten** (1974):

The scouts varied enormously in their reactions to a partner spending the night. One was disapproving, and even threatened to report the deed to the College authorities: it would have been interesting to see what would have happened, but we put a 'Do not disturb' notice on the door. Another said regretfully that she wished she were younger herself, and continued dusting. Once, a friend was caught in flagrante delicto as a scout and an electrician opened the door. Whether they were oblivious, or wanted to cause the greatest discomfort, isn't clear: they casually said, 'Don't mind us', fixed the plug and left. I have particularly fond memories of 6 Magpie Lane, where in my second year four of us created a place which had a strong feeling of being our home. We cohabited openly, cooked together, brewed beer and seemed to be able to live our lives very much as we pleased.[19]

In the meantime, debate on co-education intensified across Oxford. In 1969 Corpus appointed its first female Lecturer (though not Fellow), Rosalind Hursthouse. President **Keith Thomas** later summarized subsequent developments:

Corpus was still hesitant. The JCR was strongly in favour of admitting women, but the Governing Body was divided. In 1970 they had allowed women doing Cert Eds (PGCEs) to become associate members of the MCR, but when, in 1971, a proposal was put to change the statutes to make possible the admission of women, it was carried only by 13 votes to 12, thus failing to get the necessary two-thirds majority.

So as an alternative to going completely mixed, Corpus decided on a two-pronged strategy. They would alter the statutes to allow women to be Fellows and graduate students, but *not* undergraduates, and they would also enter into a close alliance with a women's college, Somerville, involving shared fellowships, lunching and dining rights for senior and junior members, joint MCR parties and so on.

The Corpus statutes were duly altered in 1972 and the first female graduates arrived in October 1974, the month in which the first six men's colleges went fully mixed. At first, the women graduates were on a strictly limited quota, but the passing of the

Sex Discrimination Act a year or two later put an end to that. Meanwhile, opinion in Corpus was changing rapidly. In 1977 the Governing Body, which only six years earlier had been equally divided, now voted *nem con* in favour of admitting female under-graduates (20 votes for; none against; and 2 abstentions). In January 1978 Jennifer Hornsby was elected the first woman Fellow and in October 1979 the first women undergraduates arrived.[20]

It is striking, in retrospect, how such a historic change – deemed 'unimaginable' only a few years earlier – went through as quickly as it did. Few seem to have argued for the principle of segregation. Mathematics Fellow **James Murray** initially opposed on the grounds that it involved a quota system, 'which would have resulted in the women admitted being considered second-class students. The motion was defeated. It came up again the following year without a quota and we fortunately won with a considerable majority; women were to be admitted on a purely academic basis.' President **Kenneth Dover** described the final debate as 'perfunctory, as no one now was prepared to argue against the change'.[21] For Law Fellow **Peter Cane** (1978), 'having myself come from the co-educational University of Sydney, the addition of women to the undergraduate body did not actually make much impression on me; and my memory is that there was little resistance to this move to normality even from "conservative" colleagues'. Perhaps the underlying reason was that society itself was changing. Segregation of the sexes was under challenge almost every-where, including schools, and a single-sex community now looked anomalous – not, as it had done until quite recently, the natural order. 'The single most important consideration', according to the College *Record*, was 'the fact that with every year that passes an increasing number of people find that after graduation they have to work on completely equal terms with both sexes, and an increasing number will have had the same experience also before matriculation. It is no help to them to put them, between those two extremes, into a place where all their neighbours are of the same sex.'[22]

Clive Britten (1974) was another fresher when the first women arrived:

There were six women postgraduate students, and I happened to be sitting opposite one at the Freshers' Dinner. We were either side of a table, when an elderly man came and sat down at the end seat. The woman addressed him in a loud American accent, clearly from the Deep South: 'Hiya, hon[ey], I'm Susan Hicks; what's your name?' With some hesitation, the College President, Derek Hall, made himself known, struggling bravely in the face of shattered etiquette.[23]

Dina Gold (1975) was in the second cohort:

I specifically requested a room on one of the quads. But it was decreed that no woman was to live inside the main college because the bathroom facilities were considered unsuitable. I was banished to live in the New Building. Comfortable, but definitely not the same ambience.

On my first night there was a dinner to welcome all new entrants. Being an über-trendy Londoner at the time, I naturally turned up in my smartest outfit – over-the-knee leather boots and a skirt with a split up the front. To my horror I was seated next to the President on the raised top table. A split skirt was definitely not appropriate attire to wear at High Table and caused a ripple of excitement amongst the new 'boys'.

And that is what they really were to me, just boys. I was perfectly relaxed being around lots of men. I had been to a mixed grammar school in London and I already had BA and Masters degrees behind me. In contrast, so many of these fresh-faced undergraduates were straight out of posh public schools and desperately diffident towards me.

In the first few weeks of my arrival I would turn up in the dining Hall to find myself the sole woman there. I would sit down on one of the long benches and spot that places around me filled up but no one wanted to sit directly next to me on account of excruciating shyness. I vividly remember taking the initiative to break the ice. I tried striking up a conversation with the pimply youth sitting diagonally opposite me. On asking him a direct question, as, being no shrinking violet I was wont to do, he blushed and in a flurry of embarrassment and confusion, dribbled soup all down the front of his shirt.

My experience was that Corpus women students in those early days were treated with some considerable degree of respect – and indeed reverence. The graduate students were regularly invited to lunch in the Senior Common Room and I was very aware that, as often the only woman present, I would be asked to sit next to the President. It was little honours like that which made me feel I was somehow 'special'.

Everyone at Corpus – the academics, the College staff and the students – made me feel extremely welcome. I never heard anyone object to the introduction of women and the only complaint, certainly amongst the undergraduates, was that they wanted more of us!

Quite early on, I chose largely to ignore the fact that I was one of such a small number of women. I hardly ever saw those living out of College, and during my first year there was only one other woman living in the New Building with me, but it didn't bother me in the slightest that I was so often the only woman at an event. Naturally I mixed mostly with my fellow graduate students and pretty soon I became what I would refer to as an 'honorary man'. I simply joined in whatever everyone else was doing and I never felt excluded. I frequently would go punting, like one of the 'lads', and when they threw each other in the Cherwell I got chucked in too! I vividly recall walking, sodden and caked in mud and bits of weed, back to College through the streets of Oxford!

I moved out in my second year into a College-owned shared house at 25 Boulter Street. There was something of a frisson in the Bursar's Office about my request to relocate there because the other occupant was a fellow MCR student – a male. This was treated with some trepidation by the College – perhaps times have changed! I assured the Bursar that there was nothing untoward going on which might embarrass Corpus. We were not romantically involved and there was no question of any impropriety. It turned out to be a very convenient arrangement for both of us – we could throw off any unwanted attention from the opposite sex by pretending to be a couple!

The small number of women, and the fact that they were graduates, meant that for undergraduates such as **Eugene Dainov** (1976) Corpus remained essentially male: 'In the then mercifully all-male atmosphere of the College, one could always retire to the [Beer] Cellar and lick one's wounds in company after being rebuffed by some haughty female.'[24] Only in 1979 did female undergraduates arrive. **Margaret Harper** (1979) wrote home:

> Last night Corpus Freshers were invited to a party at St Hugh's (all female). In past years this party has worked by the cattle-market effect, but this year the St Hugh's ladies were rather horrified to find that our men tended to take fright and cling to the Corpus ladies. We, of course, felt suitably sorry for the St Hugh's ladies but really found it rather amusing. Very unchristian. One young man edged up to me and said in a stage whisper: 'Are you from Corpus? Oh, that's all right then.'

Looking back on her first impressions, she recalled

> being surprised when another girl (who had been to a girls' school) was shocked that I left my underwear 'on public view' whilst it was drying. It never crossed my mind that it was something to hide because boys might see it! And being a little disconcerted by how basic the Plummer was.
>
> I didn't expect much in the way of cooking facilities but they were paltry in the New Building. When I discovered that there was a kitchen in the bottom of one of the Magpie Lane houses, I quickly got into using it, thanks to one of my male friends having a room there. He was a great cook and I remember many happy meals with him and other friends. I'm not sure how I would have managed otherwise or how other people did, seeing as we were hogging that kitchen! We ate out a lot too – back in the day, our grants stretched quite a long way!

Looking back, I think it's surprising that we were apparently randomly mixed up in the New Building, with maybe a couple of girls on each corridor. It worked fine for me – very easy for sneaking back from late night visits to my boyfriend, thank you very much! At the same time, I was pretty bowled over by the speed with which the majority of the girls seemed to partner up with the boys – but then we did have a lot of choice. I remember Valentine's Day being a bit of a dilemma. One year I baked 12 gingerbread hearts for my 12 favourite young men!

The scouts' attitude was interesting. There was one fearsome female in the main Quad who apparently refused to be scout for the girls and I remember hearing that some scouts wouldn't make girls' beds. I thought it was odd that someone should make *anyone's* bed for them but that was what happened so I let my lovely scout, Joyce, get on with it. She seemed to have no problem with girls being there. There were other scouts, however, who reported people who were sleeping together.

Finally, I remember subbing for a male cox in a men's boat. I don't think it ever crossed the stroke's mind that with a female cox it might be a good idea to wear a jockstrap or at least some pants under his rowing shorts. Every time he came forward to take a stroke, he revealed all!

Farzana Ahmed (1979) thought the College 'not completely ready for the first intake of women – there were not separate toilets for women and the associated services that go with that. There was one bathroom per corridor if we wanted to have a bath – no shower facilities.' She found the scouts 'very kind but less forthcoming to support the women – at least the one on my floor. I would clean up my room and do my bed and she would come in, sit, have a cup of tea, do a little vacuuming and then leave. I recall her getting annoyed when I left dirty cups!' **Penelope Curtis** (1979) was another in the first cohort:

Most of the 18 women in my year quickly paired off with the men whom they were later to marry. As I didn't, I found more of my friends in other colleges, through the usual activities, especially drama, but also through the Ruskin School of Art, where I spent a day or two a week. There was contempt, at the time, for the stay-at-home nature of the new first year, and it was perhaps inward-looking, but I found its modest domesticity quite reassuring. The co-educational shift was less remarkable to me than the Thatcherite turn, and the sense, already, that we were in the concluding pages of a remarkable chapter within British education.

Unexpectedly, one of the women's early successes was on the river. **Boris Rankov** (1973) recalled:

> The change to co-education at Corpus was not without its difficulties. The integration of women into the Boat Club became a sort of test case. The Women's 1st VIII saw no reason why they should not share the Club's equipment equally with the men; the men saw no reason why the best boats, which were not available to male novices, should be used by a women's 1st VIII made up almost entirely of novices. In the end there was compromise, but not before there had been confrontation over such matters as the men's monopolizing of the drying room with overripe kit. In these disputes, the College authorities understandably tended to favour the women, who were challenging the status quo. Nevertheless, at times passions ran high on both sides. The Corpus women rapidly made their mark on the river and became *the* dominant force in women's rowing at Oxford.[25]

The MCR was soon able to report that the Women's VIII, 'frightening off opponents with Icelandic curses, achieved five magnificent bumps and earned a Bump Supper for the whole College'.[26]

Despite such triumphs, the arrival of women was not always easy. For **Penelope Curtis** (1979) 'it soon became clear that the co-educational policy had been imposed against the will of the student body'. **Margaret Harper** (1979) felt

> pretty uncomfortable with the attitude of some of the men who were already resident. Interestingly, I find myself calling them

'men' and those that arrived with us 'boys'. Looking back, it feels like our cohort treated us as equals (it felt very much like we were all in this together and I really enjoyed having so many good male friends) whereas a significant number of the resident men seemed not to know what to do with us. Very few spoke to me and I found it difficult to speak to many of them. There was no such barrier with the boys in my year.

Gregory Wilsdon (1978) thought Corpus was unprepared:

The 'nastoids' who dominated the Beer Cellar came mainly from my own year, the last all-male admission. They behaved almost as if they felt the need to stand and fight the last battle for masculinity. I recall a JCR motion to purchase a 'girlie' calendar for the Beer Cellar, towards the end of the first year in which Corpus had gone co-residential. It was defeated, but only after quite a long debate. Looking back, it is astounding that people were willing to argue for such an offensive gesture.[27]

According to **Alvin Jackson** (1979),

Corpus remained an essentially male institution throughout the early 1980s. Yet the College lacked, I think, the brutal edge possessed by some of its exclusively male neighbours (such as Oriel). When I was interviewed for admission, in the autumn of 1978, some remnants of an older dispensation were still visible – dozing rowers and boozy rugby-players sprawled in the JCR and in the Television Room. But I suspect that these were always a marginal, though sometimes flamboyant skin coating the fundamentals of College society. The introduction of women did not so much undermine any macho ascendancy as reinforce these fundamentals: humanity, introversion, quietly effective scholarship.[28]

John and **Alison Vile** (1980 and 1981) thought the last all-male year showed 'more roughness/aggression, heavy drinking and inevitably more sporting ability, as the pool from which to draw the talent was larger', compared with subsequent years.[29] Even in the third year, with 60 women (approaching one-third), **Jacki Davis** (1980) questioned 'how long it will be before Corpus can actually describe itself as a mixed college' and felt that 'in some respects, Corpus sees itself and behaves as if it were still a men's college':

> Rather than being welcomed with open arms, many women who come to Corpus are aware of a certain amount of hostility towards them, which, while not intentional, can nevertheless be hurtful. Witness the first entry of a female Corpus fresher into the holy sanctity of the JCR: she is not welcomed, but instead considered rather brazen and aggressive for using College facilities in the same way as her male counterparts. The atmosphere in the Beer Cellar has improved over the last year, although some still express faint horror at the sight of a woman indulging in such 'male' pursuits as playing darts or table football! The feeling still prevails that the male members belong there and the women are guests, welcome as long as they behave in the way expected of them. It is these attitudes, perhaps exaggerated to make the point more emphatically, which make most women at Corpus look forward to the prospect of a truly mixed college, with a fairly even ratio of numbers. True integration will not occur until all those who have been at the College while there have been all-male years have left. Until then, the idea of a men's college with women in it, will still prevail – among the women as much as the men.[30]

Nevertheless, co-education was being taken more for granted. **David Wilton** (1981) was 'largely oblivious to what was then the remarkably recent move to being a co-ed college'. **Nicola Feather** (1981) thought her predecessors 'had been the groundbreakers for women in Corpus: by the time of the third year of mixed intake everything, including the Plummer, was properly arranged. We girls felt no institutional disadvantages by virtue of our gender. Among the dons, there was not a whiff of the misogyny that apparently welcomed those who had come up in 1979.' Indeed:

The only times you would see an obvious separation would be the purely functional, for example, a rowing, football or netball team gathering in the lodge. Even then, the blend of College members walking past would ensure that neither a heavily oestrogen- nor testosterone-laden atmosphere had a chance to accumulate.

I'm guessing that, by virtue of its size, Corpus has always been a tight social network with overlapping work and extracurricular relationships. There may have been a brief hiatus when women first arrived but by the time I came up friendships were largely centred on interests and personalities, with gender as a side issue.

It would be easy to assume that those who joined Corpus from co-ed schools had the easier ride because we were used to inter-acting with the opposite sex, but the picture is a complicated one. Universally charming, Wykehamists and Etonians seemed always to be entirely comfortable in mixed company. There were others who had attended single-sex schools but who were nonetheless relaxed because they had opposite-gendered siblings.

It might have been expected that extremely academic men would find it hard to relate to women, but on the level playing field of intellect, they appeared to be absolutely fine.

Having been educated in the company of the opposite sex all my life, I regarded the whole situation as completely normal. It never occurred to me until now to look beneath the surface and wonder how much effort might have had to be made to present the image of cool unconcern as regards gender.

When you add the factor of personality (gregarious or shy; womanizer/man-eater or relational; eccentric or 'normal') to school background, the matter ceases to be amenable to analysis. All you can say is that Corpus was in every way a heterogeneous society. To an equal extent, there was no pressure to segregate, to mingle or to pair off. Everyone found their natural level. I am deeply grateful to the women in the previous two years for their contribution to this state of affairs.

For me, it did not take long for gender-blindness to kick in. In the second term of my first year, I invited a school friend to stay with me. She was at a teacher-training college, preparing to teach home economics. When we strolled into breakfast, her startled (and almost certainly, envious), reaction was 'My goodness, what a lot of men!'

I had to pause for a moment to adjust my focus in order to see what she meant – yes, there were rather a lot of them – then the image faded in the time that it took me to help myself to corn-flakes. We then went to sit down with my friends and I cannot now say whether this group was mainly composed of men or women.

The JCR, however, still felt like one 'last hangover from the past' with its arcane rules. 'If you got it wrong there wouldn't just be laughter or booing, but "disembowelment by ridicule", so I sat and listened as arguments were repeated or went round in circles.' On the other hand, the women winning a Bump Supper for the whole college was a success. 'In my entire career, there was never any outrage that women were "taking" men's places, no condescension shown to us because we were "only girls", and no suggestion that we were honorary men or token females. We were Corpuscles, and that was that.'

Geraldine Herbert-Brown (1985), an Australian postgraduate, thought Corpus 'still, in ethos, an all-male college'. But according to **Camilla Byk** (1992), 'we were one of the first 50:50 intakes at Corpus and I never felt inferior or second class in any way, apart from when a female tutor berated me for changing my name when I got married in my second year. That was my first experience of meeting a feminist. Up until then I was fairly unaware of any current inequality in education.' **Debbie Welch** (1994) thought Corpus 'was about 2/3 male when I went. However, my school had been similar (again an ex-all boys' school) so I didn't really notice.'

Going co-ed created new challenges. Some were physical: **Gregory Wilsdon** (1978) thought 'the arrival of women shamed the administration into introducing measures that male undergraduates had been requesting for years: refrigerators, better cooking facilities, a higher standard of cleanliness, lighter and more imaginative food'.[31] Did they encourage cleanliness? In a letter home, **Margaret Harper** (1979) noted how a (male) friend 'hadn't washed his sheets since arriving', so she 'stuffed them in with mine'. Later she reported a joint wash with another male friend ('We swear by Persil'). **Tony Coady** (1963), a Visiting Fellow in 1983, noted that, 'when I went to wash my clothes in the College laundries, I was surprised to find that there were never any male undergraduates doing their washing. Since the male students seldom appeared in conspicuously dirty clothes, I had to assume that the women were helping them out. Not an unqualified triumph for female equality!' But stereotypes were not necessarily true. A former scout, **Margaret Scully,** recalled one female student:

> even the saucepan she had been cooking with would be on the carpet on the floor, everything was a clutter and there would be cups and saucers, plates, where she'd had them all in and every-thing just left there. You know, she was just so untidy. It was funny, the girls were more untidy than the boys! Probably they brought more things with them, more clothes, more hairbrushes, all their stuff. I think boys were pretty good. We didn't have any really untidy ones.

Co-education naturally changed social life. Parties and discos, which previously would have taken place outside College or required the 'import' of women, could now be arranged internally, on a staircase or in the Beer Cellar. As we shall see, 'sweaty bops' became a staple of College life. But as President **Kenneth Dover** observed, new issues arose:

> To speak of the 'civilizing effect' of women on the College may sound patronizing, but it is also true; the hard-drinking, glass-breaking rugger-club set dwindled away. Inevitably there have been sexual problems. While I was merely annoyed, on an annual inspection of College premises, to see that the plaster on the wall above one woman's pillows had been pulverized by the constant impact of her energetic lover's head, I was more perturbed by a woman who was completely thrown off balance by the transfer of a man's affections to another woman on the same corridor, and by a man who had to take a year off because he was obsessed by a woman who had no time for him. That kind of trouble is

more manageable when the two people concerned live in different colleges. The effect on the cleaners was also regrettable. Some were widows with a right to be jealous, and they were not well disposed towards young women who did not sleep alone; and one did not have to be a widow to resent the behaviour of men who would leave a loaded condom on the floor for a cleaner to tidy up. Those, however, were intercollegiate problems before any colleges went mixed.[32]

Inevitably, there were affairs. According to **Nicola Feather** (1981):

Some people went out with each other, and some people stayed aloof from that sort of relationship. Of the ones who had boyfriends or girlfriends, some slept with each other and some didn't. I'm sure I'm not the only one who, without imagining universal conquest, hoped to meet 'someone nice'.

On a positive note, integration meant it was possible for the romantic element of friendships to wax and wane without any major show. A woman walking into Hall was an entirely normal phenomenon: her presence there was not an occasion for others to wonder to whom she belonged, and to what extent. We had the freedom to talk to whoever we wanted, whenever and wherever we liked.

However, in the social climate of the time, this freedom had its darker side. When in my second week at Corpus I needed to put an end to unwanted advances, I turned for comfort and advice to a female third-year medic from a different college. I suppose I was ashamed that I hadn't got the hang of recognizing and taking charge of dodgy situations. For obvious reasons, I don't know how many other female Corpuscles might have suffered in this way.

Farzana Ahmed (1979) recalled that 'having boyfriends over for the night was strictly not allowed', and that after a scout complained about one friend and her boyfriend, 'I "lent" them my room but then got into trouble myself'. Despite such efforts, Corpus soon saw its first 'College babies' – one to a Corpus couple and one to a Corpus father and a mother from another college. **Margaret Harper** (1979) thought the Corpus couple had to marry to qualify for College married quarters: 'But I do feel for the College authorities – it was probably one of the things they most dreaded and they did negotiate a solution so that both the parents could continue their degrees.'

Privacy, as **Ben Whitby** (1986) recalled, was another problem:

I guess about one-third of the undergraduates were women. It wasn't a big deal by 1986, especially if you had been to a mixed school. However, in the late 1980s the invention of sexual ideological politics gave us new ways to complicate the resolution of mutual attraction between bright young hormone-filled people. In a small college with thin walls privacy was not a realistic expectation unless you went somewhere else (and news travelled), so there was plenty of gossip.

Andrew Wilson (1987) thought Corpus's size 'a mixed blessing; not only did everyone know everyone else, but they also knew who was (and wasn't) sleeping with whom. Gossip abounded.'[33] **Rachel Richards** (1993) recalled how, during a fire alarm on her corridor, 'a door slowly opens and a pair of students, evidently caught in flagrante, sheepishly emerge wearing respectively an oversized T-shirt and a bed sheet (who knew they were a couple?)' Later she went to the Lodge:

Crossing the cobbles of Merton Street, I casually scan the bikes lining the College walls and those of Oriel opposite. I look for one belonging to a second-year student, a rower in the Men's 1st VIII, who has to cycle into College daily from the Liddell Building in Iffley Road. A while ago, he asked me out – after the JCR Christmas Bop – and I turned him down. He's become a good friend since but is now seeing another girl in my year (also a friend – Corpus is, after all, a very small place) so it's not like anything could or would happen between us now. Yet every day I find myself looking for signs that he's around and, as now, when I realize his bike's not there I feel oddly deflated. I'm not entirely sure why.

Gossip remained an issue: **James Kierstead** (2006) 'briefly ended up with two girlfriends, a fact that seems to have been known to the College community at large before it had become entirely clear to me'. But many College romances were successful, as **Martin Campbell** (1992) recalled:

> Meeting my future wife in the first term certainly added to the magic of the place. Avril and I were very much in the same social circle and with Corpus being such a small friendly place, we encountered each other early on in our first term. We courted, all very properly I have to add, during our first two years at College, and then spent much of the third year apart as I was recovering from glandular fever and forced to take a year out and thus spend much of the year away from College. However, we were married in the September following Avril's graduation. At this stage we were offered one of the College's 'married flats' and took up residence in Park Town where we lived throughout the remainder of my course. We didn't see our romance at Corpus as particularly unusual; amidst the many relationships within the University there were certainly others between Corpuscles at the time we were in College.

Gail Bartlett (1996) 'met and sat next to my future husband Alex Rogers at Freshers' Dinner, and we were lucky enough, some nine years later, to hold our wedding reception in College'.

The mid-1980s saw growing recognition that simply admitting women was not enough. **Simon Preston** (1982) recalled the problem of language: 'two of my contemporaries were the first women chemists at Corpus. At a dinner for all Corpus chemists, where the invitations stated Black Tie, they were aggrieved that the wording was sexist, so they wore men's suits to make their point. Dr Gasser was not amused.' When **Jennifer Hornsby** (1978) arrived as the first woman Fellow, she did not find Corpus 'a hostile male environment'. But understanding of the challenges – not always explicit – faced by women developed and it was after her return from abroad in 1985/6 that 'women's issues came to be properly on the agenda in the College.

The self-styled Women Tutors' Group was formed at the start of that year. I was one of four founder members, all of us sole female Fellows in our respective colleges. Before very long, there were about ten of us, meeting to consider how life might be better for women in Oxford colleges.' Their concerns included sexist language, sexual harassment, access to pastoral advice from a woman, nursery provision for College employees, and maternity benefits:

> I had an easier time in Corpus than some of my colleagues in other colleges. I think Corpus was the first to have a Code of Practice on Sexual Harassment. And very soon I came to be officially the Tutor for Women Students. In my early years in that role, Tuesday 'Women's Teas', which I joined in, were arranged in the JCR. Within a couple of years progress was made under nearly every head.

The JCR established a Women's Welfare Officer; and its President, **David Miliband** (1984), reported the 'highly successful "Women's Teas" bringing many women from College together in an informal atmosphere'.[34] One group formed Les Femmes Savantes, 'a female dining society, formed for the enjoyment of pleasant company, good conversation and fine food and good wine'. Their President, **Catherine Paxton** (1985), explained that its name 'is the title of a Molière play which mocks the pretensions of a circle of learned women. By adopting it, we acknowledged the impossibility of setting up a single-sex dining society in Oxford in the late 1980s with a completely straight face.' She saw similarities with the Women's Teas: 'Our decision to exclude men stems not from hostility or a defensive mechanism, but it is a matter of consciously electing, once in a while, to meet women in a social context.'[35]

Sexual harassment was a new issue for Corpus. In 1981 **Margaret Harper** (1979) wrote home about a friend 'assaulted on the way home from a party we'd all gone to':

> She was walking on her own. I was not far behind on a bike with three men. I think she thought we were closer than we were. I didn't even know she'd set off. Anyway, by the time we found her

she was in quite a state. Robin and I took her to my room as she lives out of College and plied her with coffee and then she decided she wanted to report it so I rang for the police.

The woman concerned was quickly provided a room in College. **Jennifer Hornsby** recalled the later university-wide women's campaign on rape alarms:

I don't think there was any single event that triggered the campaign, and I'm sure no Corpus woman was involved in any of the various events that may have led to it. The Thames Valley Police offered their services to speak to women in colleges about safety (about how they might protect themselves against male violence, as the activist women would have put it). And one (male!) police officer came to Corpus to talk to the women.

JCR President **Pushpinder Saini** (1986) reported that 'the SCR has always had an open ear to the needs of the junior members. The College has provided all female members with rape alarms and the Corpus Governing Body has become one of the first academic institutions in the country to adopt a comprehensive code on sexual harassment.'

Another initiative was a 'Corpus Women's Group'. Lucy Atkins (1987) reminded fellow students that 'whether seething Thatcherite or roaring revolutionary leftie, it is your group'. It aimed to counter 'the more obvious, and all too often ignored, manifestations of the Oxford "men's club atmosphere". The Women's Officer is there to listen if you need to talk, and to help you if you wish to take action, for example, in cases of sexual harassment. She is there to act as your representative to the grandiose Powers that Be.' The Group offered support, an intercollegiate network, and opportunities to 'learn about Women's issues that effect your life now, and will effect you in the future on both a personal and career level':

Feelings of isolation, intimidation (ever been to a JCR meeting?), or fear are common to many women. The Women's Group can show you that you're not the only one who feels like this. Even if they are just a good way of picking up offensive one-liners to shout back at builders, Women's events give a sense of shared experience, of legitimization and confidence.[36]

The JCR reported in 1993 that 'Suzie Palmer, our Library Officer, has finally managed to get a Women's Books section in the Library'.[37] In the mid-1990s the MCR elected its own Women's Officer: 'This post is geared toward dealing with issues such as sexual harassment which are of concern to women graduates'.[38] **Caroline Knapp** (2005) attended a lively JCR debate on whether too few women were being offered places and what, if anything, should be done:

My year was singled out for being particularly male-dominated, something that surprised me greatly at the time since three out of the four 'freshers' in my subject (Chemistry) were women – proudly bucking the trend! Despite the numbers, I never felt like a minority, and being a woman at Corpus did have one advantage – Women's Tea. Every Sunday at 4pm, the women of the College would gather to chat over cake and hot drinks. The Corpus men were so jealous that they demanded their own free tea and cake, and the first Men's Tea was held during my third year.

Ensuring women and minorities had the support they needed continued to be a concern. The 1993 Oxford LGB Rights Week led to 'turmoil' in the JCR, as it voted overwhelmingly to support the final march but saw some officers resign.[39] The JCR subsequently created the post of LGB Officer and in 2001 this post was promoted within the JCR hierarchy.[40] In 2009 the JCR established an Equal Opportunities Committee spanning a broad range of disadvantaged groups:

They have already been active in promoting issues of these minorities in the JCR, hosting a successful Diversity Week, with a themed Hanukkah Formal Hall and an icons board of people who have contributed much to the causes of minorities. The JCR Committee has also been praised in the student press for the number of females and ethnic minorities in positions compared to other colleges.[41]

Co-education was the most dramatic change at Corpus in this period. Women remained a minority, but a growing one: by 2015 45 per cent of students were women and **Jemimah Taylor** (2014) was the fifth consecutive female JCR President. In 2000, addressing a gathering of female Corpuscles, past and present, **Keith Thomas** had reflected on their impact:

> I have no doubt whatsoever that the coming of women has vastly improved the texture of Corpus life and made the College an infinitely more agreeable and more interesting place. The achievements of Corpus women, both academically in Oxford and subsequently in the outside world, have been wonderfully impressive. But in my view the creation of a genuinely mixed society still has some way to go. Of course, the frank hostility with which some male undergraduates initially greeted the arrival of women has long disappeared. Today there's nothing odd or unusual about a woman being President of the JCR or the MCR. But there has not yet been a female President of the College, and Corpus, like the rest of Oxford, still has a relatively masculine feel about it.

Women, he pointed out, remained a minority amongst both Fellows (30 men and 5 women) and Junior Members (196 men and 107 women). The ratio of women undergraduates was below the University average, not helped by the position in the sciences and the College's decision to drop modern languages. He even questioned whether the competitive character of academic life was 'intrinsically masculine'. If so, 'perhaps the true integration of women into Oxford requires some rethinking of the nature and character of academic study itself'. But he concluded on a positive note:

> Yet, though there is still some progress to be made, we have come an enormous way in the last 25 years; the College has been spectacularly enriched and transformed by the admission of women. When I look around today and think that, if those votes in the Corpus Governing Body in the 1970s had gone the other way, then none of you would be sitting here today, I realize how much we all have to celebrate.[42]

Corpus Library, 2014. *Courtesy of Patrick Meyer Higgins (2005)*

5

'ALWAYS SOMETHING UNREAD':
UNDERGRADUATE STUDY

*Suddenly, in the spring before Finals, the fog cleared and all
seemed to make sense at last. But it was a close-run thing.*

Jonathan Dancy

Looking back, it was a sort of athletics course for the brain.

Sean O'Grady

Study was central to students' lives. Though some were more academically ambitious than others, lectures, reading, tutorials and the ubiquitous 'essay crisis' were universal experiences. Their cycles set the rhythm
of university life, culminating in the extraordinary experience of Finals.

In most universities there was a clear distinction between where
students lived – often a hall of residence – and the department or
faculty where they studied. Social life might revolve around either,
or around university clubs. In Oxford, by contrast, colleges played
a leading role in both academic and social life. Although University
faculties were vital – setting syllabi, arranging lectures, laboratories
and libraries, managing examinations – the colleges remained central
to the academic life of students, especially undergraduates. They
applied to and were selected by the college, were directed by college

tutors, and commonly – though not always – attended tutorials in college, did much of their work in their room or the college library, and worked most closely with college contemporaries in the same discipline. The degree of overlap between 'college' and 'study' varied between disciplines – and was becoming more difficult to sustain as ever-greater specialization increased the importance of faculties. Nevertheless, the college's central role in their academic life reinforced its position as the prime 'community' to which students belonged and with which they identified. It was a role Corpus took seriously.

Reputation

Corpus had a proud – indeed, formidable – academic reputation. As a Balliol student in the 1950s, **Christopher Taylor** had thought it 'a college to be reckoned with':

> I heard of men who read the *Classical Quarterly* at breakfast; perhaps the reader was the Corpus man who had an article on Parmenides published in CQ while still an undergraduate. Then there was the legendary Gerald Toomer, who was reported to run a continuous classical seminar in the Junior Library, and who certainly prepared for a vacation trip to Turkey by immersing himself in medieval Turkish epic poetry, on the ground that it was the only Turkish literature worth reading. When I arrived at Corpus in 1963 I found that it was all true.

Al Alvarez (1949), who studied English, thought Corpus 'above all a Greats college, although mathematics was acceptable and PPE (philosophy, politics and economics), history and the sciences were tolerated – more or less. English was not considered to be a serious academic discipline; it was like geology or forestry, a subject you read if you weren't up to anything more demanding.' In contrast to Balliol's 'intellectual swank', Corpus was 'studious and small':

> Classics was a four-year course: two years of Greek and Latin literature and ancient history (called 'Mods') followed by two years of

philosophy ('Greats'). Then, if your results were good enough, you sat the civil service exams and went on to run the country from the back rooms of Whitehall. It was a demanding course and it didn't leave much time for fun. In fact, it hardly seemed to leave much time for Oxford. Most of the Classics students ground away for their Mods dutifully, as though they were still at school, and once they got going on Greats they behaved as if they were already in the civil service. If they were oarsmen they got drunk at Bump Suppers, because that was the conventional thing to do, although little else seemed to brighten their lives. Perhaps Oxford and its irresponsibility hit them during the long vacation between Mods and Greats, but they weren't around in the vacations, so who could ever tell?[1]

Corpus was never simply a Classics, or 'arts', college. Even in 1950, only 70 out of 134 undergraduates studied subjects which by 2015 were classified as 'humanities'. By 2014 it was 81 out of 243, with 72 studying 'mathematical and physical sciences' and the rest spread between 'social', 'life and environmental', and 'medical' sciences.[2] But there was some truth in Alvarez's picture. Even in the 21st century, as Fellow **Tim Whitmarsh** observed, Corpus enjoyed 'worldwide fame as a hub for the study of the ancient world'.[3] And **John Harrison** (1950) recognized its sober, hard-working, reputation: 'We were, I think, a level-headed, conscientious, docile group, accepting without thought of revolt the rules of the institution and enjoying the routine of work, which in my case was little different from school.' **John Whale** (1951) thought Corpus 'a serious-minded college, peopled with intending professionals: lawyers, teachers, doctors, civil servants'.[4] 'Serious-minded' was off-putting to some but attractive to others. The *Pelican Record* noted in 1969 that 'a lot of outsiders still regard [Corpus] as a stuffy little college full of grey academics, exceptional only in its ability to scale the heights of the Norrington Table (though why this should be a black mark against it, I can't think!)'[5] **William Waldegrave** (1965) saw it more positively:

Also attractive about Corpus was a certain intellectual austerity of style. One felt this with Hardie and Nisbet, though austerity is perhaps too mild a word for Fraenkel. Corpus wasn't intellectually flash. It was very good alpha scholarship, but it didn't show off, didn't think it smart. Its mood was perhaps slightly puritan, reflecting the tone of our great Scottish classical scholars. I found this attractive and congenial.[6]

Fellow **Peter Cane** thought Corpus 'self-confident and unpretentious'. President **Keith Thomas** appreciated the College's 'atmosphere of relative ease and informality', thought the students and tutors 'hard-working and serious', and was 'mystified at the College's reputation for eccentrics'.[7] **Nick Hassall** (1989) thought Corpus 'a serious place, almost everyone worked hard and was proud of its place in the upper echelons of the Norrington Table. This was a good thing, but it also meant that Corpus definitely wasn't regarded as a "fun" college.' For **Andrew Wilson** (1987), Corpus was 'close-knit, renowned for Classics, rather left-wing and tolerant of minorities':

Corpus's reputation for Classics was one of the reasons I applied there, but I was nevertheless unprepared for seeing that reputation in action. Several times I was astonished to see a look of awe cross the face of a student – and not always a fresher, either – from another college when they heard I was a Corpus classicist. I felt something of a fraud, as I had done little personally to justify this, but at the same time I felt privileged to belong to a college that was able to create this effect.[8]

Tutorials

Tutorials formed the cornerstone of undergraduate teaching. According to **Robin Smith** (1985), they involved 'producing one or two essays per week based on the reading of a selection of material from an enormous list – the amount of work which is supposed to be covered might appear quite staggering at first'. The point wasn't to accrue information: the focus was on 'questions of fact and interpretation being grasped and analysed, criticized and evaluated but never humbly accepted at face value'. The role of the tutor was not to 'teach' the subject, as at school, but 'to teach the student the approach to the subject'.[9] History Fellow **John Watts** agreed: 'What we don't do – really – is teach. Teaching does not happen in universities, except in the rather rarefied sense that we all, as students, teach ourselves.' Learning was ultimately individual:

> Students come together to share ideas and criticisms, but they do their real work by themselves – reading, thinking, writing, evaluating their own work, realizing what it is they were trying to say, what it is they don't quite accept or understand in what someone else is saying, and so on. We learn by trying things, getting lots wrong, trying again, getting less wrong (or some things right and different things wrong). Others judge us, positively and negatively, but we really learn by forming our own judgement.[10]

Tutorials usually lasted an hour, and were held singly or in pairs. Traditionally, the student read out the essay which would be discussed, questioned and challenged. Increasingly, helped by the advent of word processing, essays would be handed in beforehand – though **Rob Batho** (1964) recalled Brian Harrison 'asking for essays before the weekly tutorial' and returning them with 'detailed typed comments' as early as the mid-1960s. Fellow **James Howard-Johnston** defended the system robustly against the charge that its time-consuming nature diverted dons from research: 'the aged brain is kept alert and sharp by the energetic and ingenious arguments of the young. Fresh ideas take shape, which may one day infuse research … Tutor and pupil are equals in discussion, save that usually, although by no means always, the tutor knows a little more.' For the undergraduate, 'there can be no better education than the regular round of reading and thinking about a topic, writing a 2,000–3,000 word essay and then discussing it with an established scholar or scientist. It is this process of ingestion, digestion, argumentation, repeated week after week for three or four years, which hones the minds of the young.'[11]

This meant lectures were less central than in most universities. All too often they were ignored. **Francis Oakley** (1950) thought 'the average Oxford lecture, however informative, came through as flaccid in construction and ineffective in delivery'. **Gerry Hughes** (1952) found them 'tedious and unappetizing. I missed the friendly interplay of the classroom and as there were few good-looking girls in the lectures I soon dismissed them as a learning mechanism. In fact after Mods I didn't attend a single lecture in my own subject, though I did go to some outside it when I knew the lecturer had a good reputation.'

Lectures, seminars and practicals were more important in the sciences. And the need to raise lecturing standards was recognized, not least by President Kenneth Dover who chaired a University review in the 1980s.[12] In retrospect, some felt they had dismissed lectures too readily. **Roger Horsfield** (1952) 'went to very few lectures, which I now regret deeply'. **Ian McNeill** (1959) concurred: 'My big mistake at Oxford was not to attend lectures in subjects outside the field of modern history. The weekly tussles between Christopher Hill and Hugh Trevor-Roper were fascinating, but how much I could have learned about law and philosophy, let alone about physics!'

The transition from school was easier for some than others. **Francis Oakley** (1950) found it 'smoother than I had anticipated'. This reflected the teaching at his Liverpool grammar school: 'as I listened to the essays of my fellow tutees and nervously gauged what I might be up against, to my surprise I came to the conclusion that I had some advantages'. For **Don Montague** (1954), 'the first-year Maths syllabus had been a doddle, thanks to Manchester Grammar School, and the first year (of only two) of engineering had been a coasting-along exercise, based on what I had done at Salford Royal Technical College'. But **for Bill Gunn** (1965),

it came as an early shock to discover that I was 'on my own', swimming in scholastic waters significantly deeper than I had anticipated, with companions who were demonstrably brighter, better prepared and harder-working than myself. Writing a weekly essay of the standard and length required was not the bland, perfunctory exercise I had been accustomed to in the sixth form, nor was it an undertaking completed in an undemanding couple of hours. How vividly I remember the rising panic which accompanied my first production, which took all of a night and the better part of a day to complete and which, while superficially stretched to what I presumed was a respectable length, was still decidedly below par in every component on delivery. That all-night session rapidly became a pattern for my early terms, working in judicious time toward deadlines never being my strongest suit, then as now. Six days of the week would pass innocuously by, before urgent reality set in on that sixth afternoon: a 24-hour slog, relieved only by a midnight trip to the hot dog van in St Giles', would then ensue before the Aston tutorial; and then, a blessed sleep.

Jim Waterhouse (1963) worried about his first tutorial.

However, it turned out to be far less of an ordeal than I had imagined, even though it was on a one-to-one basis ... there was no place to hide! Never before had I been referred to as 'a gentleman', and certainly never consulted as to what topics I might like to study for the following week, with suggestions being made – advice was offered no more strongly than that – that I might consult certain books and articles.

He was encouraged to 'read around' the subject, but found the literature vast.

When I wrote my essay for the following week's tutorial, my tutor read it and then, instead of giving me a mark, repeatedly asked me: 'Why?' 'What is the evidence for this?' I had never thought to doubt if something I had read was true, but learning (I hope) to be able to assess the worth of the written word turned out to be one of the most important lessons I ever learned.

A huge amount depended on the relationship between tutor and student. It was not always positive. According to **Geoff Dyer** (1977), 'I saw my tutor once a week – an irritating intrusion on his time and an unenlightening use of mine.'[13] **John Harrison** (1950) found Classical Mods 'a disappointment':

Prose composition and Unseens were the backbone of the work. In the few classes which we had we simply translated in turn. The emphasis in the study of special texts was largely philological. Professor Fraenkel on Horace was exhilarating, but Burton on Antigone was excruciating. We read a mass of prescribed books with no discussion of their literary interest or merit. I was very envious of my friends who were reading English, that they had so much to discuss.

Bill Morris (1964) described his academic career as 'something of a disaster':

Corpus had no Engineering Fellow and I and Peter Anderton were farmed out to any number of tutors at other colleges. As a 'foreigner' they seemed to have no interest in me and, as a result, my early enthusiasm soon evaporated, to be replaced by a sense of drudgery which was to last for the next three years. I thought then, and still do now, that the standard of teaching and lecturing was really quite dreadful. I discovered how to learn, but at no stage did I enjoy, as my friends did, the pleasure of being taught. I still envy those who had a close relationship with a single tutor; I know it would have made a big difference to me. In fact, my only pleasing memory of the Engineering Department is the view from the library on the top floor. It is one of the finest in Oxford and I sought solace there on many a dreary day.

Andrew Purkis (1967) complained about one external tutor:

Some of us were farmed out to a don at Oriel called Christopher Seton-Watson, who had perhaps lost his way. At any rate, his tutorials were very poor, with long silences punctuated by vacuous comments such as 'Bismarck – great conservative statesman', followed by renewed silence. Then we were sent out very early from one tutorial because a friend had called round on Christopher for a drink, and we complained to Brian Harrison. To his great credit, despite the embarrassment, Brian (supported by Trevor Aston) immediately 'sacked' Seton-Watson and sent us to Tim Mason, a friend of his, who had a profound impact on me and a couple of others at Corpus.

Simon Bainbridge (1968) found Mods and Greats 'duller than I had believed possible. This was nobody's fault, except perhaps my own for choosing it and then persevering with it so cackhandedly.'[14] **Richard Abernethy** (1973) stuck with Law, despite the fact that 'I never felt any real passion for my subject. The kind of learning I was doing in my political life seemed more important at the time and still does so today. Today, the area of law that I know best is employment law, which was not covered in the course.' Others, frustrated by the subject or the tutor or both, decided to switch course. **Michael Goodman** (1950) studied PPE: 'After grappling, in a rather illogical manner, with "Logic" and the writings of a gentleman named Wittgenstein, I decided I would rather change to reading Jurisprudence.' **Don Montague** (1954) found his maths tutorials 'painful'. 'Why I could not perform or get on with my tutor, Jim Mauldon, I do not know. I used to come out of tutorials feeling angry, with him or myself, and frustrated, dreading the next. In retrospect I guess he must have found me difficult and unsatisfying to deal with.' After Mods 'it was blindingly clear to me that I did not want to read Mathematics', and he negotiated a switch to Engineering. **Patrick Bourdillon** (1964) also switched from maths: 'I knew I was out of place when the real mathematicians were exchanging exciting mathematical teasers up and down the breakfast table in Hall while I was wondering about the batting order for the afternoon's game. Medicine somehow seemed more practical.'[15]

There were other criticisms. Although **Robert Lee** (1964) considered his tutors 'excellent', he benefited from the fact 'that I was genuinely interested in their respective areas of research and keen to do well':

But the dominant teaching system, whether at the College or University level, was far from perfect: in many respects the History syllabus was in need of serious reform; the quality of some of the Faculty of Modern History's lectures was sometimes poor; and the tutorial system, whatever its intrinsic academic merits, could be inflexible and counter-productive particularly if the working relationship between a Fellow and an undergraduate ever broke down. There was no emphasis on the potential benefits of teamwork or the need to acquire what today would be recognized as 'soft skills'.

Nevertheless, most Corpuscles were deeply impressed by the quality of their tutors. **Peter Waterfield** (1946) recalled that 'my tutor Michael Wallace-Hadrill set me impossible quantities of reading, but with an occasional encouraging alpha minus encouraged me to try harder and find a fascination in the complexities of medieval history'. **George Richardson** (1947) was tutored by Frank Hardie, who was 'very attentive and used to take a great deal of time over one's essays, virtually took them to pieces and didn't actually tell you how to put them together again. He was a really serious, question-asking, tutor.' **Bernard Jacobson** (1956) thought David Pears, his philosophy tutor, a 'brilliant' teacher: 'he would never, in discussing an essay, tell me anything I hadn't yet thought of, instead asking questions that would lead me to think of it myself'. **James Shelby Tucker** (1955) arrived from Yale, where he had been taught 'there were seven reasons for the French Revolution – neither six nor eight, but seven. Michael Brock taught me that history is a record of researched and conjectured opinion, not a chronology of settled facts, and changed my understanding of history fundamentally. I believe that this was my first encounter with education (*educere*, to lead out, as well as *educare*, to train).' **Mueen Afzal** (1960) observed:

When some people said, and still do, that it did not matter what college you went to as long as you got a place at Oxford, I would always disagree. Apart from its being small, intimate and friendly, Corpus was among the few colleges which managed to find very high quality tutors in all subjects, even when those were not available in the College itself.

Amongst his tutors, **Paul Quarrie** (1962) particularly recalled Gerald Toomer ('the "mighty Toomer" as he was described to me recently by Noel Malcolm'):

I remember his setting me an immensely difficult unseen from

Wilamowitz's *Griechisches Lesebuch*. It was a passage about steam engines from Hero of Alexandria. Nowhere but in Corpus and from no other person but Toomer would any undergraduate in Oxford have received such a task. None of us realized in the early 1960s how wide-ranging and profound was, and is, his scholarship, and this was, of course, true of the entire Fellowship.

Simon Squires (1962) was struck by how Robin Nisbet, Gerald Toomer, Frank Lepper, Jim Urmson and John Briscoe 'displayed the happy knack of appearing to improvise a tutorial, so that it resembled almost an impulsive exploration – even though they had done it all many times before. Admittedly, when faced with the seemingly implacable intellect of Toomer one felt it was impossible to think of any observation worth making, but Nisbet's generous reaction to the most feeble response was always encouraging.'

Good tutoring opened up intellectual vistas. **Jonathan Dancy** (1965) recalled studying philosophy with Jim Urmson:

It was really his example that sent me into academic life. I realized that I could not imagine a better way of spending my time than reading interesting books and talking about them to interesting people. Christopher Taylor was also a model, but much younger. For the first five terms of Greats I had no idea what philosophy was all about but still found it interesting and worthwhile. Jim Urmson summed this up with what he wrote about me in collections during this period: 'Mr Dancy and I meet for an hour each week to discuss philosophy, but no idea passes in either direction.' This was kindly meant; he knew I was working well enough, but also that I had little or no clue what was going on. Suddenly, in the spring before Finals, the fog cleared and all seemed to make sense at last. But it was a close-run thing.

The philosophy bug also caught **Gareth Moore** (1966): 'As soon as I began studying it I fell in love with it, became obsessed by it. It was, along with music, the most exciting thing I had ever known.'[16] **David Stogdale** (1968) discovered that, 'perhaps to the surprise of some of my contemporaries, I genuinely enjoyed most of my pure physiology. I was incredibly well taught.' **Vincenzo Morelli** (1972) described studying PPE as

> an extraordinary, truly blissful experience. Andrew [Glyn] and Brian [Harrison], together with the several other tutors they selected for me across the other colleges, patiently shepherded me through my studies, tolerating my free-market bias, poor written English and less-than-adequate maths. I was taught to structure my thought process, to look for my own sources, to usefully frame a problem, to absorb differing views, to appreciate good scholarship, to argue my case credibly, to treasure intellectual freedom, intellectual honesty and, most important of all, intellectual humility.

Beverley Patterson (1979) 'enjoyed studying biochemistry and had a good relationship with my tutor Dr Don Wild, who taught me many things including all I ever needed to know about protein synthesis. This was really my first step towards a lifelong career in science.' **David Wilton** (1981) thought studying PPE 'great':

> There was plenty going on in the relatively early days of Thatcherism against a backdrop that included the Falklands War and the Miners' Strike. The Monetarist versus Keynesian economic debate was in full flow. And Corpus was a great place to be doing the studying. I was incredibly fortunate to be tutored by Andrew Glyn, Brian Harrison, Jennifer Hornsby, Douglas Hutchinson and others. The intellectual horsepower to which I was exposed was awe inspiring.

He was impressed by his (famously left-wing) tutor, Andrew Glyn:

> At first I was taken aback by some of his views but he was invariably absolutely charming, good natured and extraordinarily convincing. I was particularly confused as an unworldly 18-year-old trying to reconcile my father's firmly held and oft-stated view that Tony Benn was nearly the incarnation of the devil to Andrew's

rational and articulately expressed view that he was not. It was a great and vivid exposure to differences of opinion and belief.

Sean O'Grady (1981) described it as 'a sort of athletics course for the brain, helping it to think a bit more imaginatively'. For **Jonathan Garner** (1983):

> My abiding memory of Corpus is of the quality of my tutors – Christopher Taylor for philosophy, Brian Harrison for politics and Andrew Glyn for economics – each providing an extraordinary commitment to teaching undergraduates on a weekly basis term in, term out. They had very different styles of teaching but as an ensemble the effect on our intellectual development in the PPE group was immense; they treated us as adults and were always interested in our point of view.

Ben Whitby (1986) was tutored by Thomas Charles-Edwards ('you could feel the passion for his subject, even if you did not share it') and Brian Harrison:

> TCE was simply a great teacher of history – he set me reading and thinking. BH saved my degree. He had been on sabbatical for the summer term and I had not been taught by him (instead his substitute and I fobbed each other off). But he agreed to mark extra essays I did in the summer vacation, and gave me the time to go through them, which sorted me out for my final year.

Eliza Pakenham (1986) recalled her first tutorial with Val Cunningham:

> When I came out an hour later, I'd blushingly lost my intellectual virginity. How had I missed the fact that my hero, G. M. Hopkins, was all about sex? And Austen too, for that matter? And how could a man with a Lenin beard be wearing a Barbour? The terrifying double act of Val Cunningham and Susan Hitch continued for my first year. Once a week I skulked outside the sunny, book-encrusted

study for a cheerful grilling by Val, knowing only that whatever I had written would never go as far as he would recommend. Or Susan's eyrie, where I sweated to conceal that I understood nothing about Anglo-Saxon gems, or Chaucer, or anything really. But I did know one thing: this teaching was a gem itself, and I was lucky to be there at all.

Camilla Byk (1992) captured the sheer excitement some experienced: 'Did I love my subject? Yes I did, I was enthralled by Pirandello's plays and Dante's *Inferno*. I loved the French philosophers and rushed to the library after each tutorial, keen to get started on the next essay. Friends would tease me for being a swot but I was genuinely fascinated and enthralled by everything in the Taylorian library.'

Despite occasional critics, the Oxford tutorial system lasted, and remained popular – contributing, for example, to high student-satisfaction scores in a 2012 survey.[17] And because it was largely college-based, it helped to reinforce students' identity with their college. However, the extent of this overlap between academic study and college life varied. Humanities and social science students could usually work in or near Corpus, in their room, the Library or the nearby University libraries. Scientists – who were increasing as a proportion of the total – spent more time away. As **David Mark Jackson** (1959) observed, medical education was 'centred on South Parks Road, so Corpus didn't feature much except for an hour's tutorial every week with David Jamison.' For him, 'Corpus became more a home and a centre for social and sporting collegiate activity'. **Christopher Bridgett** (1961) thought 'the experience of being an Oxford medical student ran parallel to being an undergraduate at Corpus. For me the great advantage of College life was the many good friends I was able to make who were reading for other degrees.' **Paul Vaight** (1963) studied chemistry, which meant 'practicals during the day':

Practicals also excluded you from socializing in the JCR and the general life of the College during the day. I particularly loathed organic practicals in the Dyson Perrins since your clothes came out reeking of pungent organic odours and washing clothes wasn't high up the priority list; Health and Safety would have a fit today. However, practicals did allow you to meet fellow chemists from other colleges since we were arranged alphabetically and even today I am still friendly with some Ts and Ws.

Students were 'farmed out' to tutors in other colleges for subjects or topics which could not be covered by Corpus Fellows. This could be a mixed blessing. **George Richardson** (1947) was sent for politics to an external tutor who was 'frankly, rather neglectful'. 'I was down to less than an hour and he wasn't really interested.' But he also had the 'good fortune' to be sent for economics to Sir John Hicks at Nuffield: 'I was very, very lucky. That was a stroke of real luck.' **Geoff Goodall** (1950) found Corpus had no Modern Language Fellows:

> So we half-dozen linguist freshmen had to assemble in the Taylorian Institution, form queues in front of the tables behind which sat the languages dons from other colleges, and wait our turn to ask them if they would tutor us in this or that special subject. One lecturer in particular, Dr Garabedian, from Keble, had special links with Corpus and so was obliged to take the lot of us for French prose composition seminars and for paired tutorials. Garabedian was a great Oxford character: eccentric, benevolently mischievous and quite brilliant. I really looked forward to his sessions.

Christopher Watson (1957), studying chemistry, had the 'huge good fortune to be "farmed out" to Dalziel Hammick of Oriel' who proved 'a superb source of inspiration. His practice was to establish at the first tutorial how much flattery you could take, and then ply you with carefully judged amounts at every subsequent meeting. I found that irresistible.' But **Ken Reynolds** (1966) regretted that, 'as a linguist in a college that didn't do foreign languages other than long dead ones, I had virtually no contact at all with the Fellows'. And **Brian Swift** (1993) was frustrated by reliance on external tutors:

> My first tutor retired at the end of my first year, leaving it to someone who was not based at College. By this I mean he was not

'part of Corpus'. This disappointed me, as I had wanted to feel more fully involved in teaching life there. Coupled with that, for French I was taught mainly by New College and the other colleges they sent me to. So I felt a bit in limbo, not fully belonging to either college academically.

Other factors affected the association between College life and teaching. The opening of the John Radcliffe Hospital in 1979 was followed by the move of medical training to Headington.[18] Syllabus reform – sometimes allowing students to mix traditionally separate disciplines – and the growth of academic specialization increased the need to look outside any one college for expertise. As **Nick Witney** (1969) recalled, Corpus had been largely self-sufficient in philosophy and Classics: 'Few of us bothered much with University life. We classicists had only to climb a staircase to learn from the best tutors of their generation (as evidenced by Corpus's dominance of the Norrington table) – Robin Nisbet, Frank Lepper, Jim Urmson, Ewen Bowie.' But Fellow **Christopher Taylor** found teaching, even in philosophy, becoming 'more specialized across the board' so that he taught more students from other colleges 'in exchange for Corpus students whom I farmed out to specialists in other areas':

Instead of seeing one's students for most of the terms in which they were taking philosophy subjects, which in the case of Greats meant seeing them for virtually every term of the seven, one typically saw them for one or perhaps two terms in total. Consequently, the continuous monitoring which was one of the most positive aspects of the old system was replaced by reliance on reports from colleagues in other colleges, who themselves lacked the ongoing familiarity with the individual student which had previously been taken for granted. This loss was to some extent balanced by the gain to the student provided by a greater proportion of expert tuition, sometimes (if one were lucky) by a world leader in the field. I remain uncertain whether the overall tendency was positive or negative.

Nevertheless, much teaching continued to be done within the

College; and even when 'farmed out', students remained the responsibility of their College tutor. Corpus took the academic performance of its students seriously, responding vigorously to occasional setbacks in performance. While the extent to which individual students' studies were based in their own college or the wider university varied considerably, the strong connection between college and academic study was sustained and remained a defining feature of Oxford and Corpus life.

Time and wider learning

Time management was a major challenge. There were two cycles: the short (weekly/fortnightly) round of essays and tutorials, and the longer cycle of exams. Regardless of discipline, the 'essay crisis' was a universal experience. When **Nicola Feather** (1981) arrived,

> I underwent a complete transformation from goody-goody to (relative) slacker. At school, I would finish my homework the day it was set. At Corpus, if I had an in-house tutorial, I would often be running up the stairs to the tutor's room as the hour was striking, with an essay completed only moments before damply attached to my sweaty hand. The chief problem was that there were too many exciting things to do, and interesting people to talk to. I'm sure I wasn't the only one who struggled with time management issues.

Often the 'essay crisis' turned into the 'all-nighter'. **Peter Jarvis** (1957) described himself as a 'night owl. Almost all my essays were written between ten at night and five in the morning, the effort being sustained by French cigarettes, black coffee brewed suicidally on an upturned electric fire, and endless Dizzy Gillespie on the record player. This must have driven others in the Quad demented, but nobody ever complained.'[19] When, years later, **Charles Overton** (1970) revisited the New Building,

> it was with regret that I noticed the wall-mounted 'anglepoise' desk lamps were no longer present. Student life involved late night working and 'essay crises' for many of us. The lamp provided a

simple communication device at one or two o'clock in the morning
… Three 'twangs' on a spring meant 'David (Charles), do you want
a cup of coffee?' Two twangs in response meant 'Yes', one twang
meant 'No'. Gold Blend was the preferred lubricant at such times.

Others used the Library. **Angus Lapsley** (1988) recalled that,

As the hours passed, an atmosphere of mutual support would
develop: Gavin in the Lodge provided company until about 2am
and after that a routine would develop involving stretches of silent
work punctuated by regular trips to the caffeine-dispensing drinks
machine in the JCR and long debates about matters more appealing
than the task at hand (which meant just about anything).[20]

The long cycle reflected the fact that Oxford students – again, unlike
most other universities – typically had only two public examinations:
'Prelims' (a pass/fail gateway) or 'Mods' (which counted towards the
degree) took place from the end of the first term to the end of the
second year, depending on the subject; and 'Finals' (or 'Schools') –
the main degree exam – at the end of the third or fourth year. In the
meantime, apart from start-of-term college 'collections' – which were
rarely taken too seriously – terms were blissfully exam-free.

This had positive academic benefits – students could explore
beyond the syllabus. **Andrew Purkis** (1967) recalled how 'Brian
Harrison responded to our interest in contemporary oral history by
co-ordinating a project based on interviewing College scouts (and
long-standing Oxford figures who could talk about how their roles had
changed). This was a Corpus special and very interesting.' It also meant
time to indulge wider, non-academic, interests: 'There was always the
third year to re-engage with the academic excellence agenda! So for
me the second year was a more important time to explore theatrical
opportunities, the lovely environment of Oxford, and social opportunities. I was relatively lazy in academic work and failed to take the
opportunities to study the Civil War in England.' But it was easy to get
the balance wrong. **David Stogdale** (1968) 'spent too many hours in the
pub, although in fairness I was not alone, and in my second, examless

year far too many essays were late and in a few cases completely missing. I deserved my "roasting" collection, but I paid heed.'

Learning was not limited to formal study. When Fellows, scouts and their families lived and dined within College, there was scope for informal contacts and hospitality. In the 1950s, as **Charles Gardner** (1951) recalled, Frank Lepper led summer reading parties in a chalet near Chamonix: 'The regime was that we were expected to work in the mornings and were free to do what we liked after lunch, mostly playing cricket and other games on the lawn and walking, and in the evenings after supper playing various intellectual games.' According to **Bernard Jacobson** (1956), Lepper 'read improving literature to us in the evenings after dinner. But as for our own reading, careful research established that the only book on the chalet shelves that every member of our group read while we were there was a bodice-ripper entitled *Vera at Mystery Manor.*' This tradition seems to have ended by the 1960s; and dons – particularly the married ones – were increasingly living out. **Thomas Charles-Edwards**, one of the last married Fellows to live on site, described the College at night from the 1980s as 'a monochrome student community'.[21] Relations with tutors remained generally friendly, and some invited students to their homes. **Anita Gilman Sherman** (1979) recalled that 'I babysat once or twice' for one. **David Sooby** (2003) described his tutors, who arranged dinners after his exams, as 'very approachable'. But informal and social contacts were becoming rarer. Although **Ben Whitby** (1986) greatly appreciated his tutors, 'I never found dons particularly approachable outside the tutorial, which was probably due to my diffidence rather than any aloofness on their part.'

More important was the opportunity for students to learn from each other. **Don Montague** (1954) described 'being surrounded by men and women almost all exploring ideas and their own and other people's minds' as 'simply marvellous'. For **David Booth** (1955), studying chemistry, mixing with other disciplines proved a major influence:

> For myself, the 'staircase system' (in those days unique to Oxbridge and Durham – although I was in what was then the Annexe with corridors) resulted in a rapid spurt in my intellectual

growth that began to set my career. Within our first fortnight, a fresher reading PPP introduced me to experimental psychology and 'linguistic analytical' philosophy. As far as I recall I had not heard of psychology or philosophy. Yet my upbringing on study of the Bible (KJV!) let me see psychology and philosophy as the disciplines studying the mechanics of human life. So I moved my Chemistry Part 1 and Part 2 as close as I could towards biochemistry and brain research, went to London for a BA in Philosophy and Psychology and a PhD in Brain Biochemistry and then made a career in Psychology departments.

Bernard Jacobson (1956) studied with Lloyd-Jones, Lepper and Pears: 'Yet, with no disrespect to those superb teachers, I think it was from my fellow students as much as from my official teachers that I did my most important learning.' **Bill Morris** (1964), studying engineering without enthusiasm, was inspired by his friends reading Greats, PPE and Modern Languages: 'I wanted to be like them. They imbued me with the desire to know about everything, to be able to hold my own in any conversation about anything with anybody anywhere. Above everything this is what I got from Corpus and it has served me well right up to the present day.' According to **Peter Buxton** (1978):

> Friendships which crossed academic boundaries were not just inevitable but highly valued. When not debating important topics such as the best way to encourage a tortoise to move quickly in order to trounce a rival college in the annual Tortoise Fair, discussions would range far and wide. The academic boundary fences set up between subjects were ignored and, when not deriding with youthful arrogance another subject for being 'lightweight' or irrelevant, connections were made and respect, albeit sometimes grudging, for another subject was engendered.

A shared academic discipline could also stimulate camaraderie, friendship and learning. For **Andrew Purkis** (1967), 'my closest friends during my time at Corpus, some of whom turned out to be lifelong, were other Corpus historians. The commitment to and engagement in the subject glued us together.' Learning from each other, and exploring beyond the syllabus, could be fostered by clubs. One was the 'Critical Society', founded by **Al Alvarez** (1949) and other Corpuscles:

> We drew up a fighting manifesto about the deplorable state of Oxford criticism and how the Critical Society was going to set it right, had 2,000 copies printed in two shades of blue and spread them all over the University. We piled them up in the lecture halls and common rooms, pinned them on all the college noticeboards and scattered them through the student cafés.
>
> Freddie Bateson was not impressed. No one will come, he told us; this is Oxford; they don't want to know. I thought his knee-jerk put-down was typically Oxford, too, and resented him for it. But secretly I believed he was right and was astonished when the first meeting was packed out and briefly the Critical Society became the hottest ticket in town ... We all wrote papers and argued ferociously, and for a time the society was what it was supposed to be – subversive and fun.[22]

John Miles (1949) was another founder: 'It was through the Critical Society that I first met William Empson, and heard of a poet called Wallace Stevens, whose oeuvre was to become a lifelong interest.'

Quasi-academic clubs seem to have ebbed and flowed over the years. In 1966 'a most successful Corpus Philosophical Society has been established as a forum for philosophical discussion among undergraduates, graduates and senior members of the College', and two years later the Tortoise Society was debating the motion 'This House regrets the Expansion of Science'.[23] In the 1980s President **Keith Thomas** 'lamented the decline of intellectual societies in the College, although [he] conceded that the modern student had a considerably bigger workload than in the past which tended to reduce time for such activities'.[24] Nevertheless, 1985 saw the foundation of a Corpus History Society ('to be of interest to historians of all periods and secondly to attract those to whom history was an interest rather than an academic subject'). It arranged talks and a 'termly "jaunt"' to historic sites.[25] **Elizabeth O'Brien** (1990) 'gave a talk on one of my excavations', and 'enjoyed several outings to various historic sites and churches'. And in 2012 Fellow **Tim Whitmarsh** could report: 'Classics at Corpus is in rude health. We have a thriving undergraduate Classics Society, which regularly pulls in crowds of over 50.'[26]

Aspirations

Academic aspirations varied. **Al Alvarez** (1949) admired 'the cult of the Brilliant First':

> It was what I wanted most of all when I went up to Oxford, wanted with the same baffled intensity as I'd wanted to play rugger for the 1st XV at Oundle. Freddie Bateson didn't approve. Because his socialism set him apart from the other English dons, the pupils he liked best and who followed his political interpretation of litera-ture never got firsts, no matter how clever they were. So when my results came through he responded with malicious glee, as though I'd tricked the examiners (whom he despised) but he and I knew better.[27]

Not everyone had such ambitions. **Roger Horsfield** (1952) found 'academic achievement required a serious investment in time but it was possible to do enough to stay out of trouble without too much difficulty. When I saw the examination results I was satisfied that I had done enough. I would have hated to have worked really hard and still only got a second.' **Philip Hamilton-Grierson** (1953) thought 'a modicum [of work] was required, although a few hours a week was all that was needed to secure a soundish PPE second, based largely on stringing together specious jargon'.

Tutors recognized that not all were academic high-flyers. **Jeremy Hewett** (1953) was taught by Theo Tylor at Balliol, 'who must have realized from day one that I was not first-class material (in fact there were only four firsts in my year) – so he set about to ensure me an honourable second, insisting that term was for savouring the joys that Oxford had to offer, not to be spent among dull books or boring lectures'. Tyler set him vacation work, meaning 'I was able to spend most of each term sailing at Port Meadow'. **Bernard Jacobson** (1956) recalled

> the surprisingly relaxed attitude of my teachers to my sometimes cavalier approach to work. When I took the Classical Moderations examination during the second year of my four-year course and earned second-class honours, my Greek tutor, Hugh Lloyd-Jones, remarked, 'I'm sure if you'd worked all the time you'd have got a first, but there are other things in life.' Two years later I took third-class honours (out of the four classes there were at that time) in the final examination of Literae Humaniores. Again, as a lunch guest in College a few months after graduation, I said to Frank Lepper, 'You were very understanding when I hadn't finished an essay on time.' His reply – 'Well, you see, I always knew you had another line, so there seemed little point in making a fuss' – has always seemed to me to embody the perfect principle of a liberal education.

Rhod Thomas (1961) was a keen sportsman, playing rugby, soccer, hockey and cricket. 'You may ask when did I find time for academics. My French tutor Reg Perman of St Peter's and German tutor Cowan from New College were tolerant of my lack of preparation for the tutorials. I did manage to get a third but that was a miracle.' Mathematics Fellow **James Murray** could also be understanding:

> Most of the students were very bright with, in one year, five firsts. Corpus, as well as its well-known Classics reputation, also had quite a strong mathematics one so I was fortunate to get a remarkable number of bright and interesting students applying to take the entrance examination. One of the brightest is Andrew Fowler who succeeded me as Fellow and Tutor in Mathematics in the College. They were a varied and generally interesting, lively group.
>
> One, who could have got a first, came to talk to me to see what I thought about his not working so hard so that he could enjoy University and College social life more. He did not want to become an academic so I thought it was a great idea. So, he

worked less hard, got a respectable second, and greatly enjoyed his undergraduate time. He did medicine after graduating. Another, Orlando Gough, a student whose tutorials were never routine, seemed to spend little time working but instead was involved in a host of extracurricular activities. Before I got to know him better I lectured him on how he could get a first if he worked harder. I was totally wrong. He didn't need to work harder and he still got an excellent first in Mods and in Schools.

Brian Harrison agreed that exams were not the sole objective:

I have never thought that success in examinations is the only thing Oxford undergraduates should aim at, and there are many clever people about who don't shine at them. The important thing, it seems to me, is for students to exploit the facilities (cultural, conversational, intellectual, sporting and recreational) that are peculiar to Oxford, while at the same time doing enough academic work to get full enjoyment from it; almost as a by-product of this, success in examinations should follow. For most academics, and for more undergraduates than ever admit it, the distinction between recreation and academic 'work' doesn't exist.[28]

Nevertheless, Corpus took work seriously. **Frank Lepper**'s rigour was illustrated in a letter to the American Jonathan Kagan (1978), who had requested advice on preparing for Greats:

Your main task in the interval between now [June] and October, as far as I am concerned, is to get to know Herodotus as intimately as you can, not only what he says (in particular about Greeks, either in Greece or elsewhere), but also what sort of a person he was, so that, if one day I say to you 'What Herodotus says here is just the sort of thing he always tends to get wrong' (or something of that kind) you can say straight away, 'Oh, he does not give me that impression at all, I think he's interested and careful about this sort of thing – after all he had some experience of it himself, and in several places he seems to go out of his way to talk at length about such matters, etc. etc... .' 'Well, bully for you, Kagan', I hope I shall say, concealing my mortification.

Kagan was advised to 'index' Herodotus' texts – not just those in the syllabus – in detail. 'Find out by experiment how many pages you can read and understand of the text per working day minus, say, one and a half hours. Devote the remaining one and a half hours each working day to flipping through the corresponding pages of How and Wells and taking note of all references to Greeks etc.' He should create an index with 'a few words in either your English or H's Greek or a mixture of the two to remind you of the essence of the passage'. Although 'all this takes time' it would be 'time well spent' since it 'forces you to think about the content, should relieve you from the need to reread the whole work again and again (no time for that), and will, in the very compilation, "programme" your memory'. He was also advised to work on his Greek by 'the old-fashioned "elimination-list"' – listing all the words and phrases which he didn't recognize and then eliminating them: 'Shortly before the examination the list has been reduced to nil.' Reading the latest books was also desirable, 'but do not spend too much time on them'. In the meantime, he was enjoined to 'please, have a good holiday', because 'when we meet, we shall meet for business: the business of getting you *your* Class in Greats. I may or may not assist, but it will be *your* Class, and my job, as I see it, is not to tell you what to say so much as to tell you how to say whatever you decide (under my criticism) to make your story.'

Corpus remained, generally, a hard-working college. **Paul Vaight** (1963) thought 'the undergraduate paradigm at the time seemed to be effortlessly to get a first without apparently doing any work whatsoever; people who conspicuously worked hard were called "grey". I don't think that I was completely grey but fell somewhere within the fifty shades.' According to **Nicola Feather** (1981):

most people simply got their heads down and worked, with regular breaks for meals. There was neither a culture of being chained to one's desk nor of flamboyant dilettantism (although one of my contemporaries had to repeat his final year, owing to his love affair with acting). It seems that the previous generation had spoken of people being 'grey' or of them 'gnoming' in the Library but those words were no longer current: we weren't in the mood to criticize those who wanted to do well through hard work. At the same time, we were realistic about our chances of getting firsts. It was acknowledged that the classicists were the most likely ones to bring home the Norrington Table bacon.

Andrew Wilson (1987) thought 'academic excellence was truly respected rather than being something which one's peers regarded as a mild aberration'.[29] **David Massam** (1989) felt it had 'attained an unprecedented paramountcy':

> arrival was followed within 24 hours by an assignment of work, and the cycle continued with a short break for Mods and some relaxation of the tempo during vacations until the subfusc-clad, carnation-sporting climax in the Fifth Week of Trinity Term in my Finals year. Which is not to say that our tutors were slave-drivers, the reverse was the case; Thomas Charles-Edwards was a firm devotee of the day-trip, and Brian Harrison happily postponed essays that we might linger over lunch at his house at Wolvercote. Nevertheless, particularly with history, there was never an attainable limit to the work one could do; it was always a question of as much reading as could be achieved in the time, rather than completing the list of texts, and such a system does not lend itself to carefree afternoons. There was always something unread to produce qualms of conscience.[30]

Striking the right balance was tricky, and some felt insufficiently challenged. President **Dover** reviewed a student survey on tutorials: 'I have forgotten all those remarks except one, which occurred several times, to the effect that some tutors were too ready with commendation and insufficiently exacting.'[31] **Debbie Welch** (1994) felt 'Corpus was more relaxed than some other colleges, for example we only had collections once over the time. Looking back, it might have been better for us to have more pressure on us, but I did enjoy it at the time.

Perhaps I should have just done more work?' But despite the distractions of College life, recalled **Caroline Knapp** (2005), 'believe it or not I spent a good proportion of my time at Corpus in lectures, in labs, or working on tutorial sheets'. And **David Sooby** (2003) looked back on the 'rigour' and 'work ethic':

> Somewhere in between my social life I managed to also do my degree, which I loved. The academic rigour in the College was higher than my previous experience and I remember tutorials in beautiful old rooms with a single white board that would be filled and wiped clear over 20 times in a single hour. The tutors were unbelievably passionate about their subjects.

Finals

The climax of three or four years of study was Finals, a fearsome prospect. **Al Alvarez** (1949) described the run-up:

> In our last year all of us went a little mad with work. It was a beautiful summer, but I saw nothing of it: no croquet on the College lawn or punting on the Cherwell or beer at the riverside pubs. I spent all my time in the Corpus Library – fourteen hours a day as the exams got closer – slogging backwards and forwards through *Beowulf*, *Havelock the Dane* and *Gawain and the Green Knight*, trying to memorize inane textual variants and emendations. The narrow wooden benches made my backside sore, my shoulders and arms ached from leaning, the dusty smell clogged my nose and permeated my clothing. And each time I looked up, the great unread leather-bound folios on the shelves seemed to peer at me reproachfully, telling me there was no end to learning and I would never know enough to satisfy the examiners.[32]

In the months before Finals **Roger Horsfield** (1952) 'worked from dawn till dusk every day smoking 40 Black Russian cigarettes a day, drinking half a gallon of black coffee, and taking Soneril to sleep at night. I caught up with years of semi-neglect of my studies and actually began to really fall in love with history.' For **Chris Patey** (1958), 'our easy-going lifestyle gave way to long hours in libraries and intense revision'. This did not always go to plan: **Philip Hamilton-Grierson** (1953) went with friends 'to a croft house in Glenbrittle on Skye where I had been rock climbing two years earlier. The theory was that it was bound to rain for weeks on end, leaving us with no alternative to some intense reading. Sadly the sun shone without cease, the sea was mirror smooth, you could almost touch the Outer Hebrides and no work was done.'

David Jory (1959) adopted a systematic approach: 'I started revising for Finals during the Easter vacation of my third year, following a plan I had drawn up. I would not go to the pub until I had completed the day's planned work. Early in Trinity Term I sometimes had to run to The Bear to get there before closing time but as time wore on I was completing my work earlier and earlier in the evening, which made me feel confident.' But some, including **Tony Carr** (1956), found the stress serious:

> the long gap between Prelims and Schools created a sense of growing unease at the magnitude of the material to be held in the mind, leading finally to depression and even something like despair. My final year was the only time in my life that I have suffered stress-related illness, including shingles, and my recollection is of being in an almost perpetual state of disabling anxiety. We took, if I recall correctly, at least ten three-hour papers in the course of six days. As a hay fever sufferer in the blazing summer of 1959 I found it a great ordeal, and I had an aversion to reading anything serious for some time afterwards.[33]

Mueen Afzal (1960) recalled how, 'as the final year wore on, the looming threat of Schools begun to prey on the mind. No matter where one was, at a dinner for one of the College dining clubs or at the Beachcomber's Bar in Piccadilly, there was the disturbing thought of the final examinations which could diminish one's pleasure.' On the first morning his friends gathered at Corpus:

As I stepped over the concave stone step outside the Lodge I looked towards the left and saw Bob Minns, a historian, staggering in from Oriel Square, dressed in subfusc. I stopped for a few seconds so that I could walk with him. Minns was a cricket blue and an accomplished hockey player. As he came near me I noticed that his face was flushed, he had shaved unevenly and his gait was unsteady. He told me that he had felt nervous the night before and had taken sleeping pills. Being unable to sleep, despite the medication, he took more pills but did not remember how many. He had not slept at all during the night and now found it difficult to walk. I took him by the arm and together we made it to the Schools barely on time. Once in the examination hall, I saw that Minns sat down on his table but was unable to write – to begin with. The staff, always helpful and prepared for such contingencies, gave him one or two cups of coffee. After about half an hour he did commence writing and, I believe, almost completed his paper. To his credit, he ultimately got his degree.

Jonathan Dancy (1965) shared digs with Rod Kent. 'In our final year we vied with each other to see who could work the longest hours. Our practice was to meet for an hour at midnight and discuss what we had read during the day; I found this absolutely invaluable because it somehow fixed things in my memory which would otherwise have faded, or at least lost their edge.' Both gained firsts, as did **William Waldegrave** (1965), who had been disappointed with a second in Mods: 'I worked for Finals with concentrated fury: six days a week, eight or ten hours a day, only Sundays off, for the best part of a year. The effort paid off.'[34] For **Andrew Purkis** (1967) too, Finals meant work came first: 'I re-engaged big time with the academic agenda in my third year, so that the other beguiling forces were not so strong as to displace the central commitment to getting that good academic result. In the end, girlfriends and emotional and sexual maturity just had to wait.' **Margaret Harper** (1979) noted in a letter home that 'since Corpus has the best reputation for Classics', the Mods finalists were 'all working much too hard in order to get their first'. She gave two of them dinner: 'It's all rather ridiculous: for six days thou shall labour and do all that thou has to do and on the seventh thou shalt crack up!'

If hard work in exam years could ensure academic success (or respectability) for many, for others it was too little, too late. **Richard Fitzalan Howard** (1972) read History 'under the ever energetic Brian Harrison and the watchful eye of Thomas Charles-Edwards. I'm afraid I was a disappointment to both of them because, having done reasonably well in Prelims, I went on to get a third despite being vivaed.' He put this down in part to having spent 'too much time on country pursuits' including beagling and fox hunting; 'another distraction which scarcely helped my academic duties was membership of the Bullingdon Club'. **Richard Abernethy** (1973), by contrast, had spent much of his time on revolutionary politics:

> I sat down in the Examination Schools to take the first paper in the normal way, but walked out about 40 minutes later. Looking back, I find it difficult to distinguish the actual reasons at the time from explanations that came later. The simplest explanation would be that I had a bad case of exam nerves. I had found revision difficult. I had not slept well the previous night. I felt ill at ease in subfusc.
>
> It was not a political protest. I arrived at the Examination Schools in low spirits but expecting to complete the exams. I never presented my action as a boycott. My friends in Solidarity were as surprised and concerned as anyone when I told them. (Where would the Left be without academia?) Still, I think there was more to it than a nervous reaction. I felt that I had made a choice, although it was spontaneous and based on an immediate and personal sense of alienation right there in the exam room.
>
> The people at Corpus responded very well. By an astute piece of detective work and enlisting the help of the student Left network, they located me within a couple of hours. They tried to persuade me to resume Finals. Later, I was offered a chance to return to Corpus the next year, or after a break of one year. I was grateful, but declined. After making a life-changing decision, I did not want to go back on it. Also I didn't want to face the same situation again. Someone suggested I might apply for an aegrotat, but I thought that would be inappropriate, as I was not ill. As for the degree, I would get by without it.

Patrick Bourdillon (1964) criticized the dominance of Finals:

The major emphasis was on the final examinations, which may have reflected the result of three years, one year or one term (or perhaps even less) of hard work. Collections were not taken very seriously and were not a part of the overall evaluation process. The result was that those who were well motivated or had other reasons for persistent hard work thrived, while those without the necessary background training in self-discipline did not thrive. This 'sink or swim' attitude to the education process perhaps has merit in weeding out those with self-discipline from those without, but it ignores the needs of those without and is in stark contrast to the intensive continuous assessment process that I have been exposed to in the United States.[35]

Danielle Sanderson (1982) agreed:

My main criticism of Oxford is the undue pressure of Finals. I don't know if the regime has changed nowadays, but we had six three-hour exams in three days, upon which depended almost the entire degree classification. (Footnote: For physics, a small consideration was also given to practical coursework.) For several girls at Corpus, the pressure of Finals was too great, with one or two suffering breakdowns, and others deferring for a year. I still have occasional nightmares during which I am about to sit Finals when I remember that I also need to revise all my second-year work too!

Finals was a rite of passage, with associated rituals. According to **Peter Newey** (1944) Frank Lepper 'had a custom before Schools of inviting his Greats group out for a long walk followed by a sumptuous country tea. He also used to suggest a few days off before Schools (I went to Bath)'. **George Guest** (1951) recalled Michael Brock taking 'two or three of us in his car into the Vale of the White Horse to give us a break from revision'. According to **David Jory** (1959), there was 'unofficial encouragement to leave Oxford the weekend before Finals and relax, preferably in some country inn with one's girlfriend;

this was called a "Schools weekend"'. He told only one friend where he was going ('otherwise we would have had a chorus singing under our window or something worse') and had a 'relaxing' weekend: 'I went into my Finals in good physical and mental shape.' By the 1970s, according to **Martin Deahl** (1975), 'there developed what almost became a superstitious cult of watching the ITV series *Emmerdale Farm*, believing this somehow imbued the audience with special powers in the Exam Schools. The JCR even wrote to Yorkshire TV to obtain a framed picture of the "farm" which adorned the wall of the TV Room.'

The ritual nature of Finals was reinforced by the special clothes ('subfusc'), often with coloured buttonholes. **Dave Yeatman,** who joined from Balliol as Head Porter, noted the role of friends:

> It was the support of other students that I found encouraging, something I hadn't seen before. On the last day of the final exam you would get upwards of probably two dozen students that came to the Lodge entrance to support the one that was going off to take the last exam and that was to settle their nerves. That was something I had not seen anywhere else. Another reason I call Corpus a really nice friendly college.

The last exam was followed by celebrations – typically involving copious champagne. According to **Martin Deahl** (1975), 'we pushed the then senior scholar back from the Schools along Merton Street (Bulldogs in hot pursuit) in a supermarket trolley (acquired from Sainsbury's expressly for the purpose) complete with fireworks attached to give an extra bit of boost'. **Rob Batho** (1964) recalled:

> Exams over, champagne drunk, cherrystones spat at varying lengths over the lawn of the Fellows' garden. A very alcoholic post-Schools reception as partner to a friend at St Anne's, immediately followed by an even more alcoholic Schools Dinner at Corpus. And then the results – early on a summer's evening two days before I was to get married – the sombre voice of a Schools' porter with the news 'you have third class, sir'. Well someone had to – but it didn't

help the Norrington result that year. And those of us who didn't get firsts know that the results don't matter anyway – except that when it came to fixing the salaries for new graduates in the aero engine division of Rolls Royce Ltd a few months later an edict was issued by the personnel director, who was my boss, that 'Oxford thirds are not to be counted as lower seconds' and it cost me £100 a year.

Eliza Pakenham (1986) recalled the special character of Finals year:

I fell into long afternoon sleeps, dreaming of romance. In the mists and darkness of an Oxford winter I tried to make sense of impossible American poets: Hart Crane, Wallace Stephens. But in spring the cherry blossoms cast a pink, reviving glow. I started to work properly; reading late into the nights, fuelled on crisps from the Buttery, and the consoling lights of fellow scribblers across the lane in Merton. As the fear of Finals descended like a fog, the pace of work grew faster, the music quieter. The College hummed like a soothing infirmary: the kitchen staff doling out extra against our pallid faces, the avuncular porters counting us in at night, the tutors giving reassuring pep-talks. And already there was nostalgia in the air; the last tutorials, the last walks amongst the fritillaries in Christ Church Meadow.

Then, almost before we knew it, Finals were over: the relief tainted with a poignant sense that something else was over too. A sense Corpus would never be ours in the same way again, and that we had grown up and must now go out into the world.

How did Corpuscles perform in Finals? The nearest objective test was the Norrington Table, invented in 1963 to provide a weighted comparison of college results. Between 1963 and 2015 Corpus topped the table six times and came second or third on a further eight occasions. But the 'score' fluctuated and Corpus ranked between 20th and 25th in 1983, 1988, 1998, 2007, 2012 and 2013. The dips caused considerable concern. In the 1980s Senior Tutor Brian Harrison headed an academic review which led to changes in admissions, collections and the Library.[36] President Keith Thomas promoted academic rigour with initiatives including lunches with students, and a revived system of presidential collections. As we have seen, however, getting into any Oxford college was becoming increasingly competitive: by the 21st century standards were more uniformly high and it was more difficult to stand out from the crowd. This didn't prevent poor results prompting serious soul-searching. According to **Binyamin Even** (2004), 'over the last two decades, Corpus has descended from the summit of the Norrington rankings to mid-table, while our neighbours rose from obscurity to the summit. Their and our library, quads, and history have not changed in this time. The ethos has: where once ours was the ferociously academic, it is Merton that is now known as the workaholic's choice.'[37] Senior Tutor **John Watts** reported on the disappointing 2007 performance:

> Corpus has always regarded itself as an intellectually distinguished place – humane, low-key, amused, tolerant, sometimes mildly lefty, sometimes not, but consistently intelligent and, at bottom, serious about producing work of high quality. It was thus rather a shock for the College to find itself in 24th place in the Norrington Table in 2007 – the worst placing anyone could remember, and far below the heights of the 1970s and 1980s when Corpus was regularly at the top. More detailed scrutiny of recent performance revealed that, while this was an exceptionally bad year, undergraduate results had been in relative decline against other colleges for some time ... From being a top-rank college, Corpus had slipped into being a top-third college, then a mid-table college and finally, in 2007, a pretend-you're-somewhere-else college.

In the ensuring academic review, tutors were asked what lay behind the change. Their answers were uncomfortable:

> a diminished work ethic, a lack of intellectual ambition, an over-indulgence in extracurricular activities, a failure to deal with miscreants and some doubts about how the College presented itself to potential applicants (was its reputation for being 'small

and friendly' making it too attractive to people with, as one tutor put it, 'small and friendly minds'?)

Students agreed with some of this: collections were often a farce, full of noise, misbehaviour and predictable questions; people who did little work for their courses seemed to face no sanctions; there was not much intellectual atmosphere in the JCR. But they also had other things to say: tutors may need to offer more help with developing skills and with helping students to manage the transition from school to university; they should mark collection papers quickly and return them face to face, with the opportunity for a proper discussion; some of them found their tutors too remote and inflexible and wanted more guidance, feedback and dialogue about progress. While we tutors are often keen for students to learn self-reliance and to figure things out for themselves, we could see that there were things for us to do as well.[38]

President **Tim Lankester** concluded that the College needed to strengthen its 'academic culture'. Proposals included 'greater celebration and increased rewards for high performance not just in public exams but also throughout the year; better monitoring and more help for undergraduates who are having difficulties; ensuring that beginning term collections are taken seriously; and a tougher regime for those who are consistently performing below their potential'.[39] The next year he reported 'a renewed sense amongst all our undergraduates that they are here to pursue academic excellence and to achieve their very highest potential'.[40] Results improved – in 2010 41 per cent of finalists got firsts, and Corpus came second in the table, though it subsequently fluctuated (25th, 13th, 10th and 16th in the years from 2013 to 2016). But with standards across Oxford now so high – few were awarded a lower second or below – the table, as President **Richard Carwardine** observed, was becoming 'a measure of insignificant differences: by way of illustration, last year's top college fell this year to 25th, but still boasted 30 per cent firsts and 59 per cent upper seconds'.[41] Corpus remained academically ambitious and high-performing – but in a university where this had become less exceptional.

Eights Week, 1951. *Courtesy of Geoff Goodall (1950)*

6

'CAMARADERIE': SOCIAL LIFE

Being small, we had to join in.

Philip Hamilton-Grierson

If one happened to be crossing the Quad at the wrong time one could find oneself in any sporting team.

Jonathan Atkinson

Oxford life was about far more than study. Indeed, one of the contrasts which struck **Marc Schalenberg** (1991), arriving from Germany, was 'the exceedingly broad range of possible extracurricular student activities'. It seemed natural to join 'at least one of the many sports clubs, play an instrument or sing, be involved in JCR debates and posts, join a more exotic society (of which there are plenty) and be a member of the Union'.[1] Such activities were not just important at the personal level: they were a crucial part of what made Corpus a community.

Much social and leisure activity was informal: coffee, beer or meals with friends; trips to the cinema or theatre; punting on the river; watching TV soaps or simply 'festering' in the JCR. Many, like **David Henig** (1990), spent 'more than a healthy amount of time in the bar'. According to **James Whitelaw** (1941), 'I did not "do" sports, having survived ten years of compulsory rugger and cricket at school, and must admit that my social focus was in The Bear, the principal Corpus watering hole.' For **Peter Newey** (1944) 'the leisure activity I can best recall is leaning in a corridor at the Buttery bar learning to drink excellent beer'. But for those interested, virtually any activity could be pursued. How did they respond?

Sport

Hal Wilson (1947) thought 'the College had a deserved reputation for scholarship, and games were played for enjoyment'. This did not mean sport was unimportant. **Tony Henning** (1948) thought that, because Corpus was small, 'most of us found ourselves taking part in many sports and club activities and having to juggle this with the essential academic work'. **Gerry Hughes** (1952) noted that, 'while I spent as much time as I thought necessary on preparing for tutorials – usually 8 hours for a philosophy or history essay, so 16 hours a week – I spent at least three afternoons playing some sort of sport'. According to **Geoff Goodall** (1950):

> In response to the Dean's exhortation to join fully in the extracurricular life of the College, I joined the 1st XV rugby team and the 1st XI cricket team, both of them very respectable performers in the college leagues. This brought me some 30 friends instantly and was a joy. Though not previously versed in either sport, I joined the Association Football XI and the 3rd rowing VIII, simply to make up the numbers. No form of training for any of these teams ever took place, except for the 3rd VIII. We just turned up and played our hearts out. With the rowing, all nine of us were complete novices.

'As a small college,' **Nicholas Roskill** (1952) recalled, 'anyone of even modest athletic pretensions was required to represent the College at any sport of which he claimed the slightest expertise. I certainly played cricket, hockey, tennis and squash for the College and on one occasion rugby football.' He also played real tennis in a court off Merton Street, representing the University in this 'rather esoteric sport'. **Philip Hamilton-Grierson** (1953) agreed: 'Being small, we had to join in. I played hockey, tennis and bridge, rowed, sailed, danced reels (Corpus and LMH organized reels in St Mary's church hall). Outside the College I joined the University Yacht Club and the Mountaineering Club.' **Don Montague** (1954) found himself 'conned' into rowing:

> Rowing certainly filled the afternoons, and gave me the chance to meet and do something with new friends. Six afternoons a week rowing didn't leave much time for other sport, but, spreading myself thin, I ran several times for the University 3rd Cross-country team, and once for the 2nd, joined the OU Yacht Club and learned to sail on Port Meadow, joined the OU Jazz Club and went up to the Queen's Hall in London to hear Louis Armstrong play, in all his glory, and joined the OU Mountaineering Club, climbed with the club during the vacs, and became editor of its journal for a term or two. This didn't leave much time for work, or women, but I did well in Maths Mods, to the surprise of some.

Not everyone joined in. **George Richardson** (1947) 'never did any sport. Partly, I wasn't very interested or good at it, but also because I wanted to move on.' **Richard Abernethy** (1973) had 'zero interest in sport'. **Dina Gold** (1975) 'was asked to join just about every club and society imaginable and the rowing team put great pressure on me to be their cox – but I was not enamoured of the opportunity to train at the crack of dawn in icy weather and I turned them down'. **Danielle Sanderson** (1982) also declined: 'I had good intentions of rowing or coxing for the College, but somehow the prospect of training at 5am held little appeal. Ironically, several years after leaving Oxford I discovered an aptitude for running, and became an international athlete, training early mornings and evenings, 100 miles per week for several years.'

But avoiding sport sometimes proved impossible. 'Corpus was not a hearty college,' recalled **Peter Jarvis** (1957), 'but sport did play an important role. It must have done, because I for one had (and still have) a hearty loathing for every game from ping-pong to football, and yet even I became enrolled.' This included rugby: 'one afternoon a flu epidemic decimated the bottom XV and even I was shanghaied. I can only recall being chased up and down a muddy field by a pack of homicidal colonial giants from Teddy Hall.'[2]

There were huge variations in talent. Corpus did produce serious sportsmen and women who won blues and other distinctions, including John Scott (1956), who played rugby for England, and Boris Rankov (1973), who achieved six Boat Race victories. According to **Geoff Goodall** (1950), 'In 1951 Corpus managed to gain quite a few blues, one for rowing (Peter Bailey), one for soccer (Ernie Tweddle – who scored the winning goal in the Varsity Match) and two for swimming (Caryl Evans-Prosser and John Carver). We even had two golfing blues (Gorrie and Lewis) and several half-blues in shooting, badminton and water polo.' **Gustaf Behmer** (2014) became 'the fifth blues golf captain in the last 50 years, proud College record'.[3] But Corpus's size meant that most participants' abilities were modest and success for College teams elusive. This didn't dampen enthusiasm. **Charles Gardner** (1951) was 'particularly pleased at being able to play for the Corpus teams at hockey, squash and tennis as that was one benefit of being a member of the smallest college in the University, even if we didn't shine in Cuppers'. **Rob Batho** (1964) took up rowing:

> we never seemed too serious, and periodic stops were required so that our cox could light another Gauloise, so that being at the bottom of our division in Torpids in 1966, and having to row the full course twice in fairly quick succession came as something of a shock; but we became very good at eating the Manciple's excellent steaks.

Kenneth Pearson (1974) recalled 'the spirit shown on the sports fields, especially rugby and cricket, in which, as a college, we failed to excel'. Some, like **Nicola Feather** (1981), surprised themselves:

> I reinvented myself, to a certain extent, at Oxford. The small number of women who could be called on to represent the College

in sports meant that I went from being a no-hoper to sometime member of the College's squash, badminton, mixed hockey (an absolutely terrifying experience: girls at school never managed to make the ball travel so far or so fast) teams, along with several rowing squads. I also learned how to cox, unthinkable to my cautious, risk-aware grown-up self. What armchair viewers of the Boat Race may not realize is the sheer power represented by a men's VIII. Even with the scratch VIII I took out, every stroke jerked me backwards and then flung me forwards in my seat like a rag doll.

According to **David Wilton** (1981):

We were enthusiastic and limited as befits a small college. I played and enjoyed football, rugby and tennis. Eager to make the most of the Oxford experience I briefly took up rowing and was a spectacularly average no. 3 in the College 2nd boat. It was entertaining and great fun. The photo of our boat on my study wall shows all five visible blades at different parts of the stroke in notable contrast to the boat in the background that is rapidly and not surprisingly catching us up.

Jonathan Atkinson (1984) agreed: 'Starting with a size disadvantage meant that our teams were often not as well stocked with talent as those of some of our competitor colleges but this never prevented Corpus engaging enthusiastically. I also recall that if one happened to be crossing the Quad at the wrong time one could find oneself in any sporting team.' **Ben Whitby** (1986) played football, rugby, cricket and mixed hockey: 'Corpus was stuffed at everything because we were too small (even with some MCR members joining in). We joined up with St Hugh's in my final year (they had just gone co-ed) and became as good as the other non-sporty colleges, i.e. we won some matches. This felt heroic after some of the thrashings.' But sometimes Corpus surprised itself. **Eric Sidebottom** (1957) played rugby during an unusually successful period:

Corpus moved in one student generation from languishing near the bottom of league 3 to near the top of league 1 and were 'runners-up' to the mighty Teddy Hall by a mere 3 points to 0. The impact of this unexpected success, in terms of team and college spirit, was immense. The team, not surprisingly, was a glorious mixture of males of all sizes, from backgrounds posh and humble, educationally and socially. But with a common purpose we all developed a fondness and respect for each other.

The University's smallest college, that bastion of academic scholarship, especially in Classics, had become a truly all-round, sporting college – and not only in rugby; we reached hockey Cuppers finals, and had representatives in University teams in rugby, hockey, cricket, athletics, rowing, golf, squash, rugby fives, fencing, even soccer and no doubt others.[4]

David Jory (1959) became rugby captain:

There was not much depth in the Corpus team in those years – perhaps a total of 20 players turned out for the College in a term. But there was talent; and a remarkable team spirit (of the good kind) which inspired players to rise above their normal playing capabilities on many occasions (some of which I remember clearly). We also out-thought and out-planned most opposing teams.

Brian Sedgemore (1958) recalled a tour to Denmark, where 'copious bottles of Carlsberg' did not prevent the team 'thrashing the Danish national side'. 'In my time,' **Chris Patey** (1958) noted, 'Corpus enjoyed a brief period as a successful sporting college. Our hockey team, of which I was a member, was in the final of Cuppers for two of my three years in residence. More than one member of the team also played rugger for the College – an example of members of a small community lending a hand where needed.' **Bill Morris** (1964) was a hockey blue along with three other Corpuscles:

Corpus really was a noted sporting college then. It seems hard to believe now, but, as well as being strong in hockey, the College could boast blues in rugby, cricket, soccer and golf, not to mention squash, real tennis, fives and ice hockey even. I would venture to suggest that there were more Corpus blues during my time than there have been in the near 50 years since.

I played in three Cuppers finals, a soccer semi-final and an unforgettable rugby Cuppers match against BNC [Brasenose] (during which I was to gain my first experience of mortal fear). In the space of three years, Corpus had three outstanding fly halves: Rhod Thomas, John Pettigrew and Bob Phillips. All could have played for the University at Twickenham but only Bob did, captaining the University twice. Rhod did open the innings against Cambridge though, having scored 135 not out against Northants in the Parks. Alex Gibson was our soccer blue and I remember him returning from training one day and being very dismissive of the new University coach, Bobby Robson, destined for a knighthood after taking England to a World Cup semi-final.

According to **David Stogdale** (1969), 'in rugby, as in the Norrington Tables, Corpus punched well above its weight, in large measure due to the Welsh'. He also played cricket, football and squash: 'in a small college these activities had a strongly unifying effect'. But success didn't last. **John Geraint Roberts** (1975) was from the Rhondda: 'Coming to Corpus, I may not have had a single discernible muscle on my entire frame, but I had the right accent for rugby, see.' Corpus lost every match – until the last. 'My parents had come to visit. They stood on the touchline to see us play Univ. There were four other spectators, not all of them canine.' Against all expectations, he scored three tries and Corpus won. 'And Dad? It was the only time he saw me play. But just four years ago, he went to his grave, still half-believing I'd been good enough to win a dozen caps for Wales.'

Mark Atkinson (1971) found the Boat Club 'at a nadir':

I had never rowed competitively but had pottered around in boats in Norfolk throughout my childhood and with visions of Boat Race glory in my head I volunteered. We spent hours in the bank tub, an oblong wooden box anchored to the bank like some primitive ergometer. Finally we graduated into the tub pair, which was reminiscent of the aforementioned boats that I had pottered about in Norfolk. By Hilary I was in the 1st Torpid along with a bunch of other freshman misfits. Torpids was a disaster; we were bumped; we were over bumped; the highlight was that one day we somehow managed to row over but I think that was because everyone behind us bumped out. Summer Eights was not much better.

In the following years Corpus rowing recovered – helped by new recruits and a strategy 'based on the premise that we might not be the most experienced crew on the river or the best looking but we would be fittest'. Four bumps, leading to Bump Suppers, were achieved in successive years. Boris Rankov (1973) started his record run of Boat Race victories, joined for a couple of years by Russell Crockford (1976), who died young in a car crash.

The most unexpected success, however, came from the women. In 1978, 'the Corpus Women's VIII by dint of terror and superior speed made an easy five bumps in Eights'.[5] This led to their first Bump Supper. Further success followed, prompting **Andrew Mason** (1979) to compose a 'Bump Supper Ode: In Honour of CCC Ladies' Boat', which concluded:

Therefore we know the gods are on our side
So praise the victors, blessed with aid divine
And let the College, filled with glorious pride,
Raise thrice three cheers to hail the famous nine
Who by this feat all ages past excel
As generations numberless shall tell.[6]

Such success was rare but not unique. In 2013 President **Richard Carwardine** observed that 'those unprepared for reports that link Corpus with sporting triumph may be startled to learn of a historic double in Hilary Term's Torpids. Both the Women's VIIIs – 1st and 2nd – made four bumps and earned not just their blades and a Bump

Supper but a unique place in College history. This inspired the Men's
1st boat to similar riverine shock and awe with four bumps in Summer
Eights.'[7]

Corpus students took part in a vast range of sports. **Peter Water-field** (1946) discovered 'a squash court round the corner of Magpie
Lane and I found some small talent for that game which lasted until
an absurd age'. As well as rowing, **Francis Oakley** (1950) 'took up
cross-country running, the start of a lifelong addiction that has left
me now with a cartilage-challenged knee'. The cricket team undertook
village tours of Kent. **Jeremy Hewett** (1952) became a keen sailor 'and
was able to spend most of each term sailing at Port Meadow'. With an
Oriel friend he knocked an hour off the walking record from Oxford
to Cambridge. Influenced by President Hardie, Corpus had a strong
golf tradition: **Brian Sedgemore** (1958) recalled the College winning
golf Cuppers 'year after year'. **Mueen Afzal** (1960) was introduced to
golf and played against the President:

> From nearly 200 yards I took a wood and had an almighty swing.
> It was a good connection. To my embarrassment, I had hit a near
> perfect shot but it was sailing slightly to the left of the green and
> straight towards President Hardie! The President, somewhat
> surprised, immediately opened the umbrella in his hands and held
> it just above his head. The ball hit the umbrella and dropped on
> the fringe of the green.

Paul Vaight (1963) played football:

> We were playing at home on our ground over the railway bridge.
> Winston Churchill had recently died and it was the day of his
> funeral. The train bringing his body for burial went past the pitch
> in the middle of the game on the way to his final resting place at
> Blaydon churchyard. Someone noticed this and shouted 'Let's stop
> for Winnie'. So we stood in silence for a minute and then recom-
> menced the game.

Richard Fitzalan Howard (1972) hunted with the Christ Church beagles. **Chris Sherwell** (1969) had been a swimmer in Rhodesia and returned to the sport:

> It meant training three times a week – two lunchtimes and one afternoon – at the depressing Cowley indoor swimming-pool. In a week I would put in as much distance as I used to manage in a day previously. I was smoking and drinking, and hopelessly unfit. But the company was marvellous, and if I hated the whole business on many occasions, I loved it on many others because of the extraordinary team-spirit and camaraderie.[8]

Jonathan Garner (1983) captained the croquet team, which 'sometimes did quite well, aided often by the home advantage of the Fellows' Building lawn' with its 'distinct inward slope'. **Jonathan Atkinson** (1984) won cycling half-blues and recalled 'an annual slow cycling race across the Quad. This occurred for two or three years and, I believe, may have replaced the previous "slow tortoise race" which by then had been discontinued due to concerns of animal health. I used to enjoy doing track stands to stay stationary in the Quad as cycling there was not otherwise permitted!' **Dave Rose** (1986) – a Canadian – won an ice hockey half-blue: 'I'll be honest – there aren't too many students of the University who can play ice hockey. If you're half competent you're in.'[9] **Camilla Byk** (1992) had played hockey and skated, 'so when I was loitering one evening at the Porters' Lodge after a party, I was invited to join the Corpus ice hockey team. Off we went at 1am to play on the town rink. I had no idea what I was doing but am delighted to say that I can now claim to be an honorary ice hockey player from an Oxford team. Corpus was great for that, as you could do OUDS, or be a rep for the CU (Christian Union) or raise money at the tortoise fair without being brilliant, you just had to be willing.' **Elizabeth O'Brien** (1990) joined the University Riding Club, until stopped by an accident, and **Nick Hassall** (1989) played polo: 'not something I advertised in College. When I arrived at Oxford I fancied my chances of a half-blue. Hardly anyone had ever played polo in those days so I thought the odds would be in my favour.' He played in the Varsity match the day after Finals: 'I was incredibly hung over, fell off at one point, and was poorly mounted, but I had finally achieved my goal of a half-blue.'

Not all games were physical. According to **Charles Thomas** (1948), 'chess and cards were in wide demand. A lot of chess was played privately in College.' There was also 'a sort of Corpus/Magdalen card-playing set, solo whist, which met in someone's palatial rooms by the Deer Park'.[10] **Mueen Afzal** (1960) played in bridge Cuppers and **Tim Stockil** (1970) recalled 'all-night bridge sessions in the Beer Cellar'. **Angus Lapsley** (1988) thought pool and table football 'the two sports that Corpus seemed to take most seriously (other than gossip)'.[11] As well as polo and rowing, **Nick Hassall** (1989) played backgammon, cards ('interminable games of "shit-head"') and table football: 'We did pretty well in intercollege competitions and I probably spent more time playing table football than writing essays during my time at Oxford.'

Corpus also featured in *University Challenge*. In 1967 they 'inflicted convincing defeats on the Universities of Exeter and Surrey, but unfortunately, in face of strong opposition from Keele, failed to survive the third game'.[12] In 2004 Corpus entered for the first time since the 1980s and reached the final, against UCL. After a slow start, according to **Charles Oakley** (1998), 'we took charge, almost thriving on the challenging questions'. The final score was Corpus 250, UCL 140.[13] Could the feat be repeated? In 2009, as the President reported, Corpus reached the final again:

> Our team's performance throughout the competition was remarkable. It was led by Classics DPhil student Gail Trimble, who scored a record number of individual points since the competition began in the 1960s and she was feted in the national press for her brilliance.
>
> In the final round, Corpus defeated Manchester (whose team included a former Corpus undergraduate), but then were disqualified on the grounds that one of our team members had left the University between the filming of the early and final rounds. The disqualification was clearly unjust since the team member in question had originally been planning to stay on for graduate

work; there was nothing in the formal paperwork to indicate that students in their final year were ineligible; and it subsequently emerged that at least three of the winners during the previous eight years had included students who had left during the filming of the competition. The Manchester team generously conceded that the real victors were indeed Corpus.[14]

Flying

Some Corpuscles took to the air. **Charles Gardner** (1951) was one of three in the University Air Squadron: 'We were enrolled as Cadet Pilot Officers in the Royal Air Force Volunteer Reserve (RAFVR), given an RAF blue uniform, and amazingly were paid to learn to fly':

> Once a week we had also to attend lectures in the evenings on aeronautics, meteorology, radio procedures and engineering at the Clubhouse. The Club was also a social centre with a bar and a café, and it was there that I was able to watch Queen Elizabeth's Coronation on a black-and-white television. Every long vacation we were required to spend a week or maybe two at an RAF airfield where we flew every day, slept in dormitories and ate in the Officers' Mess.

Deteriorating eyesight meant he was eventually grounded: 'I believed this had happened because of all the hours I had spent struggling to translate Homer's *Iliad* and the speeches of Demosthenes. Sadly I never flew again.'

Roger Horsfield (1952) joined the Army equivalent:

> In order to pay for my baby son I joined the Oxford University Officers' Training Corps, which was a unit of the Territorial Army (TA). Together with my two closest friends we joined the Armoured Corps subunit and had some amazing experiences in Daimler armoured cars and watching a huge battle on Salisbury Plain to an audience of every military attaché and foreign spy that could be invited. All the weapons in the British Army were

employed advancing at the mythical enemy, culminating in an air strike. It was probably the best piece of theatre I have ever attended, and I got paid for going.

Despite the pay, not many Corpuscles seem to have followed this path. **James Dixon** (1966) already held a pilot's licence: 'Nobody within living memory at Corpus had served with the Air Squadron, but I made a beeline for its premises in Manor Road almost as soon as I had arrived in Oxford.' Following tests and interviews,

> I went round to Manor Road to sign the paperwork, including the Official Secrets Act, and collect my uniform and fairly bulky manual for the Chipmunk. I also had to secure a National Insurance number, so that my card could be stamped – yes, this would be paid employment, but at the rate of half a crown for each hour flown, as I recall. Most people then would have paid to fly, but I was committing myself to serve in the event of some kind of national emergency, and there were some quite substantial commitments to train on the ground, and to attend camps during the spring and summer vacations.

He was not the only Corpuscle in the Squadron, but it remained a minority interest: 'Few at Corpus knew of my involvement, and even those who did know seldom asked many questions about it. Rather more Corpuscles were members of the somewhat larger army Officers' Training Corps, but even that did not seem to jell readily with Corpus traditions.'

Charles Cockell (1991) also flew, but for very different reasons. A keen moth collector, he aimed to visit Indonesia:

> My plan was simple – build a moth collecting aircraft. So no sooner had I arrived at Corpus I began raising funds and taking flying lessons. Every morning at 7am, I would make the journey to Enstone airfield, furtively gaining the experience to fly a microlight aircraft over the rainforests of Indonesia.
>
> We built the machine and in 1993 I flew it, during my summer

break, over the rainforest (how did I get away with three months off my PhD to do this? I don't know). The Barnes Wallis Moth Machine had UV lights for attracting moths, a net for scooping them from the trees and RAF infra-red night vision goggles lent to us by the Dambuster Squadron (617 Squadron), one of our patrons. Moths are best collected at dusk about 20 feet over the canopy of trees. Needless to say, I crashed the machine after clipping a tree and we resorted to collecting moths by elephant back. It provided endless hours of storytelling over Corpus dinners for the rest of my time at the College. However, it also ended up as an editorial in *The Times* by Bernard Levin and in the *Daily Telegraph* amongst other places. I had brought Corpus my own personal contribution to infamy.

Arts

The arts – especially drama and music – offered another range of opportunities. **Geoff Goodall** (1950) recalled fellow linguist Alistair McIntosh (1950) directing an OUDS production of *Twelfth Night* at the Oxford Playhouse and auditioning

A would-be young actress called Maggie Smith. Alistair was impressed and gave her the part. The second notable play was his 1951 Corpus Owlets production in the College Chapel of *Murder in the Cathedral*. This was so successful that he took the whole cast on to the Edinburgh Festival, where it was again extremely well received. Such good feeling grew among the large cast that Alistair kept them all in touch for years afterwards with an annual newsletter.

Francis Oakley (1950) described 'the vitality at that time of the musical and theatrical life of the College, informal as well as formal'. He recalled 'playing Purcell late in the evening as part of a consort of recorders that Mark Sheldon put together'; being 'taught calypsos by Eldred Jones, a lifelong friend'; 'playing the Third Brandenburg Concerto in the violin section of a rather wheezy scratch orchestra';

providing 'the instrumental accompaniment for Alistair McIntosh's rather zany adaptation as a musical of Nicholas Udall's *Ralph Roister Doister*'; and 'playing in the small musical ensemble that was given a role in Alistair's OUDS production of *Twelfth Night*'. He performed in *Murder* ('I had the privilege of delivering the first dagger blow to Douglas Duncan's doomed Becket'); 'joined a Reel Club and came to love Scottish dancing'; and 'sang in a Gregorian chant choir conducted by a Benedictine from St Benet's Hall'.

Geoff Goodall (1950) had a piano, 'which I played noisily and often. This must have disturbed my next room neighbour, Corpus's newly arrived researcher, Robin Nisbet, but he never complained, bless him. But though tape recorders were not yet in evidence, 1951 did see the first long-playing vinyl records on the market and these supplemented my large collection of shellac discs, which I played frequently on my gramophone.' **Michael Goodman** (1950) had 'a portable HMV gramophone but only 78 rpm records. My choice of music apparently did not appeal to Mr Hardie who on one occasion sent his Secretary up to my room to ask me to minimize its volume.' **Philip Hamilton-Grierson** (1953) recalled that 'pop music had not yet been invented and we were mostly avid listeners to classic composers with the occasional forays into trad jazz'.

Bernard Jacobson (1956) was close friends with fellow musicians Brian Ponsford (1956) – with whom he joined the Bach Choir – and John Moffat (1956), 'a true Renaissance man':

> I spent several terms in an intensive study of the German lieder repertoire, concentrating in turn on Schubert, Schumann and Brahms, and more cursorily on Wolf and Richard Strauss. John's piano-playing, if not unfailingly accurate, revealed the musicality of his mind – any wrong notes he perpetrated, instead of creating horrible dissonances, always fitted naturally into the harmonic context. Brian, John and I formed a close-knit triumvirate throughout our student years, enjoying many pursuits together besides studying in one or other's rooms.

Christopher Watson (1957), another musician, 'joined innumerable

College and University clubs, and became an enthusiastic, if never very advanced, practitioner in the worlds of music, theatre, poetry, rowing, wine-tasting, political debating, etc.'. Although music was his main focus, 'in my first year I helped the Corpus Owlets put on a performance of Peter Ustinov's *The Love of Four Colonels*. There was a splendid group of poetry-lovers in Corpus, and we met regularly in each other's rooms and read aloud.' **Chris Patey** (1958), who had been a member of the National Youth Orchestra, played double bass in the University orchestra and other groups. Organ scholar **Alastair Sampson** (1963) recalled an encounter with Professor Fraenkel:

> We were rehearsing Bach's Cantata No. 4 *Christ Lag in Todes-banden*, and as soon as we had finished, the door burst open, and in he came, eyes filled with tears. He grasped my hand, and said: 'I last heard this work when I was in Vienna. It was with Gustav Mahler, and he said to me ...' but I was so shocked that I had just shaken the hand of a man who had shaken the hand of Gustav Mahler, that I never really did hear what he had said to him, save that the memory of the music was so fixed in his mind that we'd just brought it all flooding back to him. We all enjoyed the moment.

David Mark Jackson (1959) recalled the lighter side: 'My sitting room became the dressing room for the end of term "Smokers" in which I featured in a few sketches with Harry Charlton, Michael Gearin-Tosh, John Kinder and others, and sang Cliff Richard's "Travellin' Light" on guitars with Peter Delin to a surprisingly silent, tolerant and attentive audience.'

For **Jim Waterhouse** (1963), there had been 'an obvious lack of "culture" in my school life and home town'. His fellow students 'seemed to have learned much more about music, the arts and the theatre'. He decided to fill some of the gaps:

> So, I went to the cinema several times a week, and looked at the work of 'serious' directors (nearly all of whom were foreign).

There was, for example, a Bergman season at the Scala Cinema [later the Phoenix Picturehouse], followed by seasons devoted to Antonioni, Truffaut, and Russian and Polish directors. I note that my present film collection is dominated by this type of cinema – a lasting legacy of my days in Oxford.

I also liked 'serious music' and went to a meeting of the Oxford Music Society … The discussion afterwards centred on (I think) diminished sevenths and augmented thirds – or was it diminished thirds and augmented sevenths? This was not for me; I went back to my LPs.

Jonathan Dancy (1965) played the bass in several ensembles:

When I arrived at Oxford I was a very bad bass player; I had had a few lessons at school, but had then been in Africa for a year on VSO (Voluntary Service Overseas) and forgotten what little I knew. But my parents had very presciently bought me a not-too-bad Czechoslovakian bass to go up to Oxford with. Armed with this instrument, I was a desirable property almost no matter how badly I played; bass players were a rare commodity. And I enjoyed myself hacking away on this bass so much that I decided in my second year to spend a small legacy on a quality instrument, which I did. With the advice of some senior players in London, I bought an early nineteenth-century bass made by Bernard Simon Fendt, which is now worth very much more than I paid for it, and which effectively taught me to play properly, since if I played it well a wonderful sound emerged, and if I played badly it sounded terrible. So I had a life outside Corpus, one that stood me in good stead when I stayed on after graduation to do the BPhil in Philosophy. I even contemplated a life as a professional musician for a while.

Musical tastes were diverse. **David Jory** (1959) recalled 'going to hear Dominic Behan sing folk songs, which inspired a lifelong but not deep interest in folk songs'. **Paul Vaight** (1963) was from Merseyside, 'the epicentre of a popular music revolution with the Cavern, the

Beatles etc. in which I was an active participant before coming up. I don't remember any of my cohort sharing my enthusiasm for rhythm and blues and Chuck Berry but love of music has stayed and developed with me.'

Drama flourished. In 1967 the *Pelican Record* reported that 'Richard Carwardine has made his screen debut with his appearance as Cornelius in *Doctor Faustus*, the film version of the 1966 OUDS production which starred Richard Burton and Elizabeth Taylor. Made in Rome, the film had its premiere in Oxford at the beginning of term and has since been in general release.'[15] A highlight of the 450th Anniversary celebrations was Frank Lepper's play *The Bees,* produced by Alistair McIntosh, with music by Sir Jack Westrup. **Simon Squires** (1962) took part:

> Very properly I was cast as a worker-bee, i.e. don, and was able to witness the current President [Richard Carwardine] playing 'the President' (which he did with the utmost *dignitas*), and Sir Jack Westrup fulminating about the musical standard from his position halfway up the tree in Staircase 6 Quad during rehearsals. In a further anticipation of the future, the roles of 'Senior Tutor' and 'Chairman of Hebdomadal Council' were taken by the man who became Mods tutor at another college. And of course the whole drama depicted a fantastical vision (as dreamt by 'the President') of a college being subjected to government regulation of student numbers and other bureaucratic interference. Naturally the humour depended on the presumption that no such thing could conceivably become reality.

Andrew Purkis (1967) was in several productions:

> Most enjoyable of all were the Owlets' Revues. We did two, which were roughly akin to the Footlights at Cambridge, but Corpus-based. We wrote our own sketches as well as acting them. Though I say it myself, they were hilarious as well as silly, with the star turn being Richard Carwardine as Elvis singing 'Good Luck Charm' with the rest of us as the Jordanaires in the background.

According to **Mark Atkinson** (1971):

Christmas 1972 saw the inaugural Owlets pantomime. Ian Wood wrote a script loosely based on *Cinderella* featuring the rugby team's front row (Brandon Jones, Martin Glass and Dave Midgley) as the Ugly Sisters; Eddie Fitzgerald as the Fairy Godmother. Other participants included myself as the Major Domo, Ian MacLean, Ray Dawkins, Jeremy Holt and Clive Burgess who went on to write the scripts for *Sleeping Beauty* the next year and for *Jack and the Beanstalk* the year after. The production was a huge success due in large part to the music played by Chris Ellicott and the chief bartender, none other than Andrew Fowler (current Fellow) who kept both cast and audience well refreshed.

Like sport, artistic success was prone to wax and wane. In 1980 **Margaret Harper** (1979) wrote home that 'Owlets, the College dramatic society, looked in danger of fizzling out completely. Nobody wanted to be President or Secretary so eventually I said I'd be Secretary which isn't too arduous (or shouldn't be).' Happily, drama continued. As **Ben Whitby** (1986) recalled, 'mostly I spear-carried in plays, with a mad rush of auditions at the end of every term for the next term's plays, as a way to get out of College and meet different people'. **Helen Eastman** (1996), President of the ETC, directed Seamus Heaney's *The Cure at Troy* at Edinburgh. The year 2001 saw Corpuscles involved in *Chess – the Musical,* which played at the Old Fire Station and Edinburgh, and the Owlets took *Cressida* to Edinburgh.[16] In 2006 'Corpus illustrated once more its dramatic blood by taking a play, written by Alec Garton-Ash, to the Edinburgh Festival Fringe'.[17] Despite 'the College's almost complete absence of any dramatic talent or experience', **James Kierstead** (2006) performed in *Doctor Faustus* in the Chapel: 'it succeeded in sending my father to the hospital with an allergic reaction to dust only a few hours after I had climactically cursed the parents that engendered me. The reaction may also have had something to do with the little red dress worn, quite unholily, by our female Mephistopheles.'

The bonds which drama could engender were illustrated, as **Geoff**

Goodall (1950) recalled, by the 1951 production of *Murder in the Cathedral*:

> Fifty years later, when a number of Old Corpuscles were keen to raise money to help schools in war-torn Sierra Leone, the idea was mooted of a rerun of *Murder*, using the same cast. The miracle is that it did actually happen and Douglas Duncan played the Archbishop in both productions. Eight performances took place in the College Chapel and Cloisters in 2001 with almost the same cast, 50 years on. This unusual event made the *Guinness Book of Records* and at the same time, enough money for the Corpus Charity – Knowledge Aid to Sierra Leone (KASL) – to be able to send a set of computers to equip their empty schools and download essential teaching materials.
>
> In 2007 the KASL Committee started to plan another rerun, this time of Frank Lepper's satyrical 1967 play about a mythical President of Corpus, entitled *The Bees*. We got as far as casting and rehearsals, but then the leading man who was to play 'the President' himself fell ill and we had to cancel. That actor was Professor Richard Carwardine. His health recovered and not long after, he was elected the real President of Corpus.

Music remained important. **Julian Weitzenfeld** (1967), an American postgraduate, described Oxford as a 'musical ferment', hearing performers as varied as Sviatoslav Richter, the D'Oyly Carte Opera Company, the Incredible String Band and 'two-fifths of the Pentangle'. **David Stogdale** (1969) reflected changing horizons:

> As an incompetent schoolboy musician I had some grounding from Bach to Beethoven. Now, in the evenings – and I'm afraid during the day as well – there was Miles Davis, Oscar Peterson, Charlie Parker, Verdi and Puccini; and while the Beatles and the Stones remained the rock/pop/R&B colossi domestically, from across the Atlantic anarchic or edgier influences included Arlo Guthrie, the Doors, Frank Zappa and the Grateful Dead.

Theodore Saunders (1975) 'spent a lot of time playing the organ, much to the annoyance, I am sure, of some library users'. With the Chaplain's support, he established a mixed choir. As well as singing in Corpus they visited local churches and spent a week at Wells Cathedral. 'Another venture which a few of the choir undertook was to sing grace one day in Hall. The bread rolls came in handy, as we were pelted with them.'

Rock also reached Corpus. **Adam Sharples** (1972) played rhythm guitar in Ugly Rumours, alongside Tony Blair (St John's). **Eugene Dainov** (1976) was a member of 'a Corpus outfit called "Dynamo Joe", which achieved a brief review in the *Oxford Times* in 1978', and was described as '1st CCC Rock and Roll performing group'.[18] **Nick Hassall** (1989) drummed for the Bushdoctors, whose first gig was at Corpus: 'Alas, we did not play at the Corpus Ball. I offered our services, but felt duly snubbed when James MacIntosh, who was on the Ball Committee, let me know that our services (which would have been free) would not be required.' **George Robertson** (1991) played in George's Big Words, who performed at several gigs, including college balls.[19] **David Sooby** (2003) recalled:

We formed a band of Corpuscles (called 'The Fuming Julias') and played near enough every venue in Oxford, mostly for free drinks, including a party to celebrate winning *University Challenge*. The fact that I had never picked up a bass guitar before that first rehearsal was irrelevant and I look back fondly on being a rock star for a couple of evenings of my life, including three balls.

I also tried my hand at comedy and ended up writing and acting in sketches, as well as stand-up comedy, which remains one of the most terrifying experiences of my life, but doing comedy with six other friends from Corpus was a huge amount of fun. One of the best quotes about Corpus during my time there was after an evening where out of six comedians performing, three were from Corpus, and the individual running the event described Corpus as 'the biggest little college in Oxford'.

Some preferred jazz. **Greg Finch** (1981) recalled **Sarah Williams** (1980):

> Her sheer creative energy and organizational ability shone through as she created a succession of bands in College and during her year abroad in France – including the Blue Blemishes, the Mahogany Hall Jazz Band, and Raindance (for whom she played bongos and drove the van!). During vacations she would play as a guest musician in her father's jazz band in Cleethorpes.[20]

Not everyone sustained their musical interests. For **Beverley Patterson** (1979), 'the only regret I have about my time at Oxford is that I did not pursue music (clarinet and violin). Despite having merit at Grade 8 clarinet and having performed in the school proms at the Albert Hall, in music I felt overwhelmed by the talent at Oxford. I was always a shy player and did not like a big audience and not having my wonderful music teachers to support me made it difficult to continue with music.' But music continued to flourish. **Annette Richards** (1984) recalled resurrecting the St Cecilia Society, concerts in the Chapel, and the sheer range of Corpus music: 'Ian Smith played bebop or Purcell on his trumpet; Val Cunningham did Louis Armstrong; the brass quartet, which included the Bursar, led the carols at Christmas; Tom Blake, my scout, sang loudly in the stairwell in the morning. The choir sang in Hall: madrigals at the Corpus Christi Day dinner and carols at Christmas, when it braved the food fight.'[21] By 2006 the choir 'reached new levels of professionalism in terms of its corporate identity, its organization and of course its new CD and website' and 'embarked upon our biggest ever tour to Canada'.[22] The 2010s saw a Corpus string orchestra and the first 'President's Concert in recent memory', at which musicians from the JCR, MCR and SCR performed.[23]

Dining

Corpus sports and arts were open to anyone interested – or who could be pressured to make up the numbers. College dining clubs were a long-standing tradition, projecting a rather more exclusive image. Corpus had several, each with a distinct ethos. **Peter Baldwin** (1941) thought the Sundial Club 'carried prestige within the College as a select discussion group, entertaining and being entertained by invited guests to lead the talk', and **Graham Binns** (1943) enjoyed its 'air of quiet gravity. People took snuff and read papers to each other – no celebrity-hunting here – and there was a sense of *quality* about their proceedings'.[24] **Charles Thomas** (1948) thought it 'too serious for anyone save Greats men'.

Philip Hamilton-Grierson (1953) was secretary of the rival Chevron Society: 'we invited dons to add intellectual tone but [it] was primarily a gourmet experience. I remember discussing with the Manciple our requirements for whitebait from the Baltic.' There was also 'the Shaftesbury Club, a joint Univ/Corpus affair, and the Meander Club, a joint Merton–Corpus dining society which sported a particularly choice salmon-pink and sky-blue tie. The grander University Scots also had their Caledonian Dining Society which rivalled the Bullingdon for bad behaviour and wore green tailcoats and purple waistcoats with silver buttons. I was not grand but scraped in through jolly friends.'

Mueen Afzal (1960) was a member of the Sundial and Wasps. 'Both clubs met termly in the Law Library (now the College Office), to eat an excellent dinner and to prolong celebrations well into the night.'[25] **David Mark Jackson** (1959) recalled:

> I was lucky enough to be elected to two of the Corpus dining clubs – the Junior Sundial and the Chevron. The dinners were absolutely superb and the wines were provided from the brilliant SCR cellar, with helpful advice from my tutor, who was the sommelier at the time. While I was President, in rotation, of the Chevron, Peter Dawkins and a few members of Vincent's were dining and as a result I 'knew a few members on the committee'. Our amicable and suitably 'refreshed' state greatly helped my election to the club in 1962 – there was no serious sporting explanation for this honour. After the dinners there used to be 'cunning plans', such as driving a herd of bullocks into Merton and locking them in.

This was borderline vandalism, yet there was something inspiring about the sight of those noble bovines thundering around Merton bellowing mellifluously as we watched from the security of the Fellows' Building.

Patrick Bourdillon (1964) described the Chevrons as 'the dining club for those who would be called in the United States the "jocks". We were in furious competition with the more intellectual Wasps.'[26] **William Waldegrave** (1965), however, thought the Wasps' 'sole function' was 'to promote long, jolly and rather drunken dinners'.[27] **Bill Gunn** (1965) recalled:

Given my subsequent wine trade career, perhaps the most formative of all my Corpus experiences was an invitation to join the Wasps. This was an awakening indeed. I look now at the menu of the first dinner I attended, in June 1966, and I marvel at its opulence. I am conscious, now as then, of the breadth of the chasm that yawned between the sophistication of what was on offer and the ability of an innocent, attuned only to Mateus Rosé, Blue Nun and wines of that ilk, to appreciate it. But I became a fast learner, and a fascination with fine food and wine, and a love of their enjoyment in cheerful, articulate company, were soon strongly embedded. We affected to look down, de haut en bas, on the 'hearty' Chevrons, whose festivities we considered barbarian in comparison, but for whose sporting prowess we held a sneaking admiration.

The gap between 'jolly dinners' and 'borderline vandalism' was fine. In 1969

A few lucky men, members of the Chevrons, were in 8 Magpie Lane to witness the debagging of 'Banger' Nash and the ritual ablution of his genitals with Teacher's whisky. On the second night it was the Wasps Club which hit the headlines when some of its young gentlemen found amusement in spraying a fire extinguisher onto the vomit one of them had left on Staircase 6 and following this up by washing down the xerox machine with a similar liquid.[28]

Not everyone was impressed. **Malcolm Underwood** (1966) found 'echoes of the past, in narrowly class-based associations such as the Wasps and Chevrons dining clubs, the chief distinction between which seemed to rest on which rank of public school their members had attended'. Some avoided them entirely. Others, including **Jonathan Dancy** (1965), formed their own alternative: 'Unimpressed (and uninvited by) the existing clubs (Wasps and Chevrons) we formed our own breakfast club, which we called the Maschalids, on the suggestion of Tony MacLean's Classics teacher from Oundle, David Gaine, who was our first guest. This club did not elect new members beyond the founding members, and faded away some years after we all left Oxford.' As **Bill Gunn** recalled, they met 'for an extended breakfast of mixed grill and champagne at The Bull in Nettlebed (our more opulent members owning cars), followed by golf at Huntercombe or a walk on the Ridgeway. The Maschalids outlived Oxford, but drifted apart in the decades that followed as wives, families and other preoccupations intervened.'

Dining clubs continued into the 1980s. **Andrew Mason** (1979) reported that the '1832 Popular Front', a group opposed to changes to evening Hall, tried to form one: 'It is to be hoped that the brotherhood will flourish for many years, and that traditional activities will continue to be honoured in Corpus, and not viewed in a polemical spirit. In this age, when Oxford daily becomes more depressingly normal, we may perhaps be forgiven for adding one more harmless peculiarity to the scene.'[29] But in 1987 **Hans Towler** (1982) reported the 'demise' of the Chevrons, describing it as

a Corpus dining society of recent years and of sordid reputation. Its membership (including the author of this article and one or two others who might wish, rather smugly, to regard themselves as 'ideologically sound') was exclusively male and was supposed to represent the sporting cream of the College. The society met three times a year – drinks parties at the end of Michaelmas and

Trinity Terms and a dinner at the end of Hilary Term – and its notoriety stemmed from the aftermath of these events and the 'qualifications' for membership. The combination of far too much booze and a collection of 'good chaps' tended to often end in a sorry display of vomiting and hooliganism. It was not always like that, but it *was* often enough for the 'Chevrons' to find themselves banned from meeting in the College precincts on a lengthy and frequent basis.[30]

By this time, however, 'such behaviour had, by and large, died out. Indeed the "Chevrons" as an institution seems to have passed away.' The reason, he thought, was the growing acceptance of women: the club had represented 'a hankering after the good old days when we were "all boys together"'. But 'as more and more female undergraduates arrived in College and as (perhaps) fewer and fewer neurotic public-school boys came up, the need perceived by some for at least one bastion of pure masculinity began to fade, and now seems, with one or two exceptions, to be virtually non-existent'.

Ironically, as noted earlier, a female dining club – Les Femmes Savantes – was established, presided over by **Catherine Paxton** (1985):

My former school is a comprehensive in Sunderland and during my time in Oxford I have participated in and chaired the OUSU Target Schools scheme. Some might argue such credentials ought to incline me to oppose an institution which epitomizes some of the more controversial aspects of Oxford, rather than actually preside over it. But, I own that it has been my goal throughout to preserve as much formality and tradition as is viable. Hence, Les Femmes are single sex; dress up, not down, for dinners; and receive invitations which are stiff, white and look nice on the mantelpiece. Dining society veterans advocated formality as a buttress which prevents the society from lapsing into a nebulous arrangement. Moreover, if the society is to continue to be the sort of experience I was looking for when I put Oxford top of my UCCA form, then this policy is clearly necessary. From a purely personal viewpoint, I see Les Femmes as compensating for the disappointing lack of formality and tradition at Corpus. In a sense, the society does cater for a need, admittedly not universally felt, but a need nonetheless.[31]

Like the reinstatement of Formal Hall and new Corpus 'traditions' such as Burns Night and Corpus Christi Day, Les Femmes was a reaction to the radical wave of the previous years. Nevertheless, the old-style, single-sex dining clubs seem to have had their day. **Colin Holmes,** Domestic Bursar between 1987 and 2014, thought that 'during my time at Corpus I cannot recall any dining clubs being active within the College. I think that they had largely died out by then'.

Parties, bops and balls

If dining clubs were in decline, Corpus remained periodically enlivened by dances, balls and 'sweaty bops'. The 1948 College Dance was said to be 'the third dance in succession after a gap of 50 years':

> The floor, while undoubtedly over the Plimsoll line by the end of the evening, provided enough space for elegant gyration in the Latin American style, to music provided by the excellent Royal Marines Band, and by an admirable solo pianist during the Band interval. The weather, while hardly conducive to pleasant dalliance in the garden, had the grace to remain at least neutral – an important condition for success for a dance in so small a Hall.[32]

Corpus had a Reel Club ('Reelers') – run, according to **Don Montague** (1954), by 'a merry gang of Scots'. Women were invited by the Committee, who 'had excellent taste in such matters':

> The Committee and friends assembled after dinner in the church hall, with a wind-up gramophone and supplies of orange squash as our frugal refreshment, and merriment broke out. I was totally incompetent at any kind of dancing (despite lessons from a buxom middle-aged lady with a steel corset in rooms down

towards the railway station), and soon earned the nickname of 'Don-The-Learner'. My instinct for playing the fool was very useful, and there were other Sassenachs almost as incompetent as I was. We had enormous fun – even the extra man, whose job it was to wind the gramophone and mix the orange squash. And we met (and in not a few cases ultimately married) some very interesting women.

Mueen Afzal (1960) recalled 'bird and bottle' parties:

Guests were expected to bring a bottle and, if possible, a girl-friend. Music was provided, with Elvis Presley, Françoise Hardy, Chubby Checker and Joan Baez great favourites for listening as well as dancing. The problem with such parties was that these had to terminate by 11pm, when women guests as well as non-residents were required to leave College. So it was usually more convenient to have these parties in digs, which belonged to friends who were not living in College. Those parties would go late into the night.

Some years there were summer balls. At one, **David Mark Jackson** (1959) performed in a cabaret: 'I thought we were brilliant, but I'm not sure anyone else did.' At another, **Bill Morris** (1964) recalled his room being 'allocated to the headline act, Mr Georgie Fame – he of the Blue Flames':

I remember him telling me that he had been born Clive Powell, had started work at 15 in a Lancashire cotton mill, had been discovered while on holiday with his mum and dad at Butlin's and was then appearing at the Flamingo Club in Soho, buoyed by a recent no. 1 in the Hit Parade. This was his first time in Oxford and he loved every minute of it. Georgie is still performing and I wonder if he remembers his evening on Staircase 12.

The College's 450th Anniversary saw a Commemoration Ball with over 1,000 guests: 'The varied music of Alan Price, Cat Stephens, Zoot

Money, the Lorne Gibson [Trio] and John Bassett provided something for everyone and the Ball Committee were pleasantly surprised to observe none, even of the more senior guests, dropping by the wayside in the small hours.'[33] A few years later **Adam Sharples** (1972) played at an 'Alternative' Ball:

'I was standing on a corner in Winslow Arizona, such a fine sight to see ...' With the Stones' hit 'Brown Sugar' the future prime minister opened the set for Ugly Rumours in Hall. It was the summer of 1974 and, rebelling against the excesses of the traditional college balls with their high prices and formal dress, Corpus was staging an Alternative Ball. It was a rough and ready affair headlined by the relatively competent student band Bluebird, with Ugly Rumours the nearest thing to a Corpus band, as warm-up.

According to **Mel Johnson** (1972), Blair 'wore white skin-tight trousers and strummed his bass guitar with far less dexterity than he now applies to politics'. The ball was 'the recreational highlight of my time at Corpus':

For a pound you heard a string quartet, a jazz band and a rock group, ate a substantial meal, drank very cheaply, saw a streaker, had a good 'bop' and still felt as if your left-wing credentials were intact. Things did go a little awry when the undergraduate barkeepers, making a protest against the market economy, bought more wine from Oriel and gave it away for nothing.[34]

Dance was another option. **David Normington** (1970) became president of the University Ballroom Dance Society:

[It] gave me a much wider circle of friends, two of whom I am still very friendly with. We used to go down to Iffley Stadium and cart the record player – that does date me! – up Iffley Road every Wednesday night and we used to put it up in a room at the top of the stands. The floor was rubber, really unsuitable for dancing: it used to make your feet and legs ache, but we had a great time.[35]

Margaret Harper (1979) took tap lessons. **Danielle Sanderson** (1982) 'dallied' with ballroom dance, 'until my dance partner spent the summer in Israel and came home very orthodox, and hence unable to dance with a woman!' But parties and 'bops' were the norm. Writing home, **Margaret Harper** described a 'brilliant' staircase party: 'It was all up and down the corridor and we had a really good bop!' At another, 'we had to wear white (I wore my posh nightie) and carry a carnation. The Beer Cellar has been painted white so it looked like something out of *Vogue*.' There was a fancy-dress party, and one 'at which I have to wear a silly hat. We're obviously all regressing. No one ever seems to have a party where one doesn't have to wear something peculiar.' **Nicola Feather** (1981) remembered a concert in the Fraenkel Room and a disco in Hall: but 'more common were the "sweaty discos" in the Beer Cellar, named for the sweat that reputedly dripped off the ceiling after a few solid hours of dancing. These private parties were fun, and anyone from College could just turn up, invited or not.'

Tim Clackson (1983) considered Corpus 'quite a conservative college as regards entertainment: videos, discos and "normal" parties were what people "voted for with their feet". "Different" events were less popular, even if the alcoholic carrot was dangled. This perhaps reflects on the nature of Corpus as a whole: people tend to spend most of their time either much involved in College events or completely divorced from them, with little middle ground.'[36] **Jacquie Kelly** (1984) tried to extend the range: 'Along with Alan Mclean, I infiltrated the JCR Committee as Social Secretary and we introduced Corpus to the delights of the alternative indie music scene, as well as the Talent Night where I did my unrepeatable impression of Madonna, a 1960s and 1970s night, and the notorious Easter Bunny Cocktail Party (we didn't know you have to dilute cocktails when you make them in industrial quantities).' For **Ben Whitby** (1986) social life tended to 'begin and end' in the Beer Cellar. There were also 'JCR "bops" (normally a disco, some kind of theme, maybe in the Hall or Rainolds Room at Xmas, mostly in the Beer Cellar) with big bowls of "punch" (I still don't like blue drinks as a result). Parties at houses. Club nights in rooms over pubs or student nights at discos in the town.' There were balls: 'Corpus ones were biennial. I went to two and really enjoyed them. At the second one, I had been elected Ball Committee Chairman. We sold too few tickets, had too many entertainments and lost what felt like a lot of money but it was a great party. And someone stole my cassette player.'

Nick Hassall (1989) helped organize an 'acid house style party' and a barn dance in the Cloister Quad, featuring 'bales of straw from a local farmer which we distributed liberally all over the Quad. We were lucky we didn't have a horrendous inferno and burn the College down given you could smoke anywhere in those days – and most people did.' **Elizabeth O'Brien** (1990) had to discourage fire risk at a 'toga party' at Liddell, 'which involved the wearing of bed-sheets as togas' accompanied by candles. **Caroline Knapp** (2005) recalled thrice-termly 'bops':

> Everyone was encouraged to dress up according to the theme, and the more elaborate the costume the better. The amount of effort put in ranged from the truly incredible to the non-existent (I was usually closer to the latter end of the scale). The Christmas bop was the main event of Michaelmas Term when, for one night only, Hall would be made over into a dance floor. When the music stopped, everyone would head out to the Front Quad for a truly anarchic rendition of the hokey-pokey around the Pelican. The biennial College ball was also a great event. I attended four Corpus balls, all of which were wonderful in their own way. I particularly remember the 2008 Heaven and Hell Ball, for which we joined forces with St Hugh's.

Alexandra Harmer (2008) presided over the 2010 ball:

> I loved the experience: getting together a great committee; convincing a rather anti-ball SCR to accept our proposal and let us go ahead with it; creating and planning the event along a 'medieval' theme; choosing a nice dress; somehow managing to get through Mods a month before the ball; dealing with last-minute electrical dramas; and then watching the whole thing unfold on the night with medieval dancing and inflatable jousting and a hog roast and excited people filling the College. It was a wonderful

opportunity not only to do one of the things I love best – organizing! – but also to work with and get to know a huge range of the people in Corpus, from JCR and MCR to SCR and other staff, all coming together to create a wonderful, happy occasion.

It is striking how many social and extracurricular opportunities Corpus offered, and how almost anyone, talented or not, could get involved. Virtually any interest could be followed. **Camilla Byk** (1992) recalled one special moment:

I was a keen painter and one snowy night I set up my easel by the Radcliffe Camera, one of my favourite buildings in the whole world, and I painted through the night, using the street lights that lit up the facade. I remember saying to myself, you will never forget this moment, and I haven't. It is one of the happiest moments I had in Oxford and I felt the privilege of being free and able to do what I wanted whenever I wanted.

The proliferation of clubs, teams and activities helped bring College members together and foster their identification with Corpus. Some limited their leisure activities to informal socializing with friends, and some preferred to spend time and energy on University-level activities. But virtually everyone spent a lot of time with fellow Corpuscles, through informal and organized activities, forming bonds which crossed personal backgrounds, academic disciplines and year groups. As **Francis Oakley** (1950), who arrived 'with much maturing to do', observed:

Had I gone to one of the larger (and, perhaps, snootier) colleges, it could all have proved to be too much and I might have been tempted to withdraw almost entirely into things academic, where I felt more secure, and to have become what in derogatory American parlance is called 'a grind'. And that would have been a great shame. The rich co-curricular life of cultural and athletic activity, and the lively social interchange among students of different backgrounds that goes with it, is an integral (and strongly educative) part of undergraduate life in a residential university community like Oxford. Not all the teaching and learning that goes on, after all, takes place in tutorial and lecture hall.

Corpus Chapel, 2014. *Courtesy of Patrick Meyer Higgins (2005)*

7

'VIVE LE COLLÈGE LIBRE': POLITICS AND RELIGION

Sometimes we broke into the hubbub of the JCR, where future statesmen argued whilst the rest of us drank and gossiped.

Eliza Pakenham

The thing I am most grateful to Corpus for is the sense of belonging to an ancient institution which has its roots in the sacred.

Sebastian Barker

One of the opportunities of university was the chance to explore and develop social, political and religious views and beliefs. Although Corpus had gained a 'lefty' reputation by the 1980s, it was never a particularly 'political' college like Balliol. And in a largely secular age, strong religious commitments appeared an exception, rather than central, to most students' lives. Nevertheless, political and religious affiliations remained very important for some, of genuine interest to others and significant for the life of the College. If the most active and committed remained a minority, they brought an important dimension not just to their own lives but also to those around them.

Politics

Political engagement took many forms. At College level it normally focused on the JCR, where small-p politics were usually more significant than Politics with a large P. At University level there were well-established clubs as well as – most famously – the Oxford Union, the proving ground for many student politicians with aspirations for the national stage. But 'politics' could extend beyond these formal structures, most strikingly in the radical movements of the 1960s and 1970s. And even amongst those with no desire to engage actively in political life, there were many who recognized its importance and were interested – even fascinated – to observe it, if only from a discreet distance.

Political life in post-war Corpus seems to have been quiet. According to **David Lewis** (1945), 'Conservative and Labour thinking were at a low ebb in College, and Communism was confined to one faculty. There were, however, a few terms in which a "Corpus Caucus", headed by Philip Shelbourne and Philip Hayes, had a strong presence in the Liberal Club.' Lewis was active in the Jewish Society (JSoc), at a time of controversy over the creation of Israel: 'This even over-spilled into Corpus; I chaired one meeting there in which I narrowly avoided the lynching of Max Beloff, who had been suggesting that there was something to be said for British government policy.'[1] But **Don Montague** (1954) was perhaps more typical: 'I was politically unconscious, and so never joined any of the political clubs.' **Philip Hamilton-Grierson** (1953) noted the absence of 'political angst':

> One of my friends even retired to bed for two weeks, suffering – the doctor said – from severe apathy (later he went on to become a Labour government minister). Churchill was prime minister and the country was recovering gently from the privations of war. There were few clouds in the sky. Indeed, Bulganin and Khrushchev visited Oxford to celebrate the temporary ending of the cold war. We spied them taking tea in Magdalen gardens. Actually I think it was hock with cucumber sandwiches. Life that summer had an almost *Brideshead*-like dream quality. Political

awakening came later in 1956 after we had gone down with Eden's ill-devised invasion of Suez and Russia's invasion of Hungary. Britain's imperial glory became a thing of the past. Oh, to have been up at Oxford when the storm broke! As it was, my faith in the Tory Party was obliterated, never to return.

David Blackmore (1956) was a freshman during Suez: 'I had never met such articulate people, and mealtimes in Hall were notable for the ferocity of opinion and debate on the Suez question which was raging at the time.' Although JCR President **Michael Barnes** (1953) resisted attempts to get the JCR to take a stance – 'because it seemed to me quite wrong that the JCR, which was purely a College forum, should adopt what was inevitably a party-political stance to some extent, no matter how deeply the issue may have divided the country' – he strongly opposed the intervention:

> Undergraduates were not supposed to go to London during term time without permission, and I can remember standing on Oxford station in unaccustomed trilby and dark glasses on my way to take part in the Trafalgar Square demonstration in order to avoid detection, which seems an extraordinary thing to have to do, looking back. It was Suez that finally made me decide to attempt a career in politics, and during my eight years in the House of Commons from 1966 to 1974 I came to be very grateful for the experience that I got in having to deal with the dynamics of JCR politics.[2]

There were Corpus radicals, including **Richard Gott** (1958): 'Political activism and internationalism were the flavour of the time, symbolized perhaps by the fact that the two largest Oxford societies in those years were the Campaign in Oxford University for Nuclear Disarmament (COUND) and COSMOS, the local branch of the United Nations Association.' John Gittings (1958) won a College prize and requested 'the collected works of Mao Tse-tung, leather-bound and embossed with the College crest – a request that was granted. He was, after all, reading Chinese.' Gott attended Campaign for Nuclear

Disarmament (CND) demonstrations in London, with the agreement of Trevor Aston (who was happy to rearrange tutorials) but the disapproval of the Dean, Michael Brock.[3] **Mueen Afzal** (1960) described Richard Kirkwood (1960) as 'on the radical Left of the Labour Party and perhaps the staunchest of CND supporters at Corpus'. He was arrested at CND demonstrations, again to the concern of Brock. But this was unusual: **Ian Wylie** (1958) described the general mood: 'Very little politics, those were the best days of Harold Macmillan; the Union was openly despised in Corpus as a lefty sink. No NUS affiliation.'

College politics centred on the JCR, though **Ian McNeill** (1959) recalled the role of The Bear: 'It was near enough to serve as a waiting room for those JCR members who disagreed with their left-wing colleagues but did not want to hear a JCR debate. They relied on Brian Sedgemore to represent the opposition until it was time for the vote, when they were summoned in time and sufficient numbers to defeat any motion deemed too "leftie".' **David Jory** (1959) recalled someone lobbying for election as JCR President:

> Such outright politicking did not sit well with some of the students so, as the time for the vote approached during the meeting at which the election was to take place, emissaries were sent to the Library, The Bear, and other places I can't remember. This resulted in a substantial influx of Corpuscles who were told to raise their hands to vote when told to and not to ask questions. They did their democratic duty, defeated the aspiring politician (who, if memory serves, reached his goal a term or two later) and went back to their previous activities.

'We lived', he thought, 'our Corpus years in an unreal world.' The Sharpeville massacre 'hardly dented the armour which largely kept the real world away from us and we were certainly not as outraged as we should have been. Still, someone started "Oxfam lunches" at Corpus at which we ate bread and cheese in someone's room and donated money to "the starving millions".' Even the Cuban Missile Crisis had a mixed impact: **Tom Hassall** (1962) remembered 'the deathly hush in Hall ... when we felt we were on the verge of World War III'.[4] But **Leslie Stevenson** (1962) 'was so excited and engrossed in the new world that was opening up to me in Oxford (coming from Northern Ireland) that I was hardly aware of the Cuban nuclear missile crisis that threatened the wider world'. **Simon Squires** (1962) remembered President Kennedy's assassination: 'I was at a formal dinner in Hall: Frank Hardie announced the fact from the High Table, a statement that was succeeded by prolonged and unbroken silence from everyone there.'

William Waldegrave (1965), who thought Corpus 'a very unpolitical college' and 'took no part in JCR politics', had ambitions on the University stage. Corpus support helped elect him president of the Oxford University Conservative Association (OUCA) and the Oxford Union:

> Corpus would always come out and support its own, whatever it was for: OUDS or OUCA or anything. This was because it was a community, which was nice. But because Corpus was very small, there always had to be an intercollegiate electoral alliance if I was to succeed in OUCA. My faction consisted of Exeter and St John's, with New College and Christ Church as the enemy. The little nucleus of Corpus Conservatives – Peter Sinclair, David Scott, Anthony Maclean – was very helpful, and my caucus made quite an effective little group. Because Corpus was a small college, and because in standing for office in University organizations you couldn't rely on a large home base, you had to go out and canvass more, which was no bad thing. It made one concentrate on the tactics of how to get elected to things.[5]

Gareth Moore (1966), who 'thought it was my ambition to become prime minister', found Corpuscles – William Waldegrave and Martin Wolf – dominating OUCA and the Democratic Labour Club (DLC). 'This supremacy was sustained partly by Corpus Conservatives being members also of the DLC, and vice versa, and both casting their votes in each other's society elections in favour of the Corpuscular candidate.'[6] He became DLC minutes secretary before losing interest and, after flirting with the Marxist Society, abandoning politics. Others, including **Bill Gunn** (1965), were non-political from the start: 'I had little interest in politics or the Union, which in hindsight I regret.'

The late 1960s saw a new student radicalism, prompted by the Vietnam War, unrest in the US and Europe, and a broader cultural shift challenging 'authority' of all kinds. In 1967 flyers appeared in pigeonholes demanding 'Democracy in Corpus'. As JCR President **Alan Goulty** (1965) reported: 'Student politics raised its ugly head in the JCR in December when, amid cries of *"Vive le collège libre"*, two Canadian freshmen sponsored a motion demanding JCR representation on the Governing Body. After impassioned debate the motion was lost by 24 votes to 23 with several abstentions, but the general feeling remains that the prairies have more wind in store.'[7] Attitudes across Oxford polarized. Unsurprisingly, **James Dixon** (1966) found 'very little sympathy for the student cause among Air Squadron members':

> Many of the student leaders were seemingly American draft-dodgers, and there was frivolous chatter amongst us how we might raid a key railway signalbox and have the special train running for the Grosvenor Square disturbances shunted into a siding. Or even a leaflet drop from overhead Oxford in the middle of the night. But it was idle chatter, and we had more interesting things to do.
>
> In the case of Corpus, the name of Grant Amyot sticks in the memory vividly. I was very much a person who enjoyed the second sitting of dinner, when the wearing of gowns was obligatory. Within milliseconds of arriving, he was protesting, but to many this was all rather pointless when he could so easily have eaten half an hour earlier, when there were no gowns. As for the locking of the main gate at midnight – was there not an easy climbing-in route, albeit that you might get waylaid by Long Tom on occasion?

But **Kenneth Reynolds** (1966), studying French, experienced the Paris *événements*:

Being a student in Paris in 1968 was quite exceptionally wonderful. I was 20 years old, had my own flat and Vélosolex and was receiving what seemed a princely salary in return for some eight hours a week of conversation classes. I regularly made my way to work past the coachloads of CRS (Compagnies Républicaines de Sécurité) mobile police units, in full riot gear, lining the rue Soufflot in front of the Panthéon. Equally regularly, I was caught up in the sometimes violent and always colourful confrontations between students and the forces of order.

Despite (or maybe because of) the constant strikes, the daily disruption, the baton charges and the flying paving slabs, Paris seemed the only place in the world to be a student in 1968. Returning to Oxford after such turmoil was a distressingly dull disappointment. Life was too ordered, too cosy, too undemanding. Proust, Baudelaire – even Rimbaud – seemed irrelevant to the upheaval shaking French society.

Although the protests failed to achieve 'anything of lasting import-ance', they left him 'marked for life, knowing that I could never find peace again among the quiet cloisters within the College walls'.

These years were marked by demonstrations and sit-ins. Fellow **Christopher Taylor**, as duty pro-Proctor, became caught up after Enoch Powell MP spoke at the Town Hall:

We left the building accompanied by a few Bulldogs. As we headed towards Corpus I heard a confused noise in front of us, and we encountered a column of perhaps 50 or so students running towards us along Blue Boar Lane. They ran, arms linked in ranks of five or six, with a curious high-stepping gait, shouting, not 'Knees up, Mother Brown', as would have suited their manner of progress, but 'Ho, Ho, Ho Chi Minh, we shall fight and we shall win'. As far as I remember, the front rank collided with some of the Bulldogs, which sufficed to break their formation, and there were a few moments in which everyone milled about the street, uncertain what to do. (Something like a medieval battle, I imagine.) Then I heard a loud clattering of hobnailed boots, and a considerable force of police rushed towards the students, pushing them back into Blue Boar Lane, which became completely blocked by the press of bodies, while the opposed front rows pushed against each other like an overgrown rugby scrum. Seized by schoolboy enthusiasm, I joined the police vanguard and pushed as hard as my academic impedimenta allowed, until after a minute or two I reflected that fighting hand to hand with undergraduates was not really appropriate for an official (even a minor one) of the University, and extricated myself from the mêlée. We left the police to it and returned peacefully to Corpus via the High and Oriel Square.

He also recalled the Clarendon Building break-in, 'in search of the great bugbear of the day, secret files which the University was supposed to hold on radical students'. One of his PPE pupils from Ruskin ('at the time a leading seminary of sedition') was accused of assaulting the University Marshal, though eventually the charge was dropped. But despite the excitements, as **Andrew Purkis** (1967) observed, life in Corpus was largely unaffected: 'Although we were aware of great events such as the anti-Vietnam War protests and the *événements* of Paris, and individuals were caught up in them, I would say that they did not greatly disturb Corpus life (or, despite some noise at Union debates and odd Trotskyite demonstrations, Oxford life more widely). We were too comfortable and embedded in making the most of Oxford.' **David Stogdale** (1969) agreed:

> In the wider world it seemed a time of protest, in America overwhelmingly against the war in Vietnam but everywhere against authority. *If* and *Easy Rider* were cinematic smash hits. The Paris student riots, Tariq Ali's protest marches and the Woodstock Festival were recent or contemporary events. In Oxford this spilled over in the form of the Clarendon 'sit-in'. To this day I am amazed it was allowed to go on so long and even that it was allowed to happen at all. Meanwhile, unperturbed by the forces of social entropy, the scouts ensured Corpus ran timelessly on.

According to **Nick Witney** (1969), 'we were resolutely apolitical, rather despising the Union and its ways; the most hotly-contested JCR office was that of Glutton, the students' tribune on College food'. But Corpus was not altogether immune. **Rob Stepney** (1971) thought students 'quite deeply divided'. The big issues for his group – 'the politically engaged, non-rowing, dope smokers' – included Barclays Bank, a scholarship for Lesotho students, access for women, representation on the Governing Body, and a university-wide students' union. **David Archard** (1969) described the JCR as

> the site of regular politicized debates about the College and the world beyond. We moved the JCR's bank account from Barclays in protest at the bank's South African connections. We abolished the ban on women entering the JCR. This, I recall, was proposed in one of the shortest JCR speeches ever by Eddie Kling, an American, with words to the effect that he disdained offering any positive arguments and simply waited to see what kind of shit could possibly oppose it.[8]

For **Richard Abernethy** (1973) radical politics was a way of life:

> I had taken to socialist ideas during my teenage years and had read some Orwell, Trotsky and Marx. None of my school friends was much interested in politics, so I was eager to meet some comrades. I was to find them in Oxford, but not at Corpus. At that time Corpus was middle of the road politically, neither radical like Balliol nor reactionary like Oriel or Christ Church. Some years later Corpus was to acquire a left-wing reputation, but that was after my time.
>
> I had to look outside Corpus for revolutionary socialism, but it was not far away. There was a vibrant Left milieu in and around the University. This small, intense world, with its many internal subdivisions and cross-currents, became my main focus, and where I made friends. During my three years as a student, I was a member of two revolutionary groups (consecutively) and three campaigns (concurrently). I attended innumerable political

meetings, conferences and demonstrations. Today I find I can remember some three dozen people from the Oxford student Left, but only half a dozen of my contemporaries at Corpus.

Eugene Dainov (1974) was another activist:

Politics started with the Workers' Socialist League (WSL, or the Weasels), whose stall at the Freshers' Fair I found irresistible. Eighteen months later I had survived too many sterile meetings attended by a wide-eyed handful, had frozen too often on picket lines during the hotel strikes, spent too many Saturday mornings selling the Weasels' newspaper outside the now defunct Woolworth's on Cornmarket – across from Corpus's Tutor in Economics Andrew Glyn, who sold *The Militant* near Boots. Then I divorced both the Weasels and their competitors, the MIGs (Tariq Ali's International Marxist Group) when a slogan appeared, painted in 3-foot letters across the Radcliffe Square side of All Souls, 'Soon to be picturesque ruins'. Ugliness, I felt, was inexcusable, even in the cause of revolution – and I declared myself an anarchist.[9]

Such activism was exceptional in Corpus, and – as the 1970s progressed – in retreat. **David Normington** (1970) was more detached:

I did take an interest in politics, but didn't participate. Perhaps I was preparing, even then, to be a civil servant. I did stand for the JCR, but didn't get elected. I did go quite a lot to the Oxford Union. It was a great period for the Oxford Union; it used to have the great political figures of the day. I was fascinated by the opportunity to observe politics and to learn about it, but it never really appealed to me to be politically active myself. To get on in Oxford politics you have to have strong political views; you have in a sense to throw in your lot with one of the political parties and I did not feel I wanted to do that.[10]

Clive Britten (1974) thought 'the general level of political awareness was minimal. There were no protest marches, no seething unrest, no sense of terrible injustice'. The 1975 European referendum 'momentarily sparked some discussion' but **Warren Finegold** (1975) described JCR meetings as 'tame affairs'.[11] President **Kenneth Dover** thought that 'student troubles were a thing of the past in 1976, and none of us had any occasion to fear sit-ins or egg-throwing'.[12] **Margaret Harper** wrote home that 'the JCR is not taken particularly seriously and meetings tend to degenerate into boozy slanging matches'. **John** and **Alison Vile** (1980 and 1981) thought their generation 'a complacent lot, politically and otherwise' and that political idealism had faded with the 'me generation'. Inquorate JCR meetings meant 'dredging the Library and friends' rooms so that votes could be taken'. Some enjoyed taking on JCR roles, while 'the rest of us were happy to let them, muttering disparagingly about "political hacks" even as we left the responsibility to them'.[13]

But Corpus could swing between apathy and enthusiasm. **Julian Roskams** (1981) described JCR debate as 'always passionate, especially during the Falklands War'.[14] **Sean O'Grady** (1981) recalled 'the great GaySoc debate' after a 'sparsely attended' JCR meeting made a grant to the GaySoc helpline. This provoked a backlash – 'in the vanguard was the Christian Union, as I think it was styled' – which in turn, 'with pleasing symmetry' provoked a counter-reaction:

> the next JCR meeting was packed, with a near 100 per-cent attendance, and long, lively, impassioned debate ensued into that Sunday night. One young Christian wondered aloud, 'Why can't they just get married and have children like everyone else?' Well, of course a few decades later the gays were able indeed to do precisely that, though not in the way the Christian Union guy envisaged.

For **Jacquie Kelly** (1984), 'this was the Corpus of the Barclays Bank boycott, the Miners' Strike protests and the JCR motion to donate funds to the ANC (African National Congress). Even Ken Livingstone (a particular hero of mine) came to speak.' The JCR had moved its bank account from Barclays, in protest at its involvement in South Africa, and campaigned for the College to follow suit. **David Miliband**

(1984) and **Jaideep Pandit** (1984) reported 'two unanimous votes at JCR meetings in favour of the withdrawal'.[15] When it came to decide, the Governing Body was evenly split: President Dover gave his casting vote to move the account.

Ben Whitby (1986) described JCR meetings as

> rowdy and knockabout, with political issues of the day (living in 'Thatcher's Britain' we took it all too seriously) being debated alongside College terms and conditions and a bunch of spurious and occasionally hilarious other motions. I remember we cared a lot, gave some money each term to good causes (I think Corpus JCR sponsored a school in India) and some people were actually doing something about social issues. I often felt in my time that we were less politically active than our predecessors (we were certainly told so by the years above) and more interested in amusing ourselves. We were busy inventing/importing 'political correctness' a lot of the time, so there was a lot of arguing about the ideological use of language, although I think we were trying to find new ways to carry on having good manners.
>
> The election for JCR President was taken seriously, and I can remember us being pleased with ourselves for electing our first woman President. The JCR President invited guest speakers. We ranged from an actress from *Neighbours* (the impact of the first generation of students exposed to daytime TV, and two big colour TVs) to Ken Livingstone. I remember watching a student called David Miliband take Livingstone apart in the Q&A at that session.

But others found JCR politics off-putting. **Nicola Feather** (1981) thought the meetings 'male-dominated affairs' and **Danielle Sanderson** (1982) felt 'intimidated by PPE students in the JCR who seemed supremely confident and worldly-wise'. According to **Eliza Pakenham** (1986), 'sometimes we broke into the hubbub of the JCR, where future statesmen argued whilst the rest of us drank and gossiped'. In 1987 JCR President **Toby Harnden** (1985) had to write to members complaining that attendance was 'pitiful'. The admonition succeeded:

Pushpinder Saini (1986) reported that 'at last Corpus JCR meetings seem to have crawled out of the pit of inquoracy which they have faced at many times in the past and have again become a forum for reasoned and quality debate on questions of both local and international concern'.[16] **Andrew Wilson** (1987) thought political sentiment was changing: 'The JCR was initially vociferously left-wing, but there was a progressive shift towards the centre during the four years (1987–91) that I was there. Debate in JCR meetings during my first two years was lively and strongly opinionated, if frequently under-informed.'[17] **Nick Hassall** (1989) was 'disappointed and not very at ease' with aspects of College life, including its politics: 'The student body was heavily political – David Miliband had been JCR President before I went up and Ed Miliband was to succeed him in my second year – I didn't share their brand of socialism or world view.' His second year was 'marred by the "room ballot" scandal overseen by the JCR mandarins' – a change in the room ballot arrangements, introduced, he thought, without adequate consultation.

Corpus politics had often combined domestic concerns with global issues. Student finance, however, had not hitherto loomed large. Even the radical **Richard Abernethy** (1973) remarked, 'One issue I don't recall protesting about was our own economic position as students. Personally, I never experienced any difficulty living on my grant. Such a contrast with the students of today, who have to contend with tuition fees and loans.' As we shall see in a later chapter, this changed and student finance, particularly rents and charges, moved increasingly centre-stage, climaxing in confrontation with the SCR over rents.

Corpus students continued to ignore, dabble or get deeply involved in wider university politics according to taste. Garth Platt (1961) became the first Corpus president of the Oxford Union since 1905. He was followed by William Waldegrave (1965), educated at Eton, and Eric Parsloe (1970), who had arrived at Corpus via Ruskin. Paul Thompson (1979), Jonathan Wolf (1993) and Helen Eastman (1996) were to follow. But most, like **Camilla Byk** (1992), were less active: 'I was a member of the Union and remember Jerry Hall, Bill Clinton and other random celebrities coming to talk to us all. The popular debates were excellent, and I only wish the Union had felt more accessible so that I could have participated instead of just being in the audience.' **Ben Whitby** (1986) was unimpressed: 'I went to the Oxford Union once for a debate in the first year, but did not enjoy it, nor all the posing. I snuck in for cheap drinks a few times in the third year. It mattered a lot to some people, whether in participating in it, or in opposing it as a bastion of privilege. Mostly I read about it in *Cherwell*.'

Others looked elsewhere. **Danielle Sanderson** (1982) 'attended JSoc regularly, and set up a branch of PJS (Progressive Jewish Students)… I attended a couple of Oxford Union events, but, in retrospect, ought to have taken more advantage of the activities at Oxford.' **Catherine Hasler** (1997) found the College 'stifling' but discovered a niche with the Oxford Reform Club, eventually serving as president. It provided 'a less formal and cheaper alternative to the Union Society with lively debate and a wide spectrum of speakers':

> If you let it, Oxford will put you right up close to the shapers of public life. At the Reform Club, we entertained such notable speakers that, thinking back now, it almost makes me pinch myself to wonder whether it is really true that I did lunch at the Grand Café on the High Street with Lord Rees-Mogg, that we really did entertain Ted Heath in front of an audience of 400 in the Town Hall, and that I really was walked by Lord Tebbit from Blue Boar Street back to College on a rainy night. It must be the arrogance of youth. I do not remember feeling nervous, or grateful, or awed: all the things I would feel now if I met these people over again. We took it all in our stride.

Politics could be fun. **Charles Cockell** (1991), a postgraduate with an 'obsession' about settlement on Mars, stood for Parliament against the prime minister:

> It was in the dining room at Corpus, two months before the 1992 general election, that several friends suggested that I should assuage this nagging passion by standing in the general election

and demanding that something be done about it. After a retreat to a near-by pub and three hours later, the Forward to Mars Party was born. Our slogan, 'It's Time for a Change, a Change of Planet', was emblazoned on my Mini, which became the election battle bus. Friends at Corpus (I'll spare them the obloquy) became election agents, shadow environment and education secretaries. We paid our deposit, got the signatures and I stood as parliamentary candidate. Corpus thus became the first institution on Earth to spawn a political party dedicated to representing the interests of explorers and settlers of another world. We campaigned hard. We took on Screaming Lord Sutch, we questioned the policies of Lord Buckethead, and we faced up to the incumbent prime minister, John Major. It was Huntingdon we had chosen to stand in. If you're going to attract attention to yourself, you might as well do the job properly.

He came second-last, with 91 votes. 'The hapless John Major, who had no choice but to hang around waiting for the count to finish, got a fifteen-minute earful from me about the lack of British involvement in space exploration.' Looking back, he described this episode, and his moth-collecting expedition discussed earlier, as

> extraordinarily self-indulgent, completely insane and utterly enjoyable. But what I think is most remarkable about them is that no one even flinched. I was never called into the President's office to ask why I was bringing such disrepute upon an old and venerable Oxford college. Not a single person asked what on earth I was doing spending my time away from my PhD studies (perhaps because my mind wasn't on Earth).

As **David Henig** (1990) recalled, Corpus in the early 1990s was known for 'a distinctly left-leaning politics. Not quite Wadham or Balliol historically leftie, but certainly in the next pack.' But times were changing 'and Corpus intakes from 1990 were decidedly less political'. **Rachel Richards** (1993) agreed: 'Corpus JCR had a reputation as being stridently political and left wing'; but this was 'rather anachronistic', since her contemporaries seemed mostly 'politically apathetic, many even cynical of party politics, at least by the reported standards of previous years':

> Responses to arguments usually tend to be moderate or pragmatic rather than militant or following any single political ideology (unless of course, as often happens, someone is seeking to be deliberately provocative or antagonistic, just for the fun of winding someone else up). The JCR motions that attract the most interest tend to relate to the acceptance of sexual orientation, personal welfare issues or, with almost overwhelming support, purchasing the subscriptions to celebrity magazines for the JCR or Library toilet.

Debates remained lively. **Caroline Knapp** (2005) 'was more of an observer of JCR meetings than an active participant, but I still enjoyed watching the debates unfold'. At her first meeting 'the room was so full that latecomers had no choice but to stand by the door – I soon learned that you needed to turn up early to the first meeting of the year, so that you didn't miss out on a seat (or the pizza)'. But the JCR was not just about debate – serious or frivolous. It offered opportunities, which some relished, to take on responsibility and develop wider skills. **Jonathan Garner** (1983) was Ball Treasurer:

> Our budget was around £20,000 which was an immense amount of money for a 20-year-old undergraduate to be in charge of. I felt a huge sense of responsibility in opening and running the bank account, negotiating with suppliers – the Corpus Manciple was by far the toughest on the cost of the meal! – and reconciling the numbers. In the end we had a great night and turned a small profit which we gave back to the JCR for their charitable donation programme.

Louise Sykes (1984) was JCR Domestic Officer:

> What did being Domestic Officer give me (apart from some good

material for milk round interviews)? Well, thanks to Kenneth Dover and the Estates Committee I learnt that all the best committee decisions are made outside the room, well in advance of the meeting itself, and long before I ever heard the awful phrase 'engaging key stakeholders' I realized that is in fact the best way to get something done.

Alexandra Harmer (2008) described running a ball as a wonderful opportunity 'to do one of the things I love best – organizing!'

Religion

If some were keen to explore their political interests, within the College or in the wider university, others were more concerned to develop their religious understanding and faith. According to **David Blackmore** (1956), 'if the political climate was intelligent and active, so too was the religious one'. But, like politics, active commitment was normally limited to a minority. **Roger Horsfield** (1952) thought 'something like a quarter of all Oxford students went to church or chapel at least once a week'. But chapel was no longer compulsory: **Norman Miners** (1952) recalled only a handful attending the daily service and **Charles Thomas** (1948) thought it 'not well attended', though 'there was a hard-core Christian group, including some destined for the Church'. He thought Christopher Evans 'an ideal college chaplain. You knew where you were with a man who dressed and acted like a straight, middle-of-the-road, C of E parson. He seemed to know names and details of everyone in College; was always pleasant and helpful and concerned, spoke to everyone, never proselytized nor introduced "God" unasked into converse.'[18]

Students often looked to local churches as well as the Chapel. **David Blackmore** (1956) visited one, where 'I encountered preaching and teaching and worship that was electrifying. By the end of term, I found myself enrolling in a student Confirmation class at St Ebbe's, to the slight disappointment of the Chaplain, Christopher Evans, who nevertheless wisely nurtured me from afar':

These early weeks and months of term were a great period of personal spiritual discovery for me. And quite soon I was learning and being formed by the openness of the Chapel community and its willingness to embrace not only Anglicans of all traditions, but free churches and indeed other groups of which I knew precious little. The Chapel also invited other preachers, and they included famously in my memory Charles Coulson, physicist and Methodist, who led a discussion evening in the Chaplain's room (probably about the danger of identifying 'God of the gaps'). And then for me came the discovery of a strange new late-night service, compline. Even now, whenever I hear the phrase 'apple of my eye', I recall a candlelit Corpus Chapel.

He recalled that 'we in Corpus enjoyed the presence in our midst of a missioner Franciscan Brother, whose name I don't recall, but whose style of life and spiritual challenge I still certainly do'. According to **David Booth** (1955), he and David Blackmore were 'leaders in turn of the Corpus OICCU Group – in succession to a Plymouth Brethren, myself a Baptist/interdenominational Nonconformist. We encouraged OICCU people to attend Chapel services. We benefited from the Chaplain's discussion groups across Christian traditions. I have retained a love of the Anglican liturgy and the freedom to be found within cycles of explicit form.'

For **Sebastian Barker** (1964) 'the truly essential thing which Corpus gave me was the opportunity to be alone in a safe environment while working on the mystery of vocation':

Clearly, there was a religious and a Christian foundation to my most intense experience of living in the College. The influence was largely subliminal, I know, but I think it was all the more embedded for that. For it was during my time at Corpus that my fate was being sealed on my way to becoming a Christian poet. It should not be thought that this was always a comfortable arrangement. The truth is, when the going got tough, the transition from undergraduate to embryonic poet to poet was terrifying. I would have to say, therefore, that perhaps the thing I am most grateful to Corpus for, is the sense of belonging to an ancient institution which has its roots in the sacred.

Religion could also offer, as **Rob Batho** (1964) found, an important social dimension:

> The John Wesley Society was a main focus of contact and activity from the beginning, and proved to be a source of lifelong friendships. More immediately, it was not only in tune with my Nonconformist background – although the College introduced me to the Anglicanism to which I was to become committed later – but also brought me into contact with a number of attractive young ladies who were happy to accompany me on my theatre trips.

Although **Paddy Griffiths** (1965) thought the Quaker Meeting House 'quite a good way to meet girls', he was drifting away from religion. He found the Chaplain, John Baker, 'inspiring as well as sympathetic, and a wonderful advertisement for a church that I was then gradually starting to lose, despite four generations of Cumberland vicars in my family tree. The OICCU storm troops who made it their business to take us personally in hand were admirable people and inspiring in their personal examples; but by their Bible-bashing charismatic approach they tended to hit the wrong target with me.'[19] Chapel had 'little appeal' to **Bill Gunn** (1965), who also 'resisted the overtures of OICCU, to which a number of my contemporaries and fellow historians signed up. "When I leave this room, God goes with me", said the unsuccessful proselytizer to one recalcitrant fellow-resident in Thomas Building. "Well, please ask Him to shut the door", was the rejoinder.' By contrast, **Gareth Moore** (1966) recalled:

> Of greatest personal significance for me throughout my undergraduate years was my gradual approach to Christianity. This had begun while I was at school, somewhat against my will, and became firmly established at Corpus. It seems that it was normal at the time for people who came up as Christians to drift away from the faith. It was hardly intellectually respectable to be a Christian.

The temper of the times was very secular and modern, and religion seemed to belong to an earlier age. 'Christianity is dead, Marxism is the future', I was once told by a fellow student. For many students, not only did their religion have to compete with a number of new interests, but the broadening of intellectual horizons meant that their former faith seemed childish and untenable. This was particularly true, I gathered, of those studying philosophy.

Despite all this, I went in the opposite direction, and found myself made more rather than less religious by philosophy. In particular, I was greatly struck by the religious temper of Wittgenstein's *Tractatus* and of his *Philosophical Investigations*, and the latter opened up an approach to religious language and practice which did not seem to compel me to think of the morally and intellectually impressive Christians I knew as either fools or liars.[20]

Christianity continued to form a significant strand of College life. **Malcolm Underwood** (1966) 'greatly valued the fellowship of the Christian Union'. For **Simon Bainbridge** (1968), 'worship has never meant more to me than when I was at Corpus. This was largely thanks to John Baker, who as a preacher and leader of worship seemed to me totally admirable.'[21] According to **Charles Overton** (1970), 'My first Sunday in Oxford saw me attend St Aldates church where Revd Keith de Berry was Rector. That service saw my life take a different direction and meaning. I am today a parish priest.' **Tom Wolever** (1973) joined 'a very lively and active Christian Union':

The Chapel was not a major focus of Christian activity at the time and only a small number went to the evening services. The city churches (St Aldates and St Ebbe's) were the major places of worship, and in both there was standing room only at the Sunday morning services. There were weekly Bible studies in various people's rooms in College which attracted ten to twelve people. Many of my evenings and late into the night were spent listening to and participating in spontaneous informal discussions of ethics, philosophy and religion with believers and non-believers.[22]

Organ scholar **Theodore Saunders** (1975) worked with the Chaplain to establish a choir. 'We met weekly, and sang at the evening service on Sunday. It was during this time that I composed my Corpus Christi Service for congregational use.' **Dina Gold** (1975) declined to join:

> Unlike several of the other women, I had failed to involve myself in any way with the religious community of the College. The Corpus Chaplain came to see me and asked for an explanation. In fact he was rather keen that I should join the choir. In those days, and perhaps still today, the Chapel played a major role in the life of the College and perhaps I missed out by not being part of it. But it was not to be.

David Atkinson, Chaplain from 1977, recalled the Chapel's 'joys and surprises':

> One of the highlights was the annual Carol Service; Chapel was full, and Brian Campbell the Bursar brought out his trumpet to provide a descant for some of the singing; Norman Beech the Steward laid on mince pies afterwards. On Corpus Christi Day, Barry in the Buttery – with great reluctance and anxiety – allowed us to use the Founder's Crozier and Chalice for the Eucharist – though he carried them from the safe to the Chapel himself. One of the oddest moments was at the end of evensong when a student (suffering, as it turned out, sadly from a psychiatric disorder rather than from alcohol) strode into the Chapel and challenged me to a duel with drawn swords. It made an interesting change of routine.
>
> Some of my most joyous Chapel moments were to conduct a marriage service in Chapel for students of the College (after they had obtained an Archbishop of Canterbury's Special Licence to allow the marriage to take place in other than a parish church). I must have taken dozens over the years. Or to baptize a child of one of the kitchen staff.
>
> Some of the most poignant were funerals. I presided at the funeral of an English student, for which Val Cunningham preached; of a former organ scholar (Andrew Fathers) who had

died in a climbing accident in New Zealand. I buried the ashes in
the College garden of one of the Eights crew [Russell Crockford
(1976)] who had a memorial bench named after him, and of Dr
Elizabeth Rawson who died teaching in China. I had spent a lot of
time with Trevor Aston in the weeks before his sad suicide, and to
take his funeral service – at which Robin Nisbet spoke – was one
of my hardest duties.

Margaret Harper (1979) tried several churches – mainly St Aldates
and St Ebbe's, but also St Clements, the United Reform Church and
the Catholic Chaplaincy. In letters home she described hearing Billy
Graham ('whom I didn't find impressive at all'), helping with OICCU
lunches and leading a CU Bible study. Her second year saw her and a
friend 'off to try St Michael's at the North Gate – we like collecting
churches!' In Hilary she reported: 'This term I'm trying out College
Chapel on Sundays which has the advantage of being short and
painless! On Sunday the Bishop of Winchester (the College Visitor)
came to preach the sermon (quite sensible).' She was 'intrigued' to
find that one of the first years 'has also given up Oxford churches in
favour of Chapel, because she was fed up with being "saved *every*
week"!'

Nicola Feather (1981) also recalled the range of choice:

A short walk from College through Christ Church would bring
you to the Chaplaincy for Catholics, St Aldates ('Snaldates') for
charismatic-leaning Protestants or St Ebbe's ('Snebbes') for more
Reformed Protestants. Equally accessible were Pusey House in
St Giles' for High Anglicans or St Clements on the other side of
Magdalen Bridge for the student needing to get away from other
students.

In Chapel, normal Sunday evening services were traditional
evensong with a choir leading hymns and psalms, and singing an
anthem. As befitted a formal service, the choir and most of the
congregation wore gowns. There was a short sermon, sometimes
from a visiting speaker but more often from the then Chaplain,
David Atkinson. At the end of the service, the congregation would

be invited to enjoy sherry in the Chaplain's rooms before dinner in Hall.

She joined the Christian Union – 'students from all year groups and most subjects' – which met weekly:

We prayed for each other, mainly, but we were capable of thinking in broader terms at least occasionally. We prayed during the Falklands War, and we prayed for David Watson, the man who had led the 1982 Mission, and who had subsequently been diagnosed with bowel cancer. For some of us, that was our first experience of grappling with a God who is certainly able to heal (we read that in the Bible, and we believed it) but who does not always choose to answer even our 'good' prayers with the answers we look for. I don't know that anyone entirely lost their faith when David Watson died, but mine was certainly dented.

Perhaps I say this because there was a dominant strand of Christianity, and I was a part of it, but it seemed to me that Corpus was a place where differing traditions were all valued and nurtured. Although some people held a 'private faith' that was uncomfortable with open discussion of religious matters, Christianity was explicitly central to the lives of many of us.

Such active Christians were a minority – the CU had about 'ten or so regular members' in the mid-1980s, though the numbers were said to be higher later.[23] According to **Ben Whitby** (1986), 'You could take it [religion] or leave it in the late 1980s. Corpus was fairly secular. I hardly ever went to Chapel, and barely knew the Chaplain (we had an introductory chat). There was always something else to do (normally academic work). But in Corpus, the Chapel opening on to the Library as it does, forever associated religion and study in my mind.'

Corpus had long had students from other religious backgrounds, who sometimes felt sidelined. 'As a Catholic,' **Patrick Marnham** (1962) recalled, 'I took no part in the life of the Chapel.'[24] As noted earlier, **Ihsan Malik** (1996) found 'it hasn't been easy living as a Muslim in Oxford University', and 'obeying the rules of God in Corpus Christi has obviously been difficult, especially with no other Muslims I know of in this college'. However, 'I have befriended many Muslims and strengthened my own faith by interacting with them. Equally, I have managed to talk about Islam with non-Muslims in a rational and educational manner, without being prejudicial (I hope!).'[25] But the CU remained the most visible religious group. The spoof Hall 'seating plan', which **Eric Dugdale** (1990) described as 'remarkably accurate', included the 'God Squad' as one of the identifiable groups.[26] And amongst her 'College Types', **Rebecca Rist** (1995) described the 'Christian-Corpuscle':

> A species surprisingly active and prevalent at Corpus. Both busily and scarily efficient where lost souls are concerned, this group is not always universally popular. Distinguishing features: (1) To be seen hurrying off on a Sunday morning to St Ebbe's while other Corpuscles lie abed. (2) Hard-working and industrious; sense of humour may need developing. (3) Regarded as quirky or just plain bizarre by others ... (4) Definitely Low Church, the species prefers not too much incense in chapel and certainly no talk of the Real Presence.[27]

Some expressed their commitments through practical social action. **Richard Abernethy** (1973), a radical socialist, 'volunteered to give English tuition to a child of an immigrant family. No background checks in those days; I was simply given the address of an Indian family in East Oxford and left to get on with it. I visited Satish one afternoon a week through my three years at Corpus. One time, I took him punting.' Similarly, **Margaret Harper** (1979), an active Christian, arranged through JACARI (Joint Action Committee against Racial Intolerance) to teach English to a girl from Hong Kong; and in her third year worked periodically at a Kilburn youth club supported by the Oxford Christian Union. Others preferred journalism, described by *Cherwell* editor **Patrick Marnham** (1962) as 'an appropriately shady occupation'.[28]

Politics and religion remained important dimensions of College life, though only a minority normally engaged actively. While some found Corpus – and Oxford more widely – an environment in which to develop and articulate their convictions, most seem to have kept a certain reserve. The 'typical' Corpuscle – if such a person existed – was probably an interested but sceptical observer rather than a committed partisan. But rarely did scepticism turn into hostility: even in these sensitive areas, Corpus generally projected a spirit of friendly tolerance.

Rent protest, 1991. *Courtesy of ITV*

8

'OVER THE SPIKES': JUNIOR AND SENIOR MEMBERS

I had behaved as a lout; yes, a lout with an anarchic streak living in delirious times.

Brian Sedgemore

Relations between junior and senior members operated at several levels. Most important was the academic relationship between the individual student and tutor, discussed earlier. Less significant in this period was the 'social' relationship which had characterized College life in earlier years, when Fellows (and married scouts) had routinely lived in College. But there was also a crucial 'institutional' relationship. The College was responsible – in loco parentis – for the care of its junior members; and although the legal age of majority was reduced to 18 in 1970, it remained responsible for the governance of the institution and the well-being all who lived and worked within it. This relationship was to change significantly, as the balance between 'discipline' and 'welfare' shifted, demands emerged for student representation in College governance, and – in a tightening financial climate – new tensions tested the College's traditionally harmonious internal relations.

Discipline

Leo Pliatzky (1937) recalled Frank Lepper reminding the post-war JCR that 'though some of us might have held positions of authority and been in command of men, we were now junior members of the College and must not think that we could ignore the College rules'.[1] **Duncan Gorrie** (1949) thought that 'rules were there to be kept (most of the time). I do not recall that we found them particularly irksome; we were on the whole a conformist bunch.'[2] There was a balance to be struck. As **Oliver Clauson** (1948) recalled, Lepper 'had been in the Army so knew just how far to allow those of us, who had been in the forces, to bend the rules. When I acquired a motor cycle, the rules laid down that one had to attach a green light for identification. Frank's response was, "Don't bother, but don't park it near the College."' Even so, according to **John Brown** (1955) 'the College took its duties of being "in loco parentis" rather seriously, despite most of the undergraduates having done national service for two years before taking up residence. Undergraduates were, nevertheless, sometimes treated like schoolchildren.'

Tony Henning (1948) and friends ran into trouble one night when they tried to climb the Martyrs' Memorial. The police intervened, 'and we were given lifts back to our respective colleges in police cars':

> At that time, the Proctors, with their bowler-hatted 'Bulldogs' rather than police, dealt with University personnel disorders. Accordingly, I found myself being dealt with by Thomas Dunbabin DSO, a Tasmanian Fellow of Corpus and Senior Proctor. He was eminently suitable for the job having been the SOE (Special Operations Executive) leader of the resistance to the German invasion of Crete. Generously, he imposed no fine but required me to stay within College for a week. I'm sure we had done nothing to seriously increase the wear on the Memorial but it had been regarded as a good climb for many years and, after our attempted climbing, it was banned and made a 'sending down' offence.

The police were reluctant to get too involved with student high jinks, as **Roger Horsfield** (1952) observed at Bonfire Night:

The High was blocked by thousands upon thousands of under-graduates, very few of them completely sober. People around me got hold of a Morris Minor and turned it upside down by the side of the road. Two policemen ambled up, looked inside and said to us, 'There are some women passengers inside, they are frightened; will you put it back on its wheels, please.' I was one of those who instantly did the same and found how amazingly easy it is to lift up a motor car when you've had a drink or two.

The Proctors and Bulldogs, by contrast, remained a hazard, as **David Jory** (1959) and friends discovered after punting to 'a field where we were carousing late at night. Suddenly Proctors and "Bulldogs" appeared over one hedge in their odd uniforms (the "Bulldogs" wore bowler hat and a morning suit with pinstripe trousers, which seemed a bit incongruous after midnight in a field). We ran for the punts and some of us got away before we could be caught.'

Most disciplinary issues, however, arose within and were handled by the College. Some were minor: **Don Montague** (1954) was fined 3*s.* 6*d.* by the Dean 'for playing Dennis Brain's interpretation of the Mozart Horn Concertos too loud, too late at night, through an upstairs window out into the Quad'. The most visible – and evaded – rules concerned gate hours. Asked if he climbed in, **George Richardson** (1947) replied: 'Never. I can't tell you what degree of athletic prowess that required. There was a certain amount of barbed wire scattered all over the place. I was pretty law-abiding.' But the practice was widespread. According to **Geoff Goodall** (1950), 'we all had even-tually to complete one of the hallowed Corpus rites of passage by climbing in through the bent-back spikes of Thomas Quad wall long after midnight, risking our manhood in doing so'. **Nicholas Roskill** (1952) observed: 'I am impressed nowadays by the manner in which we climbed in – up onto the quite high wall with a row of spiked railings: as the term went on the railings were pushed further apart, making the entry easier. If you had been to a dance or party wearing a dinner jacket it was wise to remove your jacket and throw this over first.' For climbing out, according to **John Brown** (1955), mountaineering skills were useful: 'On one of the upper floors of the staircase there was an unbarred outside window. So any late-staying mountaineer could evade the authorities by indulging in a little abseiling practice. No accidents resulted that I can recall, although I'm sure we thought it would be cissy and insulting to use a safety rope!'

Enforcement had an element of ritual. **Ian Wylie** (1958) recalled the 'ancient practices' which were 'swept away' in the 1960s: 'No more does Stan's arm reach out to grab your leg as you are climbing in over the waste bins. "Dean, 10." Dean Brock would then fine one 10s., with the immortal words which so typified Oxford in those days: "Now, Mr Wylie, at this time of day you like your sherry dry?"' **David Jory** (1959) had a similar experience:

> For reasons I can't remember, I once climbed into College 'over the spikes' (as it was called) and, along with eight to ten fellow students, was summoned to Dean Brock's office the next day. Brian Sedgemore (a stalwart of the rugby team who became a lawyer, then a 'Bennite' MP) was spokesman and the rest of us were trying not to burst out laughing. Whatever story Sedgemore told, we were all punished, I think by a trivial fine, with a warning that this had better not happen again.

The dangers were real. One night **Patrick Marnham** (1962) met Harold Dawe (1962) outside the Annexe. Seeing scaffolding, they decided to climb in over the roof:

> When we reached the crest we found there was no light at all on the garden side of the Annexe. Dawe said that we merely had to slide down the roof to find the scaffolding on the other side of the building. He did so; I followed. We gathered speed as we descended and had no means of stopping when we reached the gutter, but fortunately there *was* scaffolding in place or there would probably have been two corpses on the Dean's morning list.

They were caught and reported to the Dean, Dr Jamison. He was 'appalled by the tradition of climbing into College which in those days sometimes led to drunken undergraduates suffering serious injuries' and had therefore established an alternative, safer, route through Christ Church Meadow with a loosened spike in the railing. 'When I reported to him next morning he pointed out the loose railing, adding that because it was directly beneath his window the demands of College discipline were also – in theory – satisfied. He told me to tell everyone I knew about this loose railing. (Clearly he could not do this himself.) He then gated me for a week.'[3]

By the mid-1960s, according to **Robert Lee** (1964), 'nocturnal access via Christ Church Meadow was relatively straightforward (apart from the occasional "arrests" and warning by Stan Plumb)', though 'at least one student was seriously injured when trying to scale the railings at the front of the College'. **Bill Gunn** (1965) used both routes:

It was with the Boat Club that I often braved the spikes on Merton Street, formidable by day but somehow considerably less daunting by night and with the benefit of drink taken. It was with the Boat Club that I was introduced to the longer, less challenging after-hours route into the College, leading through the grounds of Linacre and into the Meadow, and up over the wall in the corner of the Fellows' garden, to be greeted more than once by the dreaded night porter Stan, materializing with a flashlight and a proffered invitation to visit Dean Jamison on the morrow. As carpetings go these latter interviews were mild indeed, mollified no doubt by the fact the Dean was known to be a rowing man and sympathetic to his own.

The knowledge that lock-up was not to be taken seriously was quite soon in coming. I was awoken on my second night in Thomas Building by a stream of blue language from the courtyard, where a late entrant had somehow contrived to get a spike between his face and his buttoned waistcoat and was hanging impaled like a furious Mr Toad, loudly complaining about the unfairness of the world. A small crowd was gathering to watch the fun, whence some kindly spirit kindly shimmied up to undo the offending buttons and release the captive.

The following night was interrupted by a steady stream of passing traffic, as it transpired that I had drawn a room recognized as one of the main entrances to the College after hours, giving as it did on to the footpath from Merton Street to the Meadow. I soon learned to sleep undisturbed through these nightly visitations, it presumably never entering my mind that anyone more threatening than a benighted undergraduate would appear through the window.

In 1968 a late-key system was introduced: 'Such a system is becoming increasingly common practice in Oxford Colleges. It enables those who wish on a particular night to return to College after the closing of the gate to do so by a civilized method, having applied for the loan of a key.'[4] Climbing in – or out – did not cease immediately, but was now in decline. **Martin Deahl** (1975) recalled a rather different climbing escapade: 'after an evening of alcoholic excess and for reasons which I don't quite recall', he climbed down a folding fire-escape ladder from the top floor of Staircase 12 'in front of a large audience in the Quad below. Climbing down was dangerous enough. However my foolishness was really brought home to me when, as I alighted at the foot of the staircase, the whole contraption came crashing down around me to general hilarity. I didn't appreciate how lucky I had been at the time and hope the College's health and safety policies are more robust today.'

According to **Ben Whitby** (1986), 'most of the petty rules (gowns, guests etc.) had gone by the late 1980s. We had a key to the gate which got you in to all the College buildings.'

But gate and visiting hours were not the only disciplinary issues. Bump Suppers, sometimes involving boat-burnings, were a traditional trigger for misbehaviour. **Roger Horsfield** (1952) recalled one: 'Some jumped over and through the flames, others stripped the College of its fire extinguishers and fought duels with one another as they sprayed them. Some would-be firemen found the main hose and when the Dean tried to appeal for sense and better order, they washed him literally out of the Porters' Lodge area into the street.' **Philip Hamilton-Grierson** (1953) was in the triumphant VIII:

Over-exuberance led to silliness with fire extinguishers, mark 8 thunderflashes and the removal of a complete bedroom's furnishings onto the scaffolding. Four of us were fined £5 for fascist hooliganism, then a princely sum, by Dean Mauldon while the Salvation Army (SA) band played outside in Merton Street. I forget who arranged things with the SA. Chaplain Christopher Evans mentioned an 'undesirable element' in the College at evensong. This was a somewhat overreaction as the man whose bedroom had been moved onto the scaffolding was a good friend and bore us no grudge.

As rugby captain, **David Jory** (1959) recalled a dinner 'on Bump Supper lines', at which 'somebody decided we should take the University's rugby posts to the Corpus ground and take the Corpus posts to the University ground up the Iffley Road. This, it was thought, would shame the Bursar into getting Corpus decent posts.' A group – some in dinner jackets – went to the University ground, unbolted the crossbar, and lifted out the 30-foot uprights. 'Jim Celarier seemed to have a giant's strength and was in the middle of things. One after the other they came out – to this day it seems an impossibility, but we did it – and were allowed to drop. They bounced and whipped alarmingly but luckily did not break or crack.' The posts were then carried to the Corpus ground, roughly 2 miles away, over the Isis, various roads, a 6-foot fence, and the railway bridge 'with its narrow access and right-angle turns top and bottom on both sides. How we managed to manoeuvre those 30-foot uprights over the bridge I have no idea':

> At the Corpus field we quickly took the smaller Corpus posts out, only to find that the butts of the larger University posts would not go in the holes vacated by the Corpus posts (if any planning at all had been done we would have realized this, but it really was a spur-of-the-moment thing). So we lined up the University posts next to the holes, bolted the crossbar back in place, picked up the Corpus posts and returned to the University field with them ... When we put the Corpus posts in the larger University holes they (appropriately) leaned drunkenly. We reattached the crossbar and went home to bed. Our exertions had worked off the effects of the celebratory alcohol and I slept well, if not for long.

Next morning news spread that the University's posts had been replaced by what the *Oxford Mail* described as 'a rickety, lop-sided, makeshift set'. These were soon identified as the Corpus posts, though the University posts had not yet been found at the Corpus ground. As captain, Jory 'pedalled off to the University field on the Iffley Road to ask if we could please have our rugby posts back':

> The subsequent surreal conversations were almost worthy of *Monty Python* and were a highlight of my young life. Wilcox, captain of University rugby, and Richard Sharp, secretary and a fellow Cornishman (a superb player for England and way out of my class), were among the crowd milling around the 'rickety, lop-sided, makeshift set' of posts, wondering aloud how 'they' could have got the University's uprights out of the ground as there was no sign of heavy equipment.
>
> It seemed important not to tell any lies and I did not; this was easy since nobody thought to ask me if I knew anything about what had happened. I was told that normally when the University uprights were taken down, a sloping trench was dug down to where the butts were resting and the uprights were carefully lowered to the ground by laying them in the trench. But here we had no posts and no trench. What a mystery! Then I was told how 'they' had done this and that and in which direction 'they' had gone with the posts. None of what was said was true and it was very hard not to laugh or correct the speakers ...
>
> There could have been little doubt in the minds of the College authorities as to who was responsible but luckily no questions were asked. I believe the College got new rugby posts before the next season started.

1963 saw a 'notorious' Bump Supper at which, according to **Tom Hassall** (1962),

> mashed potato was hurled about the Hall with abandon and could still be seen adhering to the panelling until it was cleaned many years later. Petrol was poured into the gutter around the Front Quad and set alight, and Oriel called the fire brigade. The 1st VIII cox, Richard Wilson, tried to climb the Sundial, failed

spectacularly in the attempt and had to spend the rest of the night in hospital. During the early hours of the morning a hapless bullock was lifted bodily from the Meadow and deposited into Merton garden.[5]

This prompted, according to **Stephen Linstead** (1959), 'a laconic reminder that climbing the Sundial was prohibited!' **Bill Gunn** (1965) found some Boat Club revelries 'embarrassing to recall':

Thank heavens for a Statute of Limitations, for one night it seemed to one befuddled group of us that rather than follow the pavement homewards down King Edward Street, which promised to be unchallenging indeed, it would be more amusing to follow the more adventurous route of a line of parked cars, clambering bonnet to tail. The mission was duly completed over all of 100 yards to Oriel Square, but I shudder to think of the multiple tracks and dents that daylight would have revealed. When I read of adolescent stupidities today, I temper my disapproval with memories (thankfully few) such as this.

Kelvin Roberts (1963) recalled another boat-burning at the 1967 Bump Supper:

A practical joker phoned the fire brigade, who sent two engines. To the background of clanging bells, two firemen entered Corpus from Merton Street, hoses gushing water. A roar of anger arose from the horde of drunken undergraduates. One Corpus man, a true man of action, grabbed a hose from a fireman, and, turning it on the gate, drove both firemen back into Merton Street. Having disposed of the firemen and still in possession of a hose in full spurt, the students turned the hose on Steward Healey and thoroughly drenched him. Mark Hagger, a fresh-faced chap who exuded an aura of clean living, helped to save the boat bonfire by 'hijacking' one fire engine and driving it down Merton Street. He was dragged out by police and firemen near Eastgate Hotel, and carried off to the police station.[6]

The Oxford Chief Fire Officer described the affair as 'a riot'; but after apologies from the JCR and Boat Club Presidents he accepted that it had been 'obviously a misunderstanding'. Over 100 students were fined, including £20 for the cox who, as **Ian Hamilton** (1966) recalled, climbed the Pelican and 'practised karate chops on her neck, all too successfully'.[7] A newly sculpted replacement was installed that summer.

Subsequent Bump Suppers were less raucous. Although 'in true Boat Club tradition the crew consumed at least 1 pint of port per person', **Mark Atkinson** (1971) described the 1973 Bump Supper as 'more subdued' than its 1967 predecessor. He and a friend were summoned to the Dean 'merely because we had chalked a Pelican on the wall outside 9.1 along with the names of the crews bumped (and in those days the walls were dark brown from years of pollution). The menu was chosen with great care by the Manciple to exclude throwable items but alas he had apparently not thought of peas being used as grapeshot.'

College rivalries prompted many disciplinary incidents. Canoeing one evening with Gordon Douglas (1949) on the Isis, **Tony Henning** (1949) spotted Hertford students trying to unmoor the Corpus College barge. They called out the Boat Club, who 'streamed across Christ Church Meadow and tossed Hertford men who had not already made their escape into the river'. They in turn were followed by the Proctors – 'in those far-off days it was an offence to be out after dinner without a gown' – who took their names. Having observed this from his canoe, he then had to climb back in:

> I was aware of the normal route over the spikes to Thomas Quad but not from the Meadow. It was pretty dark and cold by the time I found my way to the roof above the Library where I appeared firmly stuck. At a critical moment in my rather slow decision-making process, another Corpuscle appeared beside me. This proved to be Mike Westmacott of the later 1953 Everest Ascent fame. He knew a sky light which could be opened so led the way and caught me after a 10-foot drop to the wooden floor below. We were both shivering by this time but, like a future Everest climber, his room was very well provisioned and he introduced me to Green

Chartreuse. Glorious at the time but put me off it for life by the next day.

The rescue of the barge from possible destruction over Iffley Weir was, of course, known by the Dean, then Frank Lepper. So it was particularly pleasing that Frank Lepper quietly thanked both Gordon Douglas and myself for our very small part in the barge rescue with no mention of night climbing.

Peter Jarvis (1957) recalled another rivalry when Corpus reached the rugby Cuppers final against St Edmund Hall:

We launched an Oxford-wide poster campaign with the slogan 'Corpus – The Great Little College' (lifted from a contemporary campaign on the new ITV, 'Woodbines, The Great Little Cigarette'). For the day we hired two lorries and a jazz band and painted banners. Finally we raided enemy territory by stealing rugby shirts from Teddy Hall changing rooms. These we attached to the lorry tails and dragged in triumph around town. Finally, anticipating trouble from the hearty Teddy Hall supporters, we loaded up with bags of flour, water-filled balloons and the like. The battle raged on and off the pitch, and clearly Corpus won hands down both ways. Had I taken the least interest in sport in later life I might have become a successful organizer of a gang of football hooligans.[8]

Brian Sedgemore (1958) was Rugby Club secretary:

At midnight after one Cuppers final we went up to the Parks and pushed Teddy Hall's mobile pavilion all the way across the Parks whence it ran out of grass and disappeared into the river. At this point we burst into song, singing the Corpus anthem, an oratorical masterpiece with descant, denigrating St Edmund Hall. Summoned to see the Dean, Michael Brock, the next morning I was told about the incident. 'Was there any evidence as regards the culprits?' I asked. 'No,' replied the Dean, 'but the Proctors found a handkerchief in the middle of the Parks.' 'Was there anything on it to help identify the miscreants?' 'No,' said Michael again. 'Well, if there's no evidence, there's nothing we can discuss,' I said, making my excuses and leaving his chambers.

The 'Corpus anthem', recalled **Pat Dolby** (1958), went to the tune of 'Cwm Rhondda':

We don't play for adoration
We don't play for victory
We just play by inclination
Merry, merry men are we

(CHORUS)
Balls to Teddy Hall
Balls to Teddy Hall
We won't play them anymore ... anymore (crescendo)
We won't play them anymore.
We'll play BNC
We'll play BNC,
We'll play bloody BNC.

David Jory (1959) heard of another incident: 'a bunch of Corpuscles had taken pieces of stone being used to resurface parts of St Edmund Hall and in the middle of the night made a wall with cement to block the narrow entrance to the Hall. As I heard it, when the Hall porter opened the College door in the morning, he faced a wall. Luckily for Teddy Hall, the cement was not yet dry and the wall could be taken down.'

Merton was another target. As noted earlier, **David Mark Jackson** (1959) recalled '"cunning plans", including driving a herd of bullocks into Merton and locking them in. This was borderline vandalism, yet there was something inspiring about the sight of those noble bovines thundering around Merton bellowing mellifluously as we watched from the security of the Fellows' Building.' According to **Brian Sedgemore** (1958):

Regularly I was summoned to see the Dean as if I were either a Mafia boss or a snitch. One such incident occurred when Tim Mitford, an intelligence guru, persuaded a cow to walk from

Christ Church Meadow into Merton Tower where it made a bit of a mess during its overnight stay. This was I thought a not inconsiderable feat but nothing to do with me. 'I suppose we've got to take this seriously and regard Merton as a friendly college,' said the Dean. 'It is after all next door.'

Tim Mitford (1958) himself met the Dean, Michael Brock, 'formally more than once':

> The last occasion was the most nerve-wracking, when I and a band of cronies had herded about 50 cows from the Meadow into Merton by night. They ranged happily about the college all night, and there was quite a stink the next morning. Fortunately, no damage was done to cows or property, and as the Bullingdon had dined that same evening they took the can before Michael could send for us. At the time we reckoned we had achieved a double whammy, Merton and The House at a single blow, and there is an uninscribed memorial in the ferocious Iron Gates installed at the corner of the Corpus garden to prevent, I suppose, a repeat.

Oriel was another natural rival. **John Kinder** (1958) recalled how one winter evening a Corpus golfer in the Quad 'proceeded to drive a number of golf balls into the darkness in the direction of Oriel'. Some 'failed to gain sufficient altitude' but most went 'over into the main Oriel quadrangle'. **Mueen Afzal** (1960) recalled a similar feat.[9] As JCR 'Guardian of the Plummer', **Paul Vaight** (1963) was charged 'at all costs to guard the Plummer's toilet doors. Seemingly, the tradition was that after an Oriel Bump Supper (they were good at rowing in those days) the revellers descended in a drunken, bow-tied horde to pillage the Plummer's loo doors. During my reign, they did indeed have a Bump Supper, there was a lot of noise and commotion but I am pleased to say I kept Corpus's honour intact.'

Perhaps **Brian Sedgemore** (1958) best captured the spirit of this period: 'I had behaved as a lout; yes, a lout with an anarchic streak living in delirious times.' It was also reflected in an episode – reminiscent of Wodehouse – after the 1961 Varsity match at Lords. **Mueen**

Afzaal (1960) attended with Corpus friends Ed Johnson (1958) and John Campbell (1956) and 'the retired Wing Commander David Bennett, DFC, DFO Bar, who was one of the frequent visitors to The Bear and nearly always looking for some form of employment. He had served in the RAF with distinction in the Second World War in Burma.' Afzaal left early, but the others stayed on in the Tavern:

By closing time, around 10pm, the company were all fairly drunk. By this time they had been joined by a blind Scotsman of a sort not uncommon in those days. They also had the sympathies of an attractive young barmaid who had been chatted up by the Wing C. As they all came out of the pub, Ed went to the middle of the road and, with both arms raised, accosted what he thought was a taxi. Unfortunately, it was a police car. The police stopped the car and, assuming that Ed Johnson was in an advanced state of inebriation and causing a public nuisance, decided to arrest him. Ed decided to put up a fight and felt that he was not doing badly with odds of 3:1 against. By this time, the staff of the Tavern came out of the pub and witnessed the game resistance that Ed was putting up.

The attractive barmaid dared the Wing C to go to Ed's rescue which he did, being later joined by John Campbell and the blind Scotsman. At this stage, when the scuffle was reaching a stalemate, more police reinforcements arrived and the whole lot were carted off to St John's Wood police station. While John Campbell was bailed out, shortly after arrival, by his father, the rest spent the night in the police station. Later that night, the police brought in a couple of street walkers as well as some tramps who were drunk and disorderly. Ed spent the night singing Corpus rugby songs, while the Wing C chatted up the streetwalkers. He described his exploits in the Second World War to the ladies and asked them to relate their wartime experiences.

The next morning they were all presented before a magistrate and fined. The largest fine was for Ed Johnson. As they were leaving the court, the police officer who had initiated the arrest came up to Ed Johnson and thanked him profusely for a somewhat unusual but satisfying evening.

But by the late 1960s Oxford, according to **Nick Witney** (1969), was 'in transition':

> Despite occasional self-conscious efforts to picnic on quail's eggs on punts, the *Brideshead* thing was history. Yet the College was still locked at night (climbing in was via the Meadow, then over the spikes at the end of Merton Grove); and we were still required to dine some nights in Hall (in gowns, with the long Latin grace that the Classics scholars competed to rattle off). And, of course, Corpus was still all-male – a constant source of angst except for those able to import girlfriends from home.

The rules on overnight guests remained fierce in theory though, as **Rob Stepney** (1971) recalled, increasingly overlooked in practice: 'the severity of the possible punishment seemed iniquitous. There was clearly an element of College staff turning a blind eye to what was going on – to the benefit of all.' Indeed, **David Stogdale** (1969) found that 'coming from an establishment where I was once caned for crossing the sightscreen at the bowler's end, I could not believe the almost complete absence of imposed "discipline".' But what some regarded as jolly japes, and others as antisocial behaviour, continued – albeit, as **Mel Johnson** (1972) observed, in different forms:

> Heavies and freaks had their own ways of demonstrating developmental delay and indulged in antisocial behaviour which would have led to our contemporaries in Blackbird Leys being imprisoned or receiving a short, sharp shock. Those who were committed to social revolution practised by occupying the Examination Schools and the Indian Institute, ostensibly in pursuit of a central student union building. After all, we had to show solidarity with the proletariat – even if they did jeer at us as we marched through the city centre and failed to see how our momentous struggle related to their own as they bustled towards Marks and Spencers or Woolworths. Heavies were capable of wrecking the Plummer, disconnecting telephones, sprinkling glass confetti over the Quad, knocking on the doors of neighbouring colleges with cars, letting

off fire extinguishers in the faces of speakers at the Oxford Union, decorating lamp posts with bicycles or even creatively redesigning the shape of the lamp post itself. Their aggression simply lacked focus and social motivation.[10]

Richard Abernethy (1973) got into trouble for disrupting a Monday Club meeting: 'Oddly, I received two disciplinary warnings over this escapade: one from the College and the other from the International Socialists, who had not approved the action. As far as I can recall, this was my only brush with authority at Corpus.' **Martin Deahl** (1975) recalled an incident when the 'Vile Bodies' dining club – 'a less well known version of the Bullingdon' – hired a College room:

Many of us objected to their presence in College on principle so we decided to interrupt their gathering with a few choicely aimed snowballs (snow was thick on the ground). The raid met with resistance and retaliation, eventually spilling out onto Merton Street where a pitched snowball battle took place. Police became involved and arrests were made. A few days later one of our classicists appeared in front of magistrates to answer charges of causing a breach of the peace. As it happened his father, a distinguished barrister, arranged for an equally distinguished colleague to defend his errant son. Oxford Magistrates' Court erupted into laughter (justices included) and the case collapsed at the point when Counsel skilfully manoeuvred a police witness to the point where he found himself saying, 'he threw a snowball at me, your honour'. My colleague was acquitted, reputation intact, which is more than can be said for the police witness.

Many disciplinary issues were over minor issues. **Margaret Harper** (1979) was summoned to the Dean – Val Cunningham, her tutor – over a dispute with Steward Norman Beech about vacation accommodation. She reported home: 'Beech v Craven ended happily when Val interviewed me whilst he was playing at being Dean. He decided it was all a complete misunderstanding and ended up apologizing for wasting my time! Isn't he a sweetie?!' But she welcomed his intervention with the Rugby Club: 'Val has been getting himself in trouble with the JCR this week by clamping down on the activities of a small group of the Rugby Club who consistently create havoc. Unfortunately, this group dominates the JCR so are protesting that he is restricting their freedom or some such rubbish. The rest of the College, I think, would prefer to see some such infringement and the College buildings still standing!'

Kenneth Dover reflected on discipline during his time as President. Demonstrations were no longer a major problem, but book theft was increasing:

> there were [also] occasional deliberate dishonesties, such as by-passing gas meters, and plenty of thoughtlessness; the morally sturdy young woman who plastered all her walls with posters and cards presumably just didn't know what improperly used Blu-Tack can do to plaster. Vandalism was rare – and convicting the culprit even rarer. Once upon a time (I am told) a Dean could assume that wrongdoers would own up and accept their punishment. Now they don't if they can avoid it.

The disciplinary process, particularly at appeal stage, had become more formal. One hearing 'lasted from two in the afternoon until midnight, with a break for dinner':

> Once an appeal has been made and the whole affair moves on to the judicial plane, rules of evidence, which have little to do with the reasoning we employ in real life, come into force, and a college is neither trained nor equipped for the detective work needed to make a conviction stick. A year or two later I had to advise the Dean (both of us gnashing our teeth) to drop a charge of dangerous vandalism because if the suspects appealed there would be no hope of proving the case against them.[11]

From the student perspective, **Gregory Wilsdon** (1978) thought 'Decanal power was in theory practically limitless and carried the sanction of fines which, if left unpaid, would prevent the student from taking his degree. One of the reasons that these arbitrary powers had not been curbed was that in recent years the Dean's exercising of them had been uncontroversial.' But a decision to hold party hosts responsible for any damage to College property that night created 'uproar' when two girls held a 'pleasant and peaceful' party:

> The same night, some members of the College, probably unconnected with the party, got drunk and engaged in a piece of vandalism – I think this was the night somebody set fire to the tumble dryer. The culprits unidentified, the Dean told the two girls that they would be held financially responsible. His target could not have been worse chosen, since the girls were by temperament and social habits as far distanced from violence as it is possible to imagine ... Fortunately, the idiocy of this particular policy became so clear that it was soon altered.[12]

In 1991 JCR President **Edward Miliband** (1989) reported that 'letting off of some fire extinguishers' had led to every junior member being fined – causing 'great concern over the unfairness of penalizing those who were some distance from the College at the time of the incident. Fortunately, a negotiated solution, in which the JCR paid a modest fine, prevailed.'[13] But **Debbie Welch** (1994) 'never really noticed the rules and discipline. Only one I remember coming up was the amusement when the Proctors sent a notice out at exam time asking us not to throw things in "pubic" places.'

Student pranks continued, sometimes self-consciously. **Martin Deahl** (1975) recalled the 1970s 'cod war' prompting the JCR to declare 'a 200-m fishing limit measured from the Pelican, which of course included the pool in Tom Quad at Christ Church next door. Christ Church men were disgruntled to put it mildly when they awoke to find toy gunboats in their pond.' **David Massam** (1989) recalled 'the ritualistic "trashing" of emergent finalists with flour and champagne, a habit which brought a letter of condemnation from the local Chief of Police, and thus the happy realization by most of us that we were as capable of authority-provoking japes as any of our predecessors'.[14] The 2000s saw Oriel–Corpus rivalry revived when Oriel JCR attempted to hold a meeting in Corpus. 'Fortunately,' **John Suares**

(2002) reported, 'the College choir were close at hand to repulse the invaders with waterbombs from the College tower ... I can't think of any invasionary forces in history whose entire might was dashed by a belligerent choir!' Corpuscles decided to retaliate. Armed with super-soakers and water-filled balloons, the 'Corpus delta force' entered Oriel through an underground tunnel:

> With hand signals as the chosen means of communication, the assault division break-in man burst into the JCR meeting, hurling a water bomb as he braced himself to hold the door open for the remaining volley of projectiles. To the assault division's delight, the majority of Oriel JCR had seen fit to attend their meeting in dinner jackets. So having unleashed vast volumes of water over the stunned and rather well-garbed Orielenses, the assault squad retreated with haste through the tunnel and up Oriel Street to a High Street pub for a celebratory pint and cigar.[15]

Caroline Knapp (2005) recalled a 'bizarre' confrontation with Mansfield:

> At one JCR meeting, someone proposed a motion to form an angry mob and march on Mansfield College, demanding port as compensation for one of their number vomiting in our Beer Cellar. The motion passed, and so after the meeting a group of Corpus-cles marched through the streets of Oxford, shouting 'What do we want? Port! Why do we want it? Honour!' Sadly, the mob was dispersed at Mansfield without getting what it came for, but at least we came away with an amusing anecdote.

By the 2000s the older disciplinary issues – gate hours, exclusion of women and climbing in – were long gone. The porters' role also changed, as Head Porter **Mike Minns** recognized: 'my staff are less involved with undergraduate discipline than they once were'.[16] His successor, **Dave Yeatman**, agreed: 'We have not got the discipline role that they had years back but we still have to maintain a control of certain things.' But there were other concerns. Drugs – which were, of course, illegal – had become more common. According to **Gareth Moore** (1966), 'cannabis was readily available and cheaper than alcohol' and **Rob Stepney** (1971) thought 'there were those who regularly smoked dope (and inhaled) – who made up perhaps a third of the College – and those who did not'. **Chris Sherwell** (1969) thought alcohol 'was pursued to still-traditional excess' and that marijuana – 'dope' – 'was "freely" available, at least to those who had the money'; but 'if there was LSD or cocaine it was not widespread'. **Eugene Dainov** (1976) took his Russian oral finals 'in a state of mind strongly affected by an organic hallucinogen taken the night before: six packets of ground Morning Glory seeds. I sailed through with a spirited defence, in Russian, of the benefits of smoking tobacco.'[17]

It is impossible to know how widespread drugs really were. **Margaret Harper** (1979) told her parents they posed little problem, 'chiefly because they are extremely expensive and the laws concerning them are very strict. I have never been offered drugs whilst being here'; and **Nicola Feather** (1981) thought there were 'none, or at least not on show. It is true that I would not know what to look for, but I don't remember anyone behaving unaccountably strangely in public.' According to *Smallprint*, the College GP 'has seen little evidence of drug-related problems although she has to deal with occasional over-excess of alcohol, often a symptom of more fundamental difficulties'.[18] **Dave Yeatman** came across drugs, though 'not frequently':

> There were quite a number of occasions when I smelt [cannabis] – from a past job [as a member of the police] I could tell the smell – and I used to say to them, 'Cannabis', and they used to deny it. I would say, 'Look, I know that's cannabis: end of story.' And they used to come back to me and say, 'Dave, thanks for not dropping us in it but just to let you know we were just trying it.' They were a bit curious that I could pick it up and I would say, 'Well, if I can pick it up anybody can pick it up.' I felt that in Corpus drugs probably did happen but it wasn't in your face. It didn't really cause a problem that I saw.

Alcohol was more common. In 1994 the JCR Rag Officer 'displayed remarkable enthusiasm and devotion to the job by being arrested for being drunk and incapable after the Rag Pub Crawl'.[19] After Finals **Nick Hassall** (1989) and a friend

> thought it a good idea in a drunken moment of madness to shoulder barge open the door of a biochemist who had asked us to stop singing or listening to music in the Quad as he was still studying for Finals. Unfortunately, the door became completely unhinged and came crashing down. We were duly summoned to see Sir Keith [Thomas] who was very diplomatic but suggested that it might be better for all concerned if we pay for the repairs to the door and quietly leave the College.

Reflecting on his experience as Dean in the 2000s, **Jay Sexton** recalled 'no major violations of College rules or, thankfully, national or international laws. Most of the students summoned to the Dean had only left their mobile phone on in the Library (automatic £10 fine) or had failed to clean up their vomit from over-drinking (automatic £25 fine paid to the scout with the misfortune of cleaning it up).' Choosing the right punishment could be tricky – when he sentenced the rugby team to three hours mopping up the Hall and Beer Cellar after inappropriate behaviour, they proved to be 'religious attendees of lectures that began at nine each morning when their mopping duties were to commence'. However, the one issue he found 'genuinely troubling' and 'a serious problem' was 'the students' unhealthy relationship with alcohol':

> This all dawned on me at the dinner for the annual Corpus Challenge (capping off a series of competitions between Corpus Oxford and Corpus Cambridge). Nearly every student in Hall that night brought his or her own bottle of wine to dinner. At first I was confused – was this some kind of exchange of gifts to commemorate the Challenge? But I soon realized to my horror that each student planned to consume, mostly with success, his or her *entire bottle* over the hour-long dinner as if it were a can of Coke (it should be pointed out here that the dinner followed a session in the College bar and was prelude to the main event, a trip to a local

dance club). Revealingly, none of the students seemed uncomfortable drinking their bottle of wine in the presence of the Dean and the Acting President. I don't think that they think it is a problem, which is what I find most troubling. Furthermore, the most serious discipline issues I dealt with this year – the trouser-droppers at a Formal Hall, the brawlers in the Quad, the participants in a sophomoric game of intercollegiate thievery – were alcohol-fuelled.[20]

He suspected the drinking reflected the 'largely internalized' pressure 'from years of exams and school expectations and competition with peers and parental pressure. Who wouldn't want a respite in this situation?'

Welfare

Jay Sexton's observations illustrated the need to balance discipline and rules with care and support. What was the 'care' side of this equation? In the 1940s, according to **Peter Baldwin** (1941), 'Corpus made no display of caring, but conveyed care in its style, academically with objectivity and personally without sentimentality. But if, for example, any Corpuscle had to be admitted to hospital he would find the President visiting him there; and aftercare was in the hands of a comfortingly professional nurse.' Its size and intimacy reinforced the sense of a caring community. **Peter Myerscough** (1954) recalled that the Chaplain's evening discussions, which were intellectually stimulating, 'promoted bonds of friendship and mutual respect' and 'for me made Corpus Christi not just a name. Care of its members and their welfare has been, and I believe continues to be, a hallmark of Corpus.'[21]

The College provided financial support in some situations. After his second year, **Francis Oakley** (1950) was advised 'with admirable and kindly bluntness' that he needed to focus on his studies:

I was told, by way of encouragement, that I would not need to find a summer job that year and that the College would make some modest discretionary funding available so that I could stay up at Oxford over the long vacation and start in on the task of catching up on my academic work and filling in the gaps in my preparation for Schools. I am eternally grateful to the College both for the forthrightness of the counsel given me at a pivotal moment and for the support extended to make it possible for me to act on that advice. It was for me the great turning point that led me in the direction of the academic calling that I have found so deeply fulfilling.

After mentioning that he needed a summer job, **Gareth Moore** (1966) was summoned to President Hardie, who advised that vacation study was important and arranged a cheque to help. 'It was not a large cheque, but I was struck by the attentiveness of senior members to the needs of juniors, and by the care to nurture the academic life of a lowly second-year student, that it betokened. This taught me, what I had not realized before, that the College actually cared about its students and did not just process them.'[22] As a non-UK resident, **Farzana Ahmed** (1979) had to pay full fees: but when 'my parents, being Third World diplomats, ran out of cash', Andrew Glyn stepped in and 'arranged for the College to excuse fees for two semesters and also persuaded the University to excuse the University-level fees'. **Tom Ogg** (2003) was another beneficiary: 'Corpus gave me thousands of pounds to stay at Corpus during the holidays to complete academic work, because studying at home was very difficult due to my father's mental illness. For that, I was and remain incredibly grateful.'

Physical injuries or sickness were handled by the College Doctor and Nurse, though others helped. When **Paul Quarrie** (1962) was injured during a College play, Fellow David Jamison, himself a medic, 'eventually looking professionally at my head, said I should have stitches. To the Radcliffe we went in his Citroën.' When **Simon Squires** (1962) became seriously ill, 'the Dean, Ewen Bowie, went far out of his way to help and to keep in touch with my parents'. Others faced emotional problems, including homesickness. **Don Montague** (1954) 'felt decidedly lonely at first', and although **Carley Chapman** (2002) found Corpus 'a fantastic place to live and study' she felt 'quite homesick a lot of the time'. Friends were one recourse, but also College staff. **Kenneth Reynolds** (1966) found Anne Nisbet, previously the President's Secretary, 'a gentle, kind, caring lady offering a warm welcome to a rather lost peasant boy newly arrived in Oxford from the far west of Cornwall'. Former scout **Margaret Scully** recalled how some students 'brought their teddy bears, especially when they first came in, in the first year. Some of them said, "Oh, I miss my mum and I must go home every weekend."'

Psychological problems were more difficult. **Philip Hamilton-Grierson** (1952) thought one contemporary 'had just endured a harrowing time in Korea and was suffering from post-traumatic stress'. As **Eldred Jones** (1950) noted, Finals were a particular problem:

> I was shocked at the number of nervous breakdowns and even suicides that occurred just before and after this ordeal. A fellow student from another college living in the same house, usually a self-assured leading athlete, completely broke down a couple of days before the examinations and asked whether I could let him have some of my notes – we were both reading English. This was too late of course to do him any good that they might otherwise have done but I let him have something. On the first morning of the examinations, another student had to help him dress and accompany him to the bus stop, encouraging him to brace up and have a shot at the exams, which he did and got a degree. Some similar breakdowns had more tragic results.[23]

Philip Hamilton-Grierson (1953) lived in Magpie Lane, run by Bob and Mrs Dickens, where 'a previous lodger had tried to commit suicide when revising for his finals. What little revision we did was constantly interrupted by Mrs D bearing cups of hot drinks so that she could be reassured of our well-being.' As noted earlier, **Tony Carr** (1956) felt 'depression and even something like despair' at the prospect of Finals and suffered, for the only time in his life, 'stress-related illness, including shingles',[24] while **Danielle Sanderson** (1982) thought that 'for several girls at Corpus, the pressure of Finals was too great, with one or two suffering breakdowns, and others deferring for a year'.

Some carried less visible burdens, only fully manifested later. **Andrew Purkis** (1967) recalled Dave Whitton (1967), 'an able but emotionally damaged' fellow historian:

After we all went our different ways, he became a research fellow at Wolfson and converted to Roman Catholicism. His inner loneliness seems to have reasserted itself and morphed into excessive drinking and smoking, mental illness and despair, and he committed suicide. This remains a terrible shock and source of guilt, because as life had moved on I had lost touch with him. We failed to sustain the communion of our undergraduate closeness and he seems to have found none other that could make his life tolerable to him in the longer term.

According to **Gregory Wilsdon** (1978), 'Oxford is a stressful place to study. A (male) member of my year in Corpus cracked up during finals, received an aegrotat, and a few years later took his own life.' **David Upshal** (1984) wrote with shock about his friend Andrew Hopley (1985), a successful student who also committed suicide a few years after leaving.[25]

Welfare was traditionally regarded as a College matter – the 1962 University Handbook claimed there was no need for a counselling service because tutors provided it.[26] But was the College equipped to give the necessary support? **David Archard** (1969) thought not:

The pressures on students were enormous, and I do feel angry still at the lack of adequate pastoral care. This is not to say tutors did not display concern for the welfare of students and make themselves available to discuss problems. They did both. But there is an important difference between amateur concern and professional counselling. Too many Oxford students experienced serious personal difficulties which were left untended. Corpus was no exception to the general rule. One student committed suicide, and made such evident preparations in the week beforehand as to be effectively advertising his intentions. Another student visibly disintegrated mentally in the run-up to Finals. He wrote nothing in his examinations, being unable to remember his name and enter it on the script. I felt the College preferred not to acknowledge such problems, nor its obligation to provide adequate assistance.[27]

By the 1970s the University had established a counselling service, but **Clive Britten** (1974), who admitted to 'feelings of insecurity and doubt', remained unimpressed:

> After a lot of agonizing, I went and saw the University counsellor, but I think she allowed me to leave too readily, and I would have been helped if I had seen her for longer. Also, it was on my own initiative that I went to see her. I don't know whether things have changed, but it would have helped if there had been some point of reference within the College.[28]

The College took steps to professionalize its service. **Mary Campbell**, College Nurse from 1975, 'attended Counselling Courses so that I could better deal with worried and depressed students – of which there were usually a few in each intake. One student even had to be taken weekly by me to Littlemore Hospital (then the local mental hospital), and I was quite often rung up in the middle of the night and had to go down to College on my moped to deal with some crisis, usually a student in distress.' The Chaplain, **David Atkinson**, also had professional training and worked closely with her and the College Doctor: 'We used to hold a termly "Student Welfare Group" lunch to bring together us three with the Dean and the JCR President and MCR President. I think it did some useful work. The least public part of my work was counselling. Students – and sometimes, may I add, members of the Governing Body – came to see me to talk through issues that were troubling them.'

Mary Campbell praised 'the splendid staircase ladies and men who gave me so much support with the welfare of the students – they knew them better than any of us'. Former scout **Margaret Scully** explained:

> We saw a lot more of [students] than anybody. As Colin Holmes [Domestic Bursar] said, 'If you think that one of them has a problem, don't think you are sneaking on them, you are not sneaking to me about them; but if you think it's a serious problem it is very important that you can come back and just quietly say, "You know, he might be having a nervous breakdown, pressure of

exams and that, you know." But I was lucky, I never had any like that.'

Head Porter **Dave Yeatman** saw the Lodge porters as another 'listening ear':

> They can't go and talk to family whereas they can come over to the Lodge at night-time, certainly in the small hours of the morning, to talk over things and you can see they are a little bit upset and get them in, give them a cup of tea or a cup of coffee and just talk about anything and everything and half an hour later they go out a different person. Whereas if you hadn't had that environment next morning they might have self-harmed, they might have done anything, but you've managed to stop that happening by being there for them.

He too would alert the College – 'certainly the College Chaplain' – to any serious concerns. He recalled one student who had struggled with work and turned to 'booze and tablets, that was just their way out'. By bringing it to the attention of the College, 'our actions nipped it in the bud and saved that person'. The family was grateful and remained in touch.

The highest-profile tragedy concerned not a student but the 1985 suicide of long-serving History Fellow Trevor Aston. He had serious mental health issues and his colleague **James Murray** recalled how 'his mental instability, increasing heavy drinking problem, unsocial behaviour, particularly at High Table, and general unpleasant and disruptive behaviour became progressively more and more difficult to deal with'. Afterwards President Kenneth Dover 'told me how unbelievably difficult Trevor had been to deal with in College, his abusive behaviour to some of the Fellows and the staff'. Dover's later autobiography included the words: 'It was clear to me by now that Trevor and the College must somehow be separated, and my problem was one which I feel compelled to define with brutal candour: how to kill him without getting into trouble.'[29] According to **Tony Coady**, 'in fact, it isn't clear that Dover played any significant role in Trevor's death, but this part of his memoir created a sensation in the media'.[30] **Andreas Willi** (1998), a Swiss postgraduate, inadvertently touched a nerve when he later invited Dover back from retirement, to speak at a seminar on Greek comedy. Dover agreed but warned, 'You should know, however, that many in the College regard me as an evil man.' Willi had read the autobiography but 'was blissfully unaware of the waves it had caused at Corpus only a few years earlier'. The seminar 'drew a large audience from the Classics community at Oxford, but the High Table dinner afterwards, though as enjoyable as ever, was scarcely attended: word had gone round that the "evil man" was in town, and many had chosen to stay away'.

Taking stock of the welfare service, Corpus journal *Smallprint* described Oxford as 'a peculiar place', with all the emotional and psychological problems to be found anywhere compounded by 'the so-called "Oxford neurosis" (intellectual precocity plus emotional immaturity)'. The College had a welfare committee composed of the Senior Tutor, Dean, Chaplain, Nurse, Doctor, JCR President, Women's Welfare Officer, MCR President and the Women's Tutor, who met regularly. The 'pivot' was the College Nurse:

> She is the first person most people go to see about everyday medical matters which if need be she can refer to one of the College Doctors. Her room is also the place where many other worries first manifest themselves often on the pretext of or in the form of minor medical needs. The Nurse spends a great deal of time trying to find out where best a person can be helped, whether in College with the Chaplain or the Doctors or outside College with the University Counselling Service or at the Warneford Clinic. She also has regular meetings with the JCR President to keep in touch with the general atmosphere in College.
>
> A recent addition to the welfare staff is Dr Van Schaik, the female partner in the College General Practice. Like the other welfare people she finds that she is faced with a diversity of problems. She has a fair number of female patients who prefer to see a woman doctor, especially about gynaecological problems. She offers practical advice on contraception when it is requested and is also ready to listen to more general worries. Where somebody has

made their mind up what they want she can provide what is required (provided there is no medical obstacle) without the intervention of the family planning clinic. Despite recent hysteria concerning drugs Dr Van Schaik says she has seen little evidence of drug-related problems although she has to deal with occasional over-excess of alcohol, often a symptom of more fundamental difficulties.

Encouraging people to come forward in the first place could be difficult: 'Friends, scouts and the JCR President all have a role to play here but some people still go unnoticed, particularly graduates or those living out, and ultimately people must still have the choice about whether or not to seek help.' Overall, Corpus was felt to be performing reasonably well: 'Its size and the energy of the Chaplain and the Nurse mean that by and large people are not left to suffer in silence once they or someone else has drawn attention to their plight.' However,

the most striking problem we found (and one of the most difficult to combat) is what is described by the Association of Oxford College Medical Officers as 'intense and devastating loneliness'. This seems to be true of Corpus as of all Oxford colleges and is a problem which is compounded by the superficial appearance the University gives of being a place where everyone is enjoying their halcyon days.[31]

These issues were not always visible. **Ben Whitby** (1986) was 'unaware of any pastoral care although I think people like Thomas Charles-Edwards and Brian Harrison were keeping an eye on me and my progress. It did not appear to be very systematic or professional but it worked.' Following a 1996 survey, the JCR concluded that 'welfare provision is generally good, and the people responsible for welfare are, on the whole, well thought-of. An effort will be made to raise the profile of the welfare panel and make their individual roles clearer, and this will be implemented along with various other new ideas.'[32] Nevertheless, reflecting in 2015 on changes since the 1990s, Academic Registrar **Rachel Pearson** felt that 'over the years students have gradually become more anxious and less resilient to pressure'.[33]

Six per cent of Oxford applicants in 2007 were registered as suffering from some form of physical or mental disability and the University's Equality and Diversity Unit supported around 1,000 students.[34] For James Kierstead (2006), 'my experience of being at Corpus had a sort of intensity that meant that the high and low points came very close together, and sometimes coincided. Some of the times I remember with the most fondness were, I am pretty sure, periods of almost unrelieved misery at the time.' He experienced chronic pain, prompted by concussion at rugby:

> Looking back, this probably had a lot to do with my psychological state in my first year. I do remember a few days spent wandering around Oxford in that period, desperately trying to break myself out of bouts of depression and anxiety. By the time the concussion had sunk in I had begun to realize that most of the people around me were crazy too. One of my close friends in the first year was indeed certifiably so, and had spent a few weeks in the Warneford after accusing the Fellow and Tutor in Latin of downloading thoughts into children's brains using his laptop. Another close friend had begun seeing a psychologist, and arranged to leave Corpus every term a week or two early. Corpus also introduced me to the term 'self-harm'; I started identifying with more confidence the characteristic striations on the forearms of many of my acquaintances.

Fortunately, his third year proved 'something of a turning point', due in part to theatre and his girlfriend. The physical setting also helped:

> When the rain, stress, darkness and depression were in abeyance, Corpus was a beautiful place. In the summer you could take your lunch-tray out into the garden and eat yoghurt-covered flapjacks with your friends, sitting on the grass under the copper beech. You could walk around Christ Church Meadow, which probably more than any other factor was the reason I made it through my degree in one piece.

JCR–SCR relations

Ultimate responsibility for the College rested with the Governing Body – the Fellows meeting under the chairmanship of the President. Although junior members could make representations, traditionally they had no role in corporate decision-making.

These long-standing arrangements were uncontroversial in the post-war years. Recalling his own student days, **Kenneth Dover** 'found it amusing that at Balliol in 1938–40, in a JCR of which Edward Heath, Roy Jenkins and Denis Healey were officers, the notion that undergraduates might participate in the government of the College was never voiced'.[35] Corpus JCR discussed issues great and small, and the 'strop book' recorded robust views on anything. But as **Simon Squires** (1962) observed, 'there was little of what you could call "activism": JCR meetings were really quite parochial, and rarely went beyond such issues as petitioning the Dean for some relaxation of women's permitted visiting hours'.

It was therefore a shock when, in 1967, **Grant Amyot** (1967) launched a campaign for 'Democracy in Corpus'. 'By democracy,' he explained, 'we mean the representation of the junior members of the College on the Governing body of the College':

In our initial leaflet, we pointed out some of the areas in which [students] have abdicated control of their own lives: the housing situation in general; the syllabuses; the system of separate men's and women's colleges with visiting hours. Complaints about these things are often heard, but almost no one has realized that his own personal problems are closely connected with the power structures which attempt to direct his life.

The rationale of our demand for representation in College (and eventually University) government is based upon the belief that men are not fully human or fully alive if they are not active in determining the direction of their collective endeavours. (This goes for workers just as well as for students.) Democratization involves and interests the participants in the collective's activity (in this case, education), and makes it a real 'community'. It is all the more important that it be implemented in education, where people acquire the attitudes they will often retain for life.[36]

Responding, **John Ramsden** (1966) regretted that 'the peace and tranquility of our medieval community' had been 'rudely shattered' by this intervention: 'never before had such heretical plans ventured within Fox's cloistered retreat'. The leaflet, posted in every pigeonhole, had 'dangled before our fascinated eyes' reforms including 'student power, syllabus reforms and co-education in Corpus',

> but there was less than detailed discussion of the practicability of such ideas. There was the obvious and singularly unfortunate fact that the demand for an end to the midnight curfew was made on the same day that our new liberal Dean announced the introduction of the late key system. Many pointed out that this would seem to underline the adequacy of present forms of representation, at a college level, but otherwise, the reform movement was engulfed in a sudden tide of overwhelming apathy. What positive reaction there was could hardly be described in print, but it will suffice to say that the suggestions book in the JCR was seen to glow for days afterwards.[37]

A JCR motion for representation on the Governing Body was rejected by 24 to 23 votes with several abstentions, but it was agreed – 'as the only way to prevent further agitation' – to establish a committee to consider further. The upshot was that 'better liaison arrangements with the Senior College should be established and that grievances held be presented by a group of JCR members rather than the President alone'.[38]

Despite the horror which greeted 'Democracy in Corpus', its ideas proved prescient. As we have seen, the 1970s saw the admission of women. Syllabus reform became the subject of lively University debate, and changes did eventually arrive, albeit slowly. Student representation was also eventually accepted, initially limited to subcommittees. According to President **Kenneth Dover**:

> This worked so smoothly and uncontentiously that it seemed to me appropriate, after another year had passed, to put my weight

behind a renewed request from the JCR for representation on the Governing Body itself. Knowing that our sister college in Cambridge had already taken that step, I rang up Duncan Wilson, the Master, to ask him how it worked. 'I think', he said, 'that the undergraduates have had a very civilizing effect on the Fellows.' I was heartened by that, but did not report it, as it would have leaked and would not have improved the Master's relations with his Fellows.[39]

In 1983 the JCR and MCR Presidents, and JCR Secretary, were finally admitted as 'non-voting members at College Meetings. It was accepted on both sides that some items of business, essentially those which concerned the academic progress, character, finance or health of an identifiable individual, should be reserved for the Fellows alone.'[40] **Ewen Bowie** thought Corpus 'among the first colleges to have junior member representation on Committees and on Governing Body'.[41] **Sean O'Grady** (1981) was 'the first student union president' to attend Governing Body: 'We did our best to keep the charges down and the support for our studies up.' He felt 'the arrangement has thus far worked well and I am sure will in time prove a remarkably wise move'.[42] President **Dover** recalled learning pains: 'Some (by no means all) Fellows reacted to suggestions and requests from the JCR with immediate "Ah, but ...!" objections, not infrequently cast in facetious or sarcastic terms, which made me curl up.' However, 'Once Fellows had got their initial response out of their system, they often proved helpful, constructive and ready to compromise, but it was a pity that progress had to start on the wrong foot, and there were occasions when the patience and courtesy of the junior members earned my respect.'[43]

In practice, JCR Presidents like **Douglas Fraser** (1983) handled much business directly with College officers:

The President treated me with meticulous politeness and studied neutrality, only letting a blatant bias show through when negotiating charges. The Bursar sits in his office, chewing a pencil and surveying a map of Corpus's farms. His contempt for committees is barely concealed. A sherry and a chat is greatly to be preferred. The Dean shares his contempt for time-consuming committees with an equal lack of regard for the JCR and its representatives. Every letter I addressed to him was sent back with a few notes scribbled in the bottom corner, except one which he chose to ignore. On the occasions when I avoided the scribbling and went to Decanal 'hours' he wasn't there. The Steward, however, receives my sympathies. He really is the pivot of the College in that he is everybody's scapegoat. Scouts, dons, maintenance staff, and accommodation officers all look to Norman [Beech] as an intermediary in the petty squabbling of Corpocracy.[44]

Representation did not end tensions between junior and senior members. **Nicola Feather** (1981) noted 'a certain ambiguity in undergraduate dealings with the SCR. Individually, they were our tutors and we were able to form more or less good relationships with them in our tutorials, depending on where they were on the scale of "benign" to "scary". Collectively, however, the dynamic resembled more closely that of the aristocracy versus the peasants.' SCR refurbishment was one point of contention. Another was dinner: 'Nightly, we were subjected to seeing the equivalent of roast sucking pig being borne aloft to High Table.' But the most serious issue was accommodation. Initially, as JCR President **Pushpinder Saini** (1986) reported, the College and JCR were in agreement:

Unlike many other colleges the Corpus Governing Body recognizes the essential role which the JCR plays within the College. The Governing Body recognized the duty of the College to provide accommodation for all of its members and we are at present on the threshold of constructing a hostel in collaboration with Christ Church: Corpus will soon have the privilege of being one of the few Oxford colleges to house all of its members for all years of their courses. The excellent relationship between the SCR and JCR was evidenced by the speedy charges settlement of 4 per cent on accommodation and a freeze in all other charges. This agreement came from an acknowledgement by the Governing Body of the grave financial state of those who are forced to 'live out' at present.[45]

The Liddell Building opened in 1991. However, as **Andrew Wilson** (1987) recalled, a bitter dispute over rents ensued:

> The SCR proposed a percentage increase that far exceeded the prevailing rate of inflation. According to the Bursar, it was desirable to bring the College's charges for accommodation into line with prevailing market levels. According to the JCR, it was precisely *because* the College's prices were below those of the private sector that they remained affordable, the private sector being sewn up between a few firms who were widely held to charge unreasonable rents for poor accommodation. The SCR remained intransigent in the face of the JCR's counter-proposal. Feelings ran very high.[46]

The dispute – which created 'a serious breakdown in goodwill between SCR and JCR' – occurred, he felt, in the context of cuts in education funding, including grants, and growing student hardship: 'it was already impossible to get through the vacation reading because of the need to work to earn extra income, and one student at least was having to take a part-time job during term time'. According to JCR President **Edward Miliband** (1989):

> When the offer of a 39 per-cent rent increase was announced in Sixth Week, many thought simply that a decimal point had gone astray, and when it was confirmed that the proposal was 'for real' there was disbelief, and anger. At the largest JCR meeting for some years at Corpus, there was an overwhelming feeling that discussion with the College must continue, but that other means of conveying the JCR's views would be necessary. Though the benefits of the new accommodation were clearly substantial, it seemed to many a perverse logic to use this as a pretext for raising charges so colossally.
>
> The half-dozen or so protests that followed were attended by a remarkable cross-section of junior members, and were mainly silent – a stay-away from the Corpus Christi Day Dinner, action at Formal Hall etc. The two 'noisy' protests, one inside college and one in Merton St (which attracted *Central News*), were extremely tame by the standards of the real world, but seemed to cause as

much shock to some senior members as the proposed increase did to junior members. Despite this, the JCR remained absolutely united throughout the three weeks.[47]

The *Pelican Record* reported 'a vocal demonstration after breakfast outside the front gate, which drew TV cameras, reporters and made local news bulletins':

> Fellows walked the gauntlet with a mixture of reactions: stony-faced, disgusted, amused, wry. Who could tell what those dons were inwardly thinking? Chants outside the SCR at lunchtime drew a more visceral response. Six-gun Val Cunningham marched down waving pistols in the air, brandishing £100 fines, even though as ex-Dean, it may have been hot air. With the lawyer's mellifluous tones, Assistant Dean Stephen Shute brought sweet persuasion to bear. To no avail. The hubbub went on. Cottage industries appeared, T-shirts, posters, badges emblazoned with words of steel, shouts of encouragement, and gradually, imperceptibly, the College shifted a little, crumbled, first from 39 to 27, then to 22 and finally 19, and that spread over two years. At length, the long vacation emerged, a war-torn bursary surveyed the wreckage and a bitterly won peace was announced.[48]

The dispute left a sour taste. **Nick Hassall** (1989) 'took no part in the protests and thought the whole thing ridiculous'. The proposed charges were 'still far below a market rent and, therefore, presumably heavily subsidized by the College'. **David Massam** (1989) thought 'the majority of the JCR found these events ugly and depressing and resorted to them only with reluctance'.[49] **Matthew Spencer** (1988) recalled moments of humour: 'we had some lovely T-shirts made of the Pelican, so lovely in fact that various Fellows could be heard asking at the end of tutorials if there might be any spare. Well ... yessss ... for an extra 40 per cent on the normal cost!' Reviewing the dispute, *Pelican Record* saw no easy answer. The proposals would have 'set Corpus about a quarter of the way down the league table of college charges'. Nor were below-inflation increases sustainable:

The plain fact is that students are not well off, and cannot be. The College subsidizes them anyway, the only issue is to what extent that should be. But when, in ten or twenty years, there are no student grants at all, what should the College do then? Charge nothing? The charges issue is not an easy one, not easy to resolve even by dispassionate, rational arguments. It created a lot of bad feeling, a sad thing in this college.[50]

According to **David Massam** (1989) 'the JCR and Governing Body both emerged intent on an improved relationship, determined that such a marked breakdown in communications should not recur. In my Finals year the negotiations were conducted in a far more restrained atmosphere.'[51] But distrust remained. JCR President **Liz Potter** (1989) resigned after difficult discussions on charges and other issues:

> The SCR–JCR communication over these and other issues was characteristic for its inadequate debate; the suggestion that junior members were lucky to engage in Charges 'Negotiations' only served to enhance my belief that it was impossible to work within a system which questioned their right to do so. It was certainly my hope in resigning that structural changes would be sought to obviate this systematically unacceptable treatment of junior members.[52]

There were further disputes, usually prompted by financial pressures. In 1995 the JCR debated battels: 'At three meetings, including an emergency one, the College's proposals were examined and hotly debated. The JCR was, however, unanimous in its condemnation of the manner in which the proposals had been introduced, which it felt had been deliberately secretive.'[53] In 2001, after negotiating lower increases and a Governing Body commitment 'to ensuring that the very poorest members of the JCR will be able to obtain maintenance support grants', JCR President **Emmanuel Botwe** (1999) concluded that 'the whole episode demonstrated that good relations between the students and the Governing Body can only benefit the College as a whole'.[54] But the following year **Jack Clift** (1999) reported further disagreements, over JCR rights and graduate charges. He was mandated to write to each member of the Governing Body expressing the extreme unhappiness of the JCR with the situation; it was also decided that the last Formal Hall of term should be conducted in silence by junior members, and the JCR President was mandated to read out a statement. When it was discovered that a potential benefactor of the College would be a guest of the President at Formal Hall, an Emergency Meeting was called in order to modify the Formal Hall action – the JCR felt that damaging the College's fundraising prospects would be an unacceptable (if unforeseen) consequence of the original proposal, and decided to moderate the earlier plans. In times of financial difficulty for the College, active co-operation between JCR, MCR and SCR holds out the best hope for long-term success.[55]

Proposals to shorten Freshers' Week prompted a further dispute. Senior Tutor **John Watts** reported 'a series of surprisingly intense demonstrations of displeasure – hissing and chanting in Formal Hall, passionate letters, emails and personal representations to tutors, a highly vocal demonstration under the windows of the final Governing Body meeting of term ("are you *listening*?", was the repeated cry)'. The protests were unsuccessful: 'Governing Body was obdurate, and a short sharp "Freshers' Week" was held in 2005, with the JCR's honour to be saved by the despatch of a questionnaire to the victims of this putatively miserable proceeding.'[56] **Tom Ogg** (2003) took part:

I vividly recall the 2005/6 demonstrations by students in relation to the shortening (or, as the students felt, in effect abolition) of Freshers' Week. David Holtham and I were in the academic committee meeting whilst Ganan Sritharan rallied the troops in the Gentleman Commoners' Quad on a rowing megaphone: 'What do we want?' ' Freshers' Week!' 'When do we want it?' 'Now!!!!' We lost on that particular occasion, though I gather that Freshers' was substantially restored in subsequent years. Marc Stears (now tutor at University College) later told me that the last people to organize protest in Corpus were himself and one Ed Miliband over increases in rent.

JCR President **Binyamin Even** (2004) thought the SCR had left the JCR 'in the dark about the reasons for the change'. He called for more discussion, but felt tension between JCR and Governing Body was inevitable:

> Clashes over reserved business in College meetings have been simmering quietly (and, occasionally, not so quietly) for years, and will continue to do so: the belief among some JCR representatives that they should be excluded only from that which is legally sensitive is simply irreconcilable with the desire for privacy and independence among some in the SCR. The biggest source of SCR–JCR tension, regarding how the SCR should financially support the JCR with regard to rent rises, has been defused by consistently low rises in recent years; but we have not been immune from bitter clashes over this in the past, nor are we likely to be in the future.[57]

Underlying these tensions was the fact that financially, as in other ways, the environment had changed. As **Nick Witney** (1969) observed, it is 'hard to believe today that when I won my place at Corpus my local County Council wrote to congratulate me, and explain how delighted they would be to pay my fees'. By the 2010s most students were paying fees from loans, with the maximum rising substantially. It is too soon for the full effects to become manifest. According to Domestic Bursar **Colin Holmes**, it is expected 'to create a huge change from grateful students to demanding customers', but by 2014 'this has been only partially realized'.[58] Nevertheless, the gradual dismantling of financial support for students – and the universities themselves – was creating pressures which previous generations, including the 1960s and 1970s radicals, had not faced, and made sustaining the College community an ever more difficult challenge.

Postgraduate with young family: Tony Coady receives
BPhil, 1965. *Courtesy of Tony Coady (1963)*

9

'A CLASS APART'? POSTGRADUATES

*My graduate years were socially speaking lonelier than I had
expected and in many ways harder.*

Jonathan Dancy

The friendly MCR soon became my refuge.

Elizabeth O'Brien

Although less conspicuous than the arrival of women, the growth of
postgraduate study represented another fundamental change in this
period. Corpus had always been primarily an undergraduate college.
Undergraduate teaching and social activities dominated College life.
Graduates were few and not very visible – often living out. The undergraduate **Simon Squires** (1962) observed that 'one knew just about
everyone by sight, other than those very few graduate students who
rarely appeared at all'. Postgraduates in turn could feel isolated and
on the sidelines.

But graduate numbers increased markedly. In 1950 Corpus had
14 postgraduates, or 12 per cent of the 135 students. They included
individuals taking 'a Colonial service course' and others reading for a
Diploma in Education. College policy was clear:

The number of postgraduates in the University as a whole is much larger than it used to be; in some colleges it is very large; in Corpus it must remain comparatively small since we attach importance to allowing all members of the College *in statu pupillari* to lunch and dine in Hall on any night of the week. An admixture of men reading for advanced degrees is a valuable and stimulating element in the life of a college especially if the postgraduates mingle with the rest and are not a class apart. This they can hardly be in a small college when they can lunch and dine regularly.[1]

By 1960 there were still only 22 graduates, but thereafter they increased. In 1970 there were 49 (21 per cent of the total), in 1992 86 (27 per cent) and in 2015 94 (still 27 per cent). They were also more international. Corpus had always taken graduate students from abroad – mainly the Commonwealth and United States – but the number of international graduate students rose significantly, from around 18 per cent in 1970 to a quarter in 1992 and a third in 2014.[2] The increase was part of a wider reorientation of the University. Oxford increasingly positioned itself as a 'global' research-based university in which undergraduate teaching remained important but no longer as overwhelmingly dominant as in the past. Postgraduate research – and the funds it could attract, through fees and research grants – was becoming far more central to its mission. Indeed, by 2015 approaching half of all Oxford students were graduates – a much higher proportion than at Corpus, though the University figures included several graduate-only colleges.

As **Jonathan Harrison** (1942) observed, the life of a graduate student after the war could be difficult:

> In those days – and I understand things have not greatly changed – graduate students, in comparison with undergraduates, were much neglected. (Those who came from other universities were in an even worse plight). They found all their friends had gone, that they had to eat out at great expense or at what were called British Restaurants – where one could get a three-course meal plus coffee for a shilling (the equivalent of 5p), but which were dismal places.[3]

Graduate supervision – which was often by dons in other colleges – could be notoriously bad: at St John's, **Kingsley Amis** found that 'by the middle of the second term no contact of any kind' had been made by his supervisor, David Cecil (New College). He transferred to Freddie Bateson at Corpus.[4] At Corpus, **Al Alvarez** (1949) stayed on for a DPhil. This 'was supposed to be "an original contribution to learning" and you were left to get on with it as originally as you could'. His topic was metaphysical poetry:

> My supervisor was Hugo Dyson, a jolly don with a limp, at Merton College, next door to Corpus. I saw him just once. He gave me sherry, told me, between gales of laughter, that he knew nothing at all about 'metaphysical pottery' (more laughter), and suggested I went to the resident expert, Helen Gardner. I wrote to her immediately, then wrote again twice, at decent intervals, until she deigned to reply with a letter that began, 'Constant dripping wears down the stone ...' But it was another two terms before she agreed, reluctantly, to see me and I saw her precisely once more, two years later. At no point did she ever offer to read anything I had written on the subject. Eventually I ditched the doctorate.[5]

Research could be an isolated and lonely existence. The work was usually in university libraries and laboratories rather than the college. When **David Blackmore** (1956) stayed on for a DPhil 'in the Physical Chemistry Lab in South Parks Road', his 'centre of activity rather shifted away from Corpus. There were very few of us who stayed on for research degrees, and Corpus then had no such thing as a Middle Common Room.' Doing research in nuclear physics, **Christopher Watson** (1957), like other graduates, lived out: 'By now, the College was no longer able to provide accommodation, but I found a nice flat in Park Town, and later a very comfortable house on Boar's Hill, which I was able to share with congenial friends.' He divided his time between Harwell and the physics department, which did afford some comradeship:

> Life as a research student was in many ways a continuation of the

patterns established during undergraduate days – music (especially opera), poetry, university clubs, socializing with an ever-growing circle of friends etc. However, I was now assigned a desk in the theoretical physics department, and was able to share with my three immediate colleagues all the excitement and frustration of that academic discipline, where you sit at your desk, staring at sheets of paper covered with your attempts to solve some mathematical problem, most of which have ended in ignominious failure. Fortunately your colleagues are having the same experience, and you can suggest possible new approaches to each other, and share the moments of triumph. Regular seminars also convey the sense that there is light at the end of the tunnel – students who are slightly ahead of you talk as if they never had any doubt that it would all come out in the end.

Corpus attracted philosophy postgraduates from abroad. The American **Thomas Nagel** (1958), a Fulbright scholar, found it 'wonderful to be a young student in a place utterly confident of itself and teeming with creative activity and controversy':

Oxford was then at the high tide of linguistic analysis, and J. L. Austin, its dominant figure, held the White's Professorship, which was attached to Corpus. David Pears, James Thomson and G. E. L. Owen were also Fellows of the College, and it was like a dream to be put in personal contact with these people whose writings I had encountered as an undergraduate – not to mention the philosophical stars elsewhere in the University like Strawson, Hart, Anscombe, Philippa Foot, Grice, Berlin, Hare and Ryle.

He found President Hardie 'the most socially uncomfortable person I have ever encountered occupying such a public position. I had to have an interview with him every term, and he found it extremely difficult to say anything, being constitutionally incapable of producing an utterance that was either false, trivial or frivolous. I found myself reduced to babbling in self-defence.'[6]

Another American philosopher, **Douglas Long** (1958), chose

Corpus mainly for the presence of Austin and Pears. He appreciated
the College community:

> Although, as a graduate student, I was older than the resident
> undergraduates, it was important to me to be, at least to some
> extent, part of College life and to have a place to meet and socialize
> with other students. Corpus had the advantage of being small
> enough that I would not feel lost in the sea of students assembled
> from around the world. I was able to get acquainted, not only with
> students from England and Scotland, but with other Americans
> affiliated with Corpus, such as Tracy Herrick and Daniel Arnow,
> as well as Canadian Rhodes Scholars John Schioler and Gary
> Vernon. The chaps from North America seemed very naturally to
> fall into a congenial group.

Long lived in lodgings but ate in College:

> The undergraduates in Hall were very friendly and respectful of
> my graduate status. None compelled me to down a tankard of ale
> at one go, as happened to a few who were 'sconced for contuma-
> cious behaviour', such as turning up late for supper or appearing
> without the traditional black gown. I never missed a meal if I could
> help it, partly because it was already paid for, but also because I
> thoroughly enjoyed chatting with table mates and learning about
> their interests and plans.

Although he socialized and travelled, his main interests were
academic:

> I could expose myself to classes, to public lectures, and to talks
> at the great variety of clubs in any way that I deemed beneficial.
> I took liberal advantage of the classes offered by Austin, Hare,
> Hampshire, Price, Strawson, Warnock and others. Miss Anscombe
> invited me to evening meetings in her home where I met Anthony
> Kenny and her husband, Peter Geach. I literally sat at the feet of
> Gilbert Ryle.

He enjoyed Oxford's wider opportunities, heard distinguished speakers including Vice-President Richard Nixon ('who cheerfully explained that the American national debt was "just money we owed to ourselves"'), and attended the Oxford Union. 'These are only a sampling of the riches that offered broad intellectual exposure well beyond any structured course of study that I might have pursued.'

Graduates were older. For **Tony Coady** (1963), a philosopher from Australia, the immediate priority was accommodation for his young family:

> Shortly after our arrival, the Hardies sent my wife a welcoming bunch of flowers and Frank's wife, Isobel, a doctor, visited our basement flat in Park Town to see if she could help with our very young baby, then only two months old. Their friendliness was in marked contrast to the stern reception we got from various landladies in Oxford when we sought accommodation carrying (or wheeling) our son Benjamin. The hostility of such Oxford landladies (and no doubt landgentlemen) to small children was a striking and depressing feature of the times, and we only got our basement flat in Park Town when we appeared rather bedraggled in Oxford rain (with baby) before Muriel Lindsay, a woman of strong Quaker conviction, who took pity on us and waived the baby veto.

Coady's supervisor was William Kneale, 'an excellent supervisor, an authority on all areas of philosophy, and one of the most decent men I have ever met'. Oxford was 'a stimulating place to study philosophy in the 1960s for there were many philosophers whose names were a byword for work at the cutting edge of world philosophy'. 'The Oxford graduate community was also stimulating, though one never suspected at the time that many of one's new associates would go on to be significant figures in the discipline.' Philosophy also attracted **Leslie Stevenson** (1962), studying mathematics as an undergraduate:

> What I am most grateful to Corpus for was the encouragement I was given (by President Hardie, Jim Urmson and Christopher

Taylor) to make the risky change from undergraduate maths to postgraduate philosophy. I had attended some lectures on philosophy and had fallen in love with the subject. I discussed my idea with them, I wrote a trial essay on the foundations of mathematics, they recommended reading and supported my application, and I started my BPhil.

By the 1960s Corpus had established a Middle Common Room (MCR), something appreciated by **Jonathan Dancy** (1965):

When I became a graduate I was lost for a while because everyone I knew had left (other than a group of younger musicians) and I had no social circle. So Corpus MCR was a definite boon, on which I to some extent relied for a year. In my second year I became a member of Pembroke SCR (as a Lecturer in Classical Philosophy) and this gave me a second 'home'. Nonetheless, my graduate years were socially speaking lonelier than I had expected and in many ways harder. It was easy to regret the pleasantly warm support that Corpus had given me over my four years as an undergraduate.

When **Julian Weitzenfeld** (1967) arrived from Chicago, 'the few postgraduate students at the College had just recently been assigned a small common room, and there was no institutional apparatus for assimilation'. He too lived out of College, up the Iffley Road, sharing with David Goodstine (1967), another American. 'As an undergraduate, David was better integrated into College affairs than I and was my primary source of contacts with other Corpuscles. Primarily as a budgetary measure, I ate all my meals out of College, many at The Jacaranda, on Iffley Road.' He mixed mainly with other graduates:

Most of my social interaction was with other postgraduate students in psychology or philosophy. I (separately) encountered two acquaintances from my undergraduate years, one from Ghana and one from Greece, on the streets of Oxford. Soon after my arrival, together with an American at Hertford, I established the Draft Information Service to serve Americans in need of counselling about military conscription. It found a home in the Friends' meeting house, and I spent considerable time with young Friends and with other Americans. I spent more time, I think, in Linacre College (then not far down St Aldates from Corpus) than with my peers at Corpus.

The College recognized the need to do more to integrate graduates, introducing – 'after their first year of study' – the right to dine once a week at High Table. 'The motive of the innovation is simple, the desire of the President and Fellows to get to know the graduates better. But these informal meetings will be useful as well as agreeable if they lead to the discussion of matters of common concern, such as the organization of teaching and the system of Public Examinations.'[7] **Julian Weitzenfeld** found it hard going:

> I was in no position to turn down a free meal, so I showed up promptly for what was to be my first meal in Hall. President Hardie took me aside and said, 'I haven't seen you in a long while. Come sit next to me.' As he turned to lead the procession through the College, I fell into place behind him. Several paces on, he turned his head and said to me over his shoulder, 'We used to walk in order of seniority.' He paced on. As I frantically wondered how I was going to rectify my faux pas, he turned his head again and added, 'We gave that up a few years ago.' And then, as my anxiety gradually receded, 'I don't know why.'
>
> I found conversational etiquette difficult. It was explained to me that an appropriate topic for conversation at the dinner table was why people talked to each other in trains in Scotland, but not in England. Curiosity about core interests was not appropriate. Unfortunate things could happen, such as when the Classics tutor with whom I was conversing exclaimed in frustration, 'This happens every time I talk with a philosopher!'

More graduates began to appear from countries other than the Commonwealth and US. **Peter Alter** (1969) was 'one of the first, probably even the very first [post-war] graduate student from

Germany', at a time when 'the memory of the war was still very vivid in Britain'. However, he met no 'unfriendliness or resentment':

> On the contrary, the welcoming and fairness shown by everyone I met in Britain, from the President of Corpus down to the librarians and bus conductors, proved to be simply overwhelming and is something I cherish until today. In this context I must remember, in particular, the famous classicist Eduard Fraenkel, a refugee from Nazi Germany who had taken up the Chair in Latin at Corpus in 1935. With tact and patience he introduced me to College life. As he was then no longer able to travel he asked me, when he learnt that I was going home for the Christmas break, to bring back a certain brand of cigars from a certain shop in Cologne, which I gladly did. Sadly, Fraenkel died in 1970, aged 81.

Although **Peter Alter** had previously visited England, 'Oxford turned out to be a real challenge for me. The term "culture shock" would be an exaggeration but it is true to say that I was quite suddenly confronted with an academic world which until then I had not known.' In contrast to Germany, 'Oxford meant a rather restricted life; it meant regular supervisions and tutorials; in short: it meant saying goodbye to the freedoms and almost total independence that German students enjoyed in those days at their as yet unreformed universities.' Fortunately, his supervisors, Agatha Ramm (Somerville) and Tim Mason, 'knew academic life in Germany rather well and turned out to be extremely understanding and tolerant in their guidance of a slightly confused newcomer to Oxford'.

Graduates, as **Peter Alter** recognized, lived largely separate lives: 'The fact that in the late 1960s Corpus still seemed to be a college that focused on looking after undergraduates made me appreciate, in particular, the companionship and friendship of some of the graduate students in College.' Many undergraduates knew little of them. 'There is little or no news of people or events in the MCR, which is not to say, of course, that nothing has happened. We do know, for instance, that George Gandy has been very active. We have to infer that most people's time is being totally consumed by their BPhils and DPhils.'[8]

Research, with its narrow focus and without the props of regular tutorials and lectures, could be surprisingly stressful. Although it might seem a natural continuation of undergraduate study, it could prove – as **John Lanchester**, at St John's, was to discover – 'close to its opposite. Instead of being structured, with regular short pieces being produced, and evaluated, against tight deadlines, it was completely formless: I saw my supervisor only every few months, and had no other contact or support of any kind from the University. I would sit in the pub or College bar with other graduate students, as we all did a fair bit, and agree that it was like having disappeared off the cliff at the edge of the world in some primitive cosmogony.'[9] **Michael Baker** (1967) stayed on for a BLitt. But 'what was clear to me, and other graduate students at Oxford at this time, was that the University remained very much an undergraduate institution, despite the rising proportion of graduates':

> The College ceased to have the appeal or relevance it had had previously. As a graduate student I recall going into Corpus for the odd lunch, chiefly because it was cheaper, but the MCR made little impact on me (though it *was* one of the few places where you could come across women students in Corpus – this being a time when there was heated debate about colleges going co-ed). There were certainly few if any social functions associated with the MCR – by contrast, I'm told, with Oxford MCRs today, which positively fizz with parties and initiatives – and I can't ever recall going to its more formal meetings.

Living out distanced graduates from College life. Supervisors were often from other colleges. 'Inevitably, too, your social circle diminished as you became a postgraduate, losing at a stroke most of your friends made as an undergraduate as they moved on into the wider world.' There was no sense that 'someone somewhere was looking after your mental and physical welfare':

> Overall you did feel that, though still part of the University, the University was fairly indifferent towards you, leaving you in a strange sort of limbo. I don't think I was upset by this. Most

postgraduates at the time accepted it as the norm, and there was certainly no organized protest about such matters – that would come much later as fees kicked in. At the same time it left you feeling somewhat rootless and adrift. I had historian friends from Corpus doing postgraduate research at St Antony's, a dedicated postgraduate college, and they seemed much more at home.

The observation that 'undergraduates and postgraduates belonged to different tribes' therefore seems well founded.[10] The day-to-day life of the research student centred on the lab or the library. According to **Michael Baker**:

My real home-from-home was neither Corpus nor my digs but the Upper Reading Room of the Bodleian Library. It was warm when it was cold outside, you had access to many books, you could read, write up notes, meet friends, try to pick up girls, or simply (too often) dawdle and daydream. The daily routine would be to get to the Reading Room early enough to bag a place for the day, plonking your books on your chosen desk space and hanging your bag casually over the back of the chair in a carefully calculated act of proprietorship. A notebook left open at a page of scrawl was always a good touch – however old the scrawl might be. Getting there too early was definitely not cool, getting there too late risked missing out altogether on a place: ambling in unhurriedly at about 10am seemed to be the standard to aspire to.

There were compensations. 'In retrospect I can see that my horizons widened as a postgraduate, to the University beyond the College, and indeed beyond that more generally. Partly this was because you met people doing research who had not come from Oxford, whose experience was very different, or who in some cases were already working in the outside world.' As an undergraduate he had acted in Owlets but now became heavily involved in University theatre, including a 'production of *Hamlet* directed by Jonathan Miller, which toured the eastern seaboard of the US for six weeks, then came back for a three-week run at the Fortune Theatre in the West End. I must have done some research as well between all those rehearsals, but looking back now at this packed list of thespian activities over two short years, it could explain why my thesis took another four years to complete.'

Mark Atkinson (1971), who returned for research after deciding the civil service was not for him ('I spent much of the time flying to meetings in Brussels with my Assistant Secretary, the only purpose of which was to stymie approval of impending regulations'), also spent most time outside Corpus, though he shared a College house with other graduates: 'it had a kitchen and a large shared dining room in the basement where we could brew our own beer, make our own bread and begin to hone our culinary skills. I remember fondly trying to gut a goose for our Christmas Feast while someone read the instructions from Mrs Beaton's through a closed door.' University rowing took up much of his time, until his supervisor persuaded him 'it was time to focus on my research'. The award of a Studentship took him to Linacre, though he 'returned to Corpus in the summer of 1978 to take the role of Richard, Captain of Boats, in what was billed as the World Premiere (and probably only production) of *Rows by Any other Name*, a 1920s-style musical written by Sam Menefee who was still at Corpus! I have probably the only extant recording of this masterpiece.'

Supervision was slowly improving. **Michael Baker** (1967) was supervised by Bernard Richards at Brasenose, who had himself received 'very unsatisfactory supervision'. However, Richards proved 'a conscientious and inspiring supervisor', taking an active interest in his work, pointing him to relevant experts and even directing a play in which he performed. 'Some of my contemporaries, however, did complain about their supervisors being notably absent or lacking interest, so the problems of the 1950s and 1960s, if rather less the norm, had nevertheless certainly not disappeared by the early 1970s.'

Adjusting to a new environment, and the in-between status of the postgraduate, took time. **Peter Colenbrander** (1974) arrived from South Africa:

I must admit, I found the first few weeks at Corpus stressful, even though I was slightly older and supposedly more mature than most of my peers. Matters improved once, with the help of Brian

Harrison, I was admitted into the BLitt/DPhil programme. So I began to live the somewhat decentred (and often solitary) life of the Oxford postgraduate: a member of one college, with a rather remote supervisor in another, and most of my academic soulmates in a third (St Antony's) or at another university altogether (Institute of Commonwealth Studies, University of London). My association with Corpus was further attenuated after I got married in March 1975 and moved into digs on Warwick Street.

And yet, I do have fond memories of Corpus. For one thing, I got married there (more precisely, we got married at the commissioner's office, but thanks to the good and enlightened offices of Jim Minchin, the Australian Chaplain of the day, the union was blessed in the College Chapel).

For another, I met many bright and lively companions there and struck up some lasting friendships. In particular, I recall David Winter, another, but older, mature student, who had previously been a bus conductor in Leeds and a union activist, and who had got into Corpus via Ruskin College. For David, who died in early 2013, Corpus was a truly transformative experience. As he reminisced not long before his death, he knew there had to be more to life than what he had experienced before going up to Oxford, and Corpus proved him right. He had a compendious knowledge of British history, but more importantly he introduced me to a colourful cast of students, from Ruskin and other Oxford colleges, on the extreme Left of the British political spectrum. Exposure to them, and more especially David's more thoughtful political observations and insights, left its mark. Simply put, I came to Corpus a fairly conventional South African liberal, and returned to South Africa a social democrat.

The Corpus MCR was also becoming more significant. The 'communal warmth of that rather down-at-heel little salon' was appreciated by Australian **Ian Britain** (1974):

I visited grander, much better-appointed MCRs in the larger colleges, but they all seemed much more perfunctory in their social tone. Mind you, we were particularly fortunate in our MCR's MC of the mid-1970s: the wonderfully-named Sturtevant Ford Weiskittel III, who through the force of his wide-smiling charm, the example of his manic energies, and the good-humoured forbearance and support of his wife (Harriot) made conviviality all but compulsory.

The smallness of Corpus also made for much easier relations between the MCR and JCR; certainly, in my circles, there seemed little sense of the apartheid or generation gap one noticed in other colleges. As well as sporting and cultural links, close friendships could be forged that disregarded differences in age or nationality. It was partly through the shared recreational activities that these friendships would be formed – in my own case, theatrical activities.[11]

The first Corpus women were postgraduates. **Anthony Gould** (1973), a trade unionist who had studied at Ruskin, was MCR President at the time:

We (myself and another Ruskin student who had been a miner) were enrolled as members of the MCR, being at least ten years older than 'normal' undergraduates. Somehow I ended up as President of the MCR after an election in which the other contestant was an American. I had been on the successful 'Left' ticket and as a consequence of election was privileged to be part of a welcoming party for the first four women students at the College. They were all graduates of other universities and so were admitted members of the MCR. This very welcome development at CCC as one of the first non-female Oxford Colleges to admit women further demonstrated that CCC was widening its entry criteria!

Dina Gold (1975), in the second cohort, took the situation in her stride: 'Naturally I mixed mostly with my fellow graduate students and pretty soon I became what I would refer to as an "honorary man". I simply joined in whatever everyone else was doing and I never felt excluded.' And the MCR continued to expand, in 1978 reporting 'improved facilities, continued growth in activities, and further increase in financial turnover, and a consistently high level of support from a membership now totalling 120'. Turnover – largely at the bar – reached £7,000; there were trips to Stratford and London, wine-tasting, cheese-tasting, and 'an excursion to a brewery'. Sport included squash, ice hockey, bar-billiards and the Women's VIII who earned a Bump Supper for the whole college.[12] The following years saw a similar mix of activities, including parties and speaker events, sometimes jointly with the SCR. In 1985 President **Robert Peden** (1979) reported:

> the MCR has continued to expand this year, and now contains about 80 full-time members engaged in research (of one form or another); Associate Membership has increased; and the College's policy of admitting Visiting Students to study for a year has also livened up our intake. In step with this, the MCR has acquired a second computer and printer, which should ease the crush on its existing facilities while enabling more of its members to use these invaluable tools.[13]

The MCR hosted speaker lunches and joint dinners or parties with other colleges. 'Relations with the SCR have been good. Joint meals and social events are always welcome and enjoyable; but perhaps the most important link forged between the two Common Rooms was a Senior Scholarship, introduced to help a graduate in the fourth year finish off a thesis. A system of College Advisors is being experimented with, to give new graduates a firmer foothold in College life.'[14] As part of his effort to get closer to graduate students, newly appointed Keith Thomas joined the MCR President and members for lunch and, as **Mary Myerscough** (1985) recalled, introduced presidential collections:

> Every graduate student had to attend one or two of these each year. As a student in a scientific field I found these fairly low-key. Students in the humanities found presidential collections rather more trying. I think this was partly because doctorates in the humanities took rather longer to complete then and there was pressure to shorten the time taken to finish and partly because,

given Corpus's areas of specialization, it was more likely that one of the senior members at the collection was expert in the area of the student's work.'[15]

'Despite people's expressions of fear and loathing', MCR President **Michael Bowie** (1985) thought graduate collections 'turned out to be quiet affairs for most of us'.[16] Corpus now had a Tutor for Graduates and offered more accommodation. Indeed, **Mary Myerscough** (1985) chose Corpus partly because it offered accommodation for all three years – though while she thought some houses 'quite adequate', others 'were reputedly worth living in as only a last resort'. Coming from Australia, she found the college system, combining academic and social roles, 'a strange combination of functions, particularly as almost all my formal study and interactions with others in my field took place outside College':

> There were no other graduate mathematicians in the MCR at Corpus. Most of the people I met and came to know through Corpus MCR were graduate students in the humanities. In Australia my friends had been almost exclusively science and engineering students, so Corpus friendships considerably widened my horizons. I made the discovery that philosophy had a rigour and logic comparable to that of mathematics, and was encouraged – by Paul Robinson and Marjorie Swann in particular – to read and enjoy more modern English literature.[17]

Twenty years after the MCR's establishment, its President **Michael Bowie** (1985) could reflect, 'we find ourselves an established fact of College life, the main social facility for one-third of Junior Members, looking like nothing so much as an ageing and world-weary JCR'.[18] But not all members were happy. **Geraldine Herbert-Brown** (1985), an Australian who had learned Latin as an adult, found Oxford was 'not so well acquainted with the idea of older students, especially females, and especially females in Classics. I attracted quizzical looks from Dons whose lectures I attended, but that was of no consequence':

The same cannot be said for the Corpus MCR. My fellow graduates, predominantly male, were all younger than I, and far more self-confident and competitive. They, too, were influenced by their culture and values. My singularity was noticed and attracted unsolicited attention. Perhaps, by defying classification, I confounded a tribal need to slot me into a category. As a conciliatory gesture I was candid about having been an adult beginner. Not a good idea. Unlike other disciplines in the humanities, one's entire credibility in Classics seems to rest upon having been initiated into the mysteries as a child, with Latin at the age of ten. The later you started, the less street cred you had; if you had started later, you didn't own up. My Achilles heel was targeted with military precision. The uncongenial atmosphere became a severe challenge to my resilience. After about six months, I ceased visiting the MCR, or dining in Hall.

She was helped by her College flat, by 'the magnificent Corpus library', but above all by her moral tutor, Elizabeth Rawson. She had been 'in awe of her scholarly reputation' and was 'amazed' when told to use her first name: 'back home, all lecturers were addressed as Professor this or Doctor that. In those days, before the scourge of Publish or Perish had become an imperative for academics, I had never, before coming to Oxford, met the author of an academic book. To have a scholar of Elizabeth's calibre treat me as an equal was inspiring.' Shockingly, Elizabeth Rawson died unexpectedly in Hong Kong. Her memorial service was held in Chapel:

> Witnessing the tiny box containing her ashes being borne up the Chapel aisle was harrowing. I could not suppress the tears when Professor Nisbet, visibly moved himself, declaimed Lucretius' *De Rerum Natura* 3.1024–45. I had never heard Latin like this. His delivery, and the sonority of the poetry, overwhelmed me. My reaction must have seemed out of all proportion to Elizabeth's far more controlled family and colleagues. But grief is inherently selfish. I had lost a mentor and well-wisher in what was still, in ethos, an all-male college. She made me welcome and restored

confidence in my own abilities at a time when I was feeling constantly under siege.

Robin Nisbet became her moral tutor. Although appearing 'a gentlemanly old fogey, set in his patriarchal ways', she found him to be 'affable, self-effacing, and entirely approachable':

> When I told him I had passed the Viva for my DPhil, his face lit up like the sun. He actually pre-empted a little joke I had in mind to play on Keith Thomas, then CCC President, who conducted collections for graduate students. Mr Thomas (as he then was), routinely asked two things: 'How many words have you written?' and 'When will you be finished?' For my last collection I planned to announce that I had reconsidered my whole research and was about to start again, when Professor Nisbet steamed in ahead of me and proudly proclaimed my success to the President.

Continuing concern about the position of postgraduates led to a University inquiry chaired by John Roberts, Warden of Merton. Corpus found its findings reassuring. The report 'recommended measures which every college should take to enhance [graduates'] welfare and ensure their fuller integration. We noted, with pleasure, if not complacency, that at Corpus virtually all the recommended steps had already been taken. We are proud of our MCR and the part it plays in the life of the College.'[19] MCR President **Jeremy Trevett** (1982) welcomed the report but thought there was more to do:

> Oxford graduates have found themselves for once the centre of solicitous attention. The rapid recognition that we were faring considerably better than many of our contemporaries in other colleges was tempered by the realization that there is still ample scope for improvement. A committee was set up to consider the College's provision for graduates in the light of the report. Its recommendations have been modest, yet welcome for all that. The book grant scheme, which previously was open only to under-graduates, is being extended to graduates; at the instigation of

my predecessor Ute Wartenberg the adequacy of the provision of cooking facilities in the hostels was examined, and improvements have been agreed; photocopying facilities are to be upgraded. There has also been a slight improvement in the availability of meals during vacations. All of this is to the good. Yet the fact that for almost the whole of the long vacation no evening meal was available shows that there is some way to go before graduates receive the same consideration as undergraduates. Only when that happens will we be wholly satisfied.[20]

The quality of graduate supervision was still a concern. But **Krystyna Bartol** (1988), from Poland, was delighted with Ewen Bowie: 'he taught me, with his empathy and wit, to have no fear or shame of expressing my ideas, to avoid being narrowly focused on unimportant things and to build my own views on an intellectual grasp of others'. She recalled 'the vivacious get-togethers at his house (with the garden easily accommodating the group of guests) in Wendlebury, where I had (and still have) the opportunity to meet people, all of whom were mighty names to me'. A further inquiry in 1997, chaired by Sir Peter North, proposed more changes at both University and college level to improve the supervision of and support for postgraduates so that, according to the University's most recent historian, 'by the end of the 1990s it was difficult for postgraduate students to slip through the net and doctoral supervision had greatly improved'.[21] **Ana Olivetti** (2007) certainly appreciated her supervisor: 'I do not have words to express my gratitude to Prof. Zedner. She has not only been an inspiring academic figure throughout my years as a graduate student. She has also been supportive and always ready to provide advice during times of uncertainty and despair. She has been a magnificent tutor.'

Adjusting to postgraduate life could still be difficult. **Elizabeth O'Brien** (1990), a mid-career Irish archaeologist, lived in a College house :

Nothing prepared me for the culture shock that I experienced when I realized that for at least a year I would live in one small room, sharing a bathroom with several male undergraduates, and with access to a tiny kitchen. I soon realized that in order to retain my sanity (not to mention sanitation) I needed to be first into the bathroom each morning. The scout, Mrs Pomeroy, was kindness itself, and it was a novelty for me to have someone do my 'housework'. The acute homesickness I felt during my first year was somewhat alleviated by my busy schedule of lectures, seminars and classes. The friendly MCR soon became my refuge. Monday lunch in the SCR was a weekly highlight.

Things improved when she became Warden at the newly opened Liddell complex:

The prospect of being responsible for 54 students (42 undergraduates and 12 graduates) was somewhat daunting but I soon became accustomed to it. One great advantage was the change in accommodation as the Warden's accommodation was comprised of a large bright airy room, with en-suite facilities (bliss!) in the Red House. I do realize that at first I was perhaps a little over-diligent in my responsibilities and I am aware that I acquired several nicknames among the students. For instance, I was referred to at one stage as 'the midnight prowler', 'an iron fist in a velvet glove' and by Eric Dugdale in the last *Corpuscles* as the 'rather over-zealous if affable warden'. However, as I settled into the position my approach became rather more relaxed, but I never ceased my nightly 'rounds' at 11pm. Over time I became a sort of agony aunt or mother figure to some of the undergraduates, and I like to think that I was of some help to them.

Graduates' involvement in Corpus naturally varied. **Ana Olivetti** (2007) 'did not spend a significant amount of time in College. Hence my "College experience" was not a very rich, intense one. I spent only the first year in College accommodation. The remaining three years, my husband and I moved to private accommodation.' She felt Corpus was 'not well prepared to receive overseas students and to cater for their specific needs', and was unhappy with its response to a break-in at her apartment. But she was grateful for 'the kindness of staff, particularly Rachel Pearson, and for the support and recognition of my achievements – I was given a prize following my performance in the MSc, offered a small amount of money to cover my academic expenses and a scholarship that contributed towards the fees. Although I could not attend as many High Tables as I would have liked, I praise the quality of the cook and food and drinks served.'

But for those who wanted it, the MCR offered a social setting and support in the sometimes strange and isolated world of the postgraduate. In 1993, according to **Kassie Smith** (1992), 'the MCR elected a welfare officer who has been instrumental in setting up a revamped welcoming procedure for new graduates. For students who have not experienced Oxford before, especially those from overseas, it can be daunting and confusing. We have produced an information pack to be sent out to new MCR members and have set up a system of volunteers to welcome people on their arrival.'[22]

Meals played an important role. **Matthew Dovey** (1990) recalled the MCR 'perk' of Monday lunch in the SCR. 'Officially this was to allow the graduates to meet with the Fellows. However, most of us saw this as an opportunity to sample better food than that served in the main hall.' On one occasion he was introduced, unexpectedly, to the Queen of Sweden: 'I now recall very little of our conversation as I was concentrating on trying not to make some fundamental faux pas: the etiquette of lunching with royalty was not a subject that had ever been covered at school!' For **Caroline Knapp** (2005), joining the MCR involved 'exchange dinners, High Table dinners, graduate adviser lunches, cheese and wine evenings, welfare brunches ...' In 2014 MCR President **Skye Montgomery** (2011) reported 'a concerted effort to strengthen the bond between the Middle and Senior Common Rooms through the much-beloved SCR–MCR lunches (SCRunches to their adherents) and the Graduate and Supervisor Dinners'. There were also joint lunchtime seminars, an MCR champagne brunch for new matriculants, a 'Dress as Your Thesis or Supervisor Bop', a joint ceilidh with the JCR and 'a *University Challenge*-style trivia game between teams representing the students, Fellows and staff'.[23]

Things had moved on from the days when graduates' needs seemed scarcely recognized. They now formed a larger and more visible part of the student body and of College life. Nevertheless, the significant differences between them and most undergraduates in age, lifestyles and academic focus meant they often still inhabited separate, if over-lapping, worlds. For **Krystyna Bartol** (1988), 'although I took part in some extracurricular activities at Corpus I was spending most of my time reading voraciously. I devoured the books in the evening in the College Library (when the Bodleian and the Ashmolean were already closed) accompanied by Bishop Fox's stern glance which seemed to assure me that his ghost is wandering somewhere between the shelves.' **Elizabeth O'Brien** (1990) did much of her research in the Ashmolean Museum Library, 'with forays out to the History Faculty Library and the Sackler', and worked in the computer room in the Institute of Archaeology. The work itself, in contrast to undergraduate studies, was often laborious, relatively isolated and tightly – even narrowly – focused. But it could be exciting. **Grant Schoenebeck** (2004), an American postgraduate mathematician, reflected how a year studying theology, 'something of which I had very little prior knowledge', had expanded his horizons: 'The sheer knowledge that I gained of the Christian thoughts, philosophies, and experiences helped me to better understand the richness of the Christian tradition. By studying this new subject which really has no boundaries, I learned of new ways to think about mathematics too. I have a much better appreciation for how a particular theorem and its proof fit in with the larger goal of understanding.'

There was no Norrington Table to measure graduates' academic performance. The increase in numbers, combined with high fees, led some to ask whether standards were being diluted. Fellow **James Howard-Johnston** noted that competition for places was less intense than for undergraduates: 'While there are many stars among [post-graduates], I doubt whether they amount to more than 30 per cent of the total.'[24] But Corpus Presidents, including **Tim Lankester**, regularly expressed pride in their achievements:

> Our graduate student body have long played an important role in reinforcing a culture of excellence in the College, and we continue to attract outstanding individuals at this level. Twelve students

were awarded their DPhils; and of those who sat for postgraduate exams this year, and for whom at the time of writing we have the results, 13 out of 20 got Distinctions. All three of our candidates for the Philosophy BPhil achieved Distinctions, and Gaurav Khanna was placed first in the University in the MSc in Economics for Development.[25]

Although Corpus remained a predominantly undergraduate institution, postgraduates were both more numerous and playing a more important and visible part of its life. Academically and socially, they were being taken more seriously, given more support and seen as an important, rather than marginal, part of the College community. They represented a significant expression of the way in which the College had become not just larger but more diverse in its membership and wide-ranging in its activities.

Reunion. Newly appointed President Steven Cowley (1978) and
Beverley Patterson (1979) return for the Corpus Biennial Dinner,
2016. Steven's was the last all-male year and Beverley was one of
the first undergraduate women. *Courtesy of Nick Read (2012)*

10

'ALL CORPUSCLES TOGETHER': LEAVING AND LOOKING BACK

We had grown up and must now go out into the world.

Eliza Pakenham

What a privilege, as well as monumental pleasure, to have been there. One never really leaves the place.

Ian Wylie

University was an important, but transitional, phase. As she departed, **Christina Lee** (2011) reflected, 'I will miss the pair of overweight wood pigeons outside my window, the gentle glow of the Pelican under the moon, and, of course, the friends and colleagues with whom I have shared the journey. As the porter closed the ogre-sized wooden gate behind me, the Golden Age of undergraduate studentship officially came to an end. The world is before us. Where to choose – who knows?'

The relationship between student and later life was rarely clear-cut. According to Fellow **James Howard-Johnston**, 'the University's chief contribution to the country and to the wider world is a regular annual discharge of undergraduates, fully formed as critical, independent-minded, reasoning individuals, ready to apply their wits to multifarious tasks'.[1] But as **Simon Squires** (1962) asked, 'how far did Corpus prepare one for a subsequent career?'

> I would have to say that, at least at the time, neither the College nor the individual really regarded this in practical terms as part of what was expected. The abiding memory is that the intellectual experience was 'made available' for each man to take advantage of (or not) as he chose, without any intrusive supervision. Reading for a degree was not a form of training, certainly not in my subject.

David Jory (1959) agreed:

> My years at Oxford and Corpus were sliced out of real time and the real world. We did things we would not have done during the rest of our lives; the environment – scouts, sconces, dining in Hall, the JCR, but also many hours of slogging study and essays to write – was unreal. One of our number opined that we took trivial matters seriously and treated serious matters as trivial; I think he was right. We learned much about life which prepared us well to face reality in our post-Oxford years but nobody pretended that Oxford life was 'relevant' or 'training for the job market'.

But as Finals approached, life beyond Corpus loomed. According to **Jacquie Kelly** (1984), 'You can divide finalists into two groups: those who have sorted themselves out good and proper with a job. And those [who] haven't.'[2] Some, like **George Richardson** (1947), were 'keen to get on and get a good degree and get a job and get out the door'. **Bernard Jacobson** (1956) was so clear about his future he almost left early:

> When I told David Pears, three years into my course, that I had decided to leave Oxford without waiting to complete the fourth year, because I had realized that I had to work in music, I was convinced by his wise response: 'Bernard, why don't you wait another year? You'll have a degree, which won't do you any harm, and music will probably still be there.'

Then, in the spring of 1960, an advertisement appeared in the
New Statesman magazine calling, as one could do in those days,
for a young man, preferably under 35 and unmarried, to work for
Philips Phonographic Industries in the Netherlands as sleeve-note
writer. Going to Mr Lepper for advice, I said I supposed there
would be little point in my applying, since there would obviously
be candidates much more experienced than I. 'Well,' he said, 'if
you don't try, you'll never know, will you?' So I responded to the
advertisement, fulfilled the various test writing assignments I was
sent, and was invited to Baarn for an interview. I got the job, and
the rest is (my) history.

Simon Squires (1962) distinguished between 'those who had
obviously mapped out a future career for themselves already and those
who approached Finals without any very clear idea of the next step,
of whom I will admit I was one'. Studying Greats, 'one saw one's own
circle disperse in two instalments, at the end of one's third and fourth
year, but a significant few of us might well remain in Oxford without
entirely obvious means of support while the purposeful ones hastened
off to their appointments in the law or in academic life.'
Mark Atkinson (1971) was uncertain about his future:

I did reasonably well in Finals, the equivalent of an upper second
I was assured. I had pursued a number of potential career opportunities during the year as, like many undergraduates, I really had
no idea what I wanted to do with my life. I had applied to some
Far Eastern trading companies for reasons now long forgotten
but probably related to some outdated romantic ideas. They went
nowhere which was probably for the best. I applied to the BBC and
got interviewed and even 'auditioned' reading the World Service
News but that also went no further. I took the civil service exam
in the hope of getting into the diplomatic service and by some
miracle passed the exam and the First Selection Board. At that
point President Hall, despite his illness, was gracious enough to
coach me on what to expect in the Final Selection Board. I have
nightmares of being quizzed in a huge darkened room somewhere

in the deep recesses of the Admiralty on topics such as how I would solve the problems with Ian Smith and Rhodesia. A few weeks later I learned that I was accepted but alas not in the diplomatic service, instead in the Ministry of Agriculture, Fisheries and Food. Not quite the same, but I had always enjoyed food so why not?

But the civil service proved unsatisfying:

It became clear to me that I did want to do research and spoke with Eric Sidebottom who was associated with Corpus. The result was that I ended up in the office of Professor Henry Harris in the Dunn School of Pathology one spring Saturday morning. At the end of our talk Henry offered me an MRC (Medical Research Council) studentship with the statement 'that anyone willing to give up an index-linked civil service pension to do research is either dedicated or stupid … and we will find out which'. I returned to Corpus.

For those aiming for academia or teaching, the link between study and career was clear. **Geoff Goodall** (1950) described his time as a 'massively helpful preparation for my subsequent life. What a boon my Oxford MA proved to be when I decided to apply for attractive teaching posts. Thanks to Corpus I acquired sufficient confidence, sufficient aspiration and a sufficiently trained mind to enable me to aim high.' He enjoyed a distinguished teaching career: 'None of this could I have attempted without my early grounding at Corpus, that nursery of scholarship and high achievement, for which I am for ever grateful.'

Douglas Long (1958), an American postgraduate, felt his year at Corpus 'influenced my subsequent research, writing and teaching at UCLA (University of California at Los Angeles) and the University of North Carolina at Chapel Hill for years to come. It enabled me to explain to students and colleagues the views of important philoso-phers with whom I had discussions or whose lectures I had heard.' It was 'clearly the single most important period of preparation for my life's work as a teacher of philosophy'. For **Tony Coady** (1963), 'Corpus has been a distinctly beneficial influence on my academic career and personal satisfaction, as I know it has been for so many others'. **Robert Lee** (1964) became a professional historian: 'in academic terms I undoubtedly benefited from the opportunities which the College offered, particularly as a result of the quality of teaching by the two outstanding History Fellows and their continued commitment to support the intellectual development of their students'. **Peter Alter** (1969) agreed: 'The experience of Oxford had a deep impact on my ensuing career as an academic historian in Germany. Modern British history became the focus of my research and teaching.' **Krystyna Bartol** (1988), a postgraduate from Poland, thought it 'obvious that the stay at Corpus helped me in my career and academic life. Leaving Oxford I felt, as a classicist, integrated into this famous scholarly centre, believing that now I could achieve much more than before. While at Corpus I made important acquaintances and friendships, some of which endure.' And **Paul Elbourne** (1989), who went on to the Massachusettes Institute of Technology (MIT), stressed 'how well Corpus prepared me for my future [academic] career':

> MIT prides itself, at both undergraduate and graduate level, on getting its students to do a really very large amount of work. 'Drinking from a fire hose' is now they frequently describe their philosophy. Some of my fellow first-years in the PhD program in Linguistics were quite shocked by how much they had to do. But to me, who was used to two essays a week in Greats, with Ewen Bowie, Stephen Harrison and Christopher Taylor, it was just business as usual.

Students of medicine or law could continue down the vocational route. Others found openings linked to their discipline. **Martin Deahl** (1975) thought his biochemistry degree 'opened the door to medical school in London and, thanks to Corpus, I went on to achieve my dream'. **Rhod Thomas** (1961), who studied languages, found 'my knowledge of French and German helped me get a job with Reuters'. Others were influenced by family or other connections – and by their extracurricular enthusiasms. The RAF wanted **James Dixon** (1966), a member of the University Air Squadron, to enlist:

But was I going to enlist in the regular service? I had other ideas, and I was heavily swayed against it by the experience of my godfather, who at that time was leaving the Army as a full colonel in his mid-40s, having had as his last posting an appointment in Trinidad to help set up a regular force there, as it gained independence. With a pension of sorts, he had no professional qualification to his name, and he was studying to be a priest at Cuddesdon just as I was reading history at Corpus. Having narrowly defeated Pete Lampl to become the Treasurer of the JCR, my inclination was to enter the world of chartered accountancy.

Helen Eastman (1996) found her vocation through student theatre:

We went up to the Edinburgh Festival with a production of *The Cure At Troy*, which was very much a student affair at the time. It was one of those rare things that happens at the Edinburgh Festival where one reviewer decides they particularly like a production and reviews it and then everyone else comes to see it and suddenly some small production in a very small theatre, in a very obscure part of the Edinburgh Festival, becomes incredibly high profile, and spectacularly manages to launch six people's careers. I remember reading an interview with myself in, I think, *The Independent*, and being referred to as 'Director Helen Eastman says this …' and I thought, 'Oh, OK, well they think I'm one so maybe I can be one …' It was literally the first time it had ever occurred to me that I could be a director. It was something relegated in my head as being a hobby, and I was so busy doing my milk round and thinking about whether I wanted to be a barrister and doing my mini-pupillage and thinking maybe I wanted to work at the BBC – I'd no conception of making a career in the theatre really until that point.[3]

For those without a clear direction, the Oxford University Appointments Committee (known as the 'Disappointments Committee') was available. **Paul Vaight** (1963) thought it 'particularly amateurish', though the College, as **Ken Reynolds** (1966) discovered, found it difficult to advise on non-academic careers:

I was invited to a meeting with Robin Nisbet in my final year, when I was applying for jobs with various commercial organizations. He was Senior Tutor and I believe it must have been part of his job to write references for members of the College. The poor chap had no idea who I was, couldn't understand why anyone would want to study French and German, and couldn't imagine what it must be like to work in business. He looked at the papers on his desk and said to me: 'Why do these people think I can write anything that may be of use to them? I know nothing at all about the world of commerce. Indeed, I'm sure you know far more than I do.' And that was just about it. I left unsure that a Corpus reference would do anything to further my career prospects in that mysterious universe beyond the College gates.

According to **Bill Gunn** (1965), 'Trevor Aston was dejected at my choice of a wine trade career, which he was convinced would be "short of intellectual stimulation". Happily, it has not proved to be so, and has given me experiences (and a collection of friends) for which I can only be grateful.' However, the inability of colleges to offer professional career advice was recognized, and the 1970s saw significant improvements in the University Careers Service (as the Appointments Committee was renamed). The proportion of finalists registered rose from around 60 to 80 per cent between 1970 and 1983.[4] Nevertheless, **Nicola Feather** (1981) found it 'could offer me no advice beyond the obvious career choices suggested by my degree: if not barrister or solicitor, then banker, accountant or company secretary'.

By the 1980s **James De Waal** felt the professions had lost their lustre: 'Medicine, Law, Academia (!), all requiring further periods of poverty and squalor to complete their mastery, are somehow not as glamorous an idea after three years already spent in this way, while other traditional ideas – the Army, the Church – are definitely not what they used to be.' Instead, 'what usually follows in Michaelmas and Hilary Terms is what is always rather unappetisingly known as "the milk round", a series of presentations and talks, where various companies and institutions try to seduce (recruit) undergraduates with the aid of considerable quantities of food and drink'.[5] **Andrew Meads** (1984) described the process:

> A whole manner of potential options was spread in front of me, such as the glories of accountancy, banking, industry. My first shock was to discover that all the entries said 'We want ambitious/dynamic/highly motivated young graduates', hence begging the question of what happened to apathetic/lazy/unmotivated slobs such as myself. However, upon reflection, I've known many people worse than me get a job, hence it would seem worth a try.[6]

The hoops consisted of

- application forms ('make it sound as if you were walking down the road and there was a flash of light and the voice of God boomed out "Go forth and be a chartered accountant"');
- company 'presentations', usually at The Randolph, where after the talks, 'vast amounts of food and drink appear and the starving hordes swoop. Indeed I know some who come for this alone';
- the interview ('I had one with a US consulting firm which was much like a mental assault course. At the end of the interview the man grinned and said, 'Tell me a joke'. The motto of this story is be ready for anything'); and finally,
- the second interview: 'Some of the banks will ask you to attend 24 assessment centres where your every move will be scanned for management potential. Other firms sometimes take you out to lunch with the intention of seeing how you handle yourself when you have a large amount of free booze placed in front of you.'

The state of the job market was important. For much of the post-war period, graduates were few and could be reasonably confident of finding interesting jobs. This became less certain. **Geoff Dyer** (1977) was unemployed: 'There was, of course, a degree of continuity. If there is one thing Oxford perfectly prepares you for, it is life on the dole.' The transition from weekly tutorials 'to signing on once a week – then once a fortnight, then once a month – felt as natural as sleeping in till ten in the morning.'[7] **Penelope Curtis** (1979) thought 'the strong sense of impending unemployment had focused the minds of many, from the outset, on getting a job. Ironically, they went on to benefit from what became a boom in the financial sector in the following decade, allowing many of them to retire preternaturally early.' **Pushpinder Saini** (1986) described the late 1980s as 'the so-called "boom years" in which jobs (especially in financial services) seemed ten a penny. I remember seeing finalists leave Corpus in those years with highly paid jobs in management consultancy or merchant banking. It really seemed as though having an Oxford degree (no matter what class) was a passport to success. The contrast between those years and the position today (1993) cannot be greater.'[8]

Not everyone followed Mammon. Realizing in her third year that 'now they're trying to throw me out into the nasty, wicked world', **Jacquie Kelly** (1984) asked, 'what am I going to do for the rest of my life? And before you say it, no, I don't want to be a teacher. Nor do I want to do any of the things English graduates are meant to want to do. In fact I could give you a lovely long list of the things I don't want to do.' Going to Oxford, she felt, was a privilege and 'personally that makes me feel like I should do something useful with my advantage'. Her conclusion? 'I'll tell you what I do want to be when I'm grown up. A social worker, a mother and a pop star.'[9]

In the past, as **Al Alvarez** (1949) observed, the academic and business worlds were far apart:

> University was for budding professionals – academics, scientists, civil servants or diplomats in the making – or for the leisured few who wanted a blue to take with them to the Stock Exchange or the merchant banks. It had nothing to do with the business world. Even my cultured grandpa Alvarez could see no real connection between higher education and making money, and the Levys prided themselves on their lack of schooling, as though it made their wealth more glamorous and deserving.[10]

Nevertheless, **Philip Hamilton-Grierson** (1953) and others preferred business to the blandishments of the professions:

> Michael [Brock] was a covert recruiter for the civil service. He introduced me to a mandarin who over a glass of port and some Madeira cake tried to seduce us into the service. (The Roman Catholic Church used a Monsignor in similar fashion.) He and Michael assured us that the pay was poor but we would be in congenial company unlike in the vulgar world of industry on which we were bent.

Would-be entrepreneurs were more unusual. **Kit Molloy** (1955) recalled Bob Saward – 'my most admired contemporary' – who 'spent most of his time in Essex, where he had started a small transport business'.[11] **Martin Campbell** (1992) was another:

> It was for the start that Corpus gave me in business, rather than for my academic qualifications, that Corpus extends the biggest influence into my life now. Having held a couple of truly horrendous holiday jobs, I decided that I could do far better in generating extra income by using some skills in desktop publishing and database software to respond to some opportunities in-house. Brian Harrison, who was my wife's tutor for a time, provided my first serious piece of database work where I began the project of converting his decades of card index and word processor records into a manageable database. The database was to grow and evolve over the years, be published in searchable form on the Internet, and evolve into something of a legend and live on now far past the point where I've said goodbye to it. Through Brian's recommendation I was introduced to authors and GPs Ann McPherson and Aidan Macfarlane and to venture capitalist Mike O'Regan, and began work on several projects to bring their published and future works to the then fledgling Internet.

He recalled a 'very scary' conversation with his wife in his final year:

It was time to decide which 'milk round' opportunities I wanted to push myself towards. Would it be engineering, the consulting or accountancy firms that court Corpus students during their final year? In the end I decided to go it alone and build on the opportunities that Corpus had already presented. It turned out that the late 1990s were the perfect time to be at the edges of the new frontier of the World Wide Web, and that a combination of design and technical skills, backed up with a little academic focus and rigour, were good ingredients to start what became a specialist Web agency catering to charities and publishing organizations which I founded, grew and later sold to a US software company.

The relationship between Oxford and subsequent career success was hard to pin down. **Paul Vaight** (1963) joined BP (British Petroleum):

Did Corpus prepare me well for my subsequent career? I think the honest answer to this is not really. I think the primary purpose of Oxford at the time (and should still be today) was to reproduce academics, a process at which it has a huge competitive edge because of the quality of the dons and intake coupled with the tutorial system. Since I'd had my fill of chemistry during my doctorate none of my acquired knowledge was directly relevant to my subsequent career in commerce. A single-sex college precluded easy relationships with half the population; there was no emphasis on teamwork, only individual performance – *both* skills are vital to leadership in business.

It seemed to **Gerry Hughes** (1952) that his experience working at Butlins was equally relevant: 'only a small proportion of graduates use the particular expertise they studied, while nearly all need social skills when they become managers. If I learned analytical skills at Corpus, I learned how to handle people at Butlins, where I learned more about life in all its facets than I did in the rarefied academic atmosphere at Oxford.' **Gregory Wilsdon** (1978) 'exercised my brain and improved my bluffing technique' at Corpus. But 'I would also have got more out of it if I had received training in the tools of the trade. As it was, I had to get into the world of business before I learnt to discard marginally relevant data; and I had to wait for business school to discover the virtues of brevity.'[12]

Others stressed the value of their Corpus experience. **Eric Sidebottom** (1957) thought team games 'a great preparation for life in the real world outside' and noted how many team members 'made a considerable impact on the world; from captains of industry such as Christopher Harding and Kit Molloy, barrister and MP Brian Sedgemore, headmaster Laurie Rimmer, entrepreneur John Scott, surgeon Gary Hampson, Oxford Dons Brian Atkins and myself. These are just the ones I know about.'[13] Others highlighted the relevance of their Corpus training in clear reasoning, crisp presentation and meeting deadlines, not least for the civil service. **Antony Walker** (1947) 'spent many years in the Malayan Civil Service where my training in logic seemed to greatly impress my superiors'. **Stephen Linstead** (1959) felt that 'as an academic discipline, history fitted me excellently for my later career in the civil service. It involves drawing defensible conclusions, usually to a tight timescale, from a mass of facts, some of which are more certain than others, and presenting one's conclusions to those who are more than likely to be sceptical of them: "Yes, indeed, Minister!"' After working in consultancy **David Henig** (1990) also joined the civil service: 'what is a brief for a minister if not an Oxford essay, slightly cut down?' **David Normington** (1970) reached the top of the Home Office:

A lot of what I have done in my civil service career has been about trying to get to the core of an issue by analysing evidence; by taking in evidence from different sources – written and oral and so on – and trying to come to a view. In the civil service it is still important to express yourself very clearly and set out what you do very clearly.

But what Corpus also does is give you confidence in your life. It widens your experience; it brings you in touch with lots of different people; it took me away from my home; it therefore gave me a completely new experience. It exposed me to views and interests and people that I would not have otherwise met and in many ways it is *that* that prepared me most for work. So the combination of the discipline I studied and the socializing effect of university was very powerful on me. I was a nervous, shy person from a northern grammar school for whom Corpus Christi College was the making.[14]

Ian Wylie (1958) found Greats useful in the 'then nascent' computer industry: 'using computers in business or government is less technical than logical, calling for the ability to think logically ... Not surprisingly, there were many Greats men in the industry then.' **Ian McNeill** (1959) found that 'economic history engaged my interest to such an extent that I continued studying it by going into banking':

The Economic History syllabus covered a wide range of economic theories. Reading about the consequences of these theories, it seemed that they were often held with the same sort of passion and tenaciousness as religious dogmas. Sometimes the results were equally disastrous. It appeared also that banking was the bridge between economic theory – as put into practice by governments, bankers and central bankers – and industry, commerce and citizens who had to exist within the current economic environment. So I became a banker and enjoyed nearly all of it, including three recessions, but retiring before the lunatic gambling, mispricing and mis-selling that brought about the 2007/8 credit crunch. What I had learned about trying to get all available information before making a decision, and about the importance of primary sources, was invaluable.

'Rather surprisingly', **Richard Fitzalan Howard** (1974) discovered 'an interest in history has been useful in the investment world in which I have been employed (by the same firm) for the last 38 years. Researching companies and markets, studying previous economic cycles, understanding investors' fear and greed and what has happened in the past, have all been important elements in making judgements about the future, which is what investment is about'. **Bill Gunn** (1965), who made his career in the wine trade, thought 'CCC, through Trevor

Aston, Michael Brock and others, taught me to express myself, in speech and on paper, to think independently and to challenge the easy consensus. I owe it a debt I can never repay.' **Anthony Gould** (1973), a former Ruskin student, returned to trade unionism:

> Looking back I am sure that my education at Corpus indirectly helped me in the rest of my life's work with the trade union movement such as the ability to meet deadlines in writing articles (think of the agony involved in getting essays in on time) for example. However, there was no directly obvious benefit – you do not need to be in possession of an Oxford degree to obtain employment in the trade union movement. I took my final exam one Thursday and started work the next morning.

'What did I learn at Oxford?' asked **Theodore Saunders** (1975). 'Probably the most important thing was to think for myself – I have been suffering the consequences of this ever since – it is not really wanted in many walks of life, sadly – but it is better to be able to do this than not to do it.' **Peter Buxton** (1978) could recall only one of his lectures – '"Parturition in Sheep". A more supremely irrelevant lecture to the practice of medicine would be difficult to imagine.' He continued,

> If I have apparently failed to remember many medical facts from my time at Oxford, did I learn anything of enduring value? Has my success as a consultant radiologist, as someone who led a team to develop telemedicine or put a CT scanner in the middle of a desert got anything to do with what was taught? Was the genesis of my current archeological work or academic study of international relations some, now-forgotten, caffeine-fuelled discussion with fellow Corpuscles? When were the tutorials that showed me, as a senior officer in the Royal Navy, how to command more than 1,500 individuals or run a multimillion pound budget? The answer, of course, is that there were no such lectures or tutorials.
>
> But that does not mean that my time at Corpus did not prepare me for such things. Education is not confined to these formal

periods, but encompasses the whole experience of College life. The value of education is not the number of lectures one attends or the facts one half remembers, but the exposure to a broad sweep of knowledge and experience that lays down strong foundations upon which any number of later careers can be built. The gift Corpus gave me was not a vast store of didactic knowledge but an ability to think; a realization that education is discovering new facts, not just memorizing old ones.

David Wilton (1981) concurred: 'I learnt a huge amount including, most importantly, how to think.' **Sean O'Grady** (1981) thought the tutorial and exam systems, requiring the quick assimilation and regurgitation of lots of material, were 'good for politicians, barristers and journalists; maybe less use for others'. Overall, 'I got more out of [Corpus] than I put into it. All-night essay crises, finals, tutorials – all helped one learn how to deal with stress and the golden rule that the best is the enemy of the good. For me, it was a great place to learn the skills I needed to follow a career in journalism, though I didn't know it at the time, and did no student journalism.' For **David Sooby** (2003), 'the analytic, presentation and attention to detail necessary to pass my degree, as well as the work ethic, have stood me in good stead and make up for the fact that I'm no longer involved in physics'.

Not everyone pursued a conventional career. When **Jeremy Hewett** (1953) graduated,

> 1956 was still a bleak time to be in England – food scarce, heating sparse – but I had seen the London production of *South Pacific* (Sean Connery made his stage debut in the male chorus of Seabees). They had 'sunlight on the sand ... moonlight on the sea ... mangoes and bananas you can pick right off the tree'. Instead of eating my legal dinners at the Temple, I signed on to crew a yacht to New Zealand, jumped ship in Tahiti, sailed all over the Pacific and ended up in Victoria, Canada.

Nicola Feather (1981) also eschewed a conventional career:

It is hard to say how much my time at Oxford has led to my current position, that of mother, housewife and career volunteer. On the one hand, I am responsible for the sort of household tasks that some think should be beneath my trained brain. On the other hand, I have always found plenty of (too many!) worthwhile, intellectually stimulating things to do in life without pursuing a specific profession.

One legacy which Corpus students of these generations did *not* usually face when they left was student debt. As **David Henig** (1990) recalled, 'I left in 1993 with no job to go to and no particular idea of what to do. But thankfully not either with particularly high debts as at least fees were still paid in those days.' By the new millennium this was changing, as loans increasingly replaced grants. How far this would influence the career choices of later generations remains to be seen.

But for many former students the most significant impact of Corpus was not the knowledge or skills they learned, or the career opportunities opened up: it was their broader personal development, the friends they made, the sense that they had grown up, widened their horizons and discovered new possibilities. **Oliver Clauson** (1948) spoke of 'the friendships, which have endured, and the intellectual stimulation after the barrenness of army life'. **Peter Waterfield** (1946) 'made lasting and wonderful friends, I discovered my own talents such as they were and I went down a more confident person, full of hope for the future. Now at nearly 90, I have outlived nearly all those dear friends.' **Geoff Goodall** (1950) described his time at Corpus as

among the happiest and most fulfilling of my life, and not just because I was fit, young and able to share my final year there with the woman of my dreams. If I had died the day after graduation, those years would have been richly worth it. To enjoy a profound acquaintance with the greatest French and German writers was an immense delight. To be guided through these languages and texts by some of the sharpest minds in Europe was a special privilege. They taught me to think clearly, to analyse sharply, to respond sensitively and to feel deeply. To rub shoulders with scores of able and interesting fellow students was such an invigorating experience, leading to countless rewarding friendships, ten of which have lasted almost to this very day. To live in Bishop Fox's magnificent ancient buildings, to read great literature in the beauty of the College garden and then to stroll down to the river through Christ Church Meadow, and perhaps go punting – was very heaven.

For **John Harrison** (1950) Corpus was 'life-changing':

I was grateful to have four years, time to grow in assurance and to feel I had gained what I could from Oxford. I had friends in Somerville and other colleges. It was for me a time of ever-widening horizons, a privileged opportunity to explore and develop new interests, a multifaceted, enriching, life-changing experience which I relished and which informed my subsequent life. Central were the discipline and appeal of academic work, which I so enjoyed that I began to wonder if it should be my future. I didn't quite manage to get a first but, in the end, after two years in the Navy learning Russian, I did become a schoolmaster.

Eric Sidebottom (1957) reflected how, in his time, 'the University's smallest college, that bastion of academic scholarship, especially in Classics, had become a truly all-round, sporting college': 'I suspect that each generation of undergraduates at every college believes that it is special and surely that is a good thing, but one can't help feeling ever so slightly smug in believing that the Corpus of the late 1950s and early 1960s was better than average.'[15] As **Ian Wylie** (1958) observed, 'What a privilege, as well as monumental pleasure, to have been there. One never really leaves the place.'

Friendships were often the most lasting legacy. After 60 years, according to **Philip Hamilton-Grierson** (1953), 'what has remained is the friendships one made'. **Gerry Hughes** (1952) 'made some excellent friends – most of whom I have stayed in touch with'. **Don Montague** (1954) recalled one:

At Corpus I was lucky enough to hit it off with John Lambert, and we met and laughed and walked and argued together for many years, until his final illness smote him down. He became a European International man, speaking eight or nine languages and having friends everywhere in Europe, of every political persuasion – and when we met again, after months or years of parting, we simply picked up where we had left off, putting up ideas, pulling each other's arguments apart, drinking and laughing together. A lovely man.

For **Chris Patey** (1958),

What I remember best about Corpus is its setting, with buildings on a human scale – a quiet refuge in which to pursue one's life free from threats or too much direction. Knowing just about everyone in College brought great advantages. It seems to me that to achieve anything worthwhile it is necessary to make relationships with others in order to take them with you on your journey. Corpus was a place in which you could not help making relationships, and close friendships too. In March 1961 Michael Brock wrote me a letter in which he said: 'I look on your generation as something of a Golden Age.'

Every December I organize a lunch in London for Corpus men of broadly my vintage. Attendance averages 35. Many of us are now in our mid-70s. But we are still part of that close-knit community in which we passed an intense formative period of our lives and learnt to share our experience of the rare privilege of being a Corpuscle.

Simon Bainbridge (1968) recalled Frank Lepper 'saying in an irresistible tone of foreboding as he looked round the table at the Greats dinner marking the end of Finals: "I suppose you realize these are the friends who are going to stay with you?" And they have, and I'm not complaining.'[16] **Robin Clarke** (1955) was more nuanced:

Looking back at my three years at Corpus, I made few friendships that endured for a lifetime; development of an ability to analyse data and draw conclusions from them, which has been the basis of my professional life, happened later, at Cambridge and elsewhere. My time at Corpus was not always happy, but this is almost certainly true of all undergraduates, everywhere; Oxford makes one aware of one's limitations, both intellectual and physical, and relationships with others, including tutors and love life, are sometimes stressful. But Corpus gave me many of the intangible benefits that make life richer: respect for other disciplines, tolerance, a love of fine gardens and buildings and music and literature. A visit to England is incomplete without at least a night spent within the College walls, and a walk round its gardens.

Not everyone made their most important friendships within Corpus. As a medical student, **Christopher Bridgett** (1961) 'made excellent friends at other colleges', and 'subsequently stayed in closer touch with them than with my friends at Corpus. Medics had a reputation for sticking together, regardless of college or subsequent career – perhaps the shared experience of coping with multiple hurdles over many years forged bonds that continue to make now regular reunions particularly important and enjoyable.' For **Stephen Linstead** (1959), 'while I did not make many close friends during my stay at Corpus, I made many acquaintances, and it is always a great pleasure to meet up with them during College reunions'. Others, such as **Rhod Thomas** (1961), found they drifted apart: 'I have lived in the USA since 1980 and have lost contact with many of my Corpus friends.' And **Tim Stockil** (1971) observed that, as a linguist returning after time abroad, 'you had to make a whole new set of friends. Did the year away make those friendships shallower, though? I still have many friends from my schooldays, but there are only a very few Corpuscles I now see.'[17]

Mueen Afzal (1960) took three main lessons from his Corpus experience. One was humility: 'it did not matter at all who your parents were or what social background you came from. In the end, it was your hard work and ability that counted.' The second was 'the ability to think and express oneself clearly. In my case, as a civil servant initially and later as a corporate board member, I found that my education at Oxford helped me enormously in defining points at issue in a case and in building up a logical argument.' But third was 'the forging of lifelong friendships. A small college, with a cloistered environment and a great diversity in its student body, enabled one to make friends for life.' 'Meeting a Corpus man in later life', he felt, 'was like meeting family – you never wasted any time on pleasantries and small talk.' He recalled an evening in 1992 in his Islamabad office:

> I was told by the secretary that a 'Mr Ingrams' wanted to speak to me. I said to myself that it could not possibly be the Ingrams I knew at Corpus. It was. When Leonard's unmistakable voice came over the phone I asked him what on earth he was doing in Islamabad. He said, 'I had come to see you today but discovered you were busy all day. I am now flying back to Karachi by the 7pm flight.' I asked him to immediately cancel his flight and come for dinner to my house. Over dinner that evening we discussed everything but business. In fact we reminisced about Corpus. We had actually not met since I went down in 1963. After that evening in Islamabad we continued to meet regularly in Washington, London, Lahore, Bahrain, Madrid and in his lovely manor house in Garsington.

Peter Stafford (1960) 'made many friends during my stay and still meet a number of them annually at various official and unofficial functions'. For **Paul Quarrie** (1962), 'the friends we made then remain friends, even if meetings are rare, just like friends made at school. Youth always has this capacity for friendship based partly on inexperience (I suppose) and on the fact that one is exploring the world in every sense.' But for **Jim Waterhouse** (1963), 'when I left Oxford, it was clear to me that an important part of my life had ended':

> I have not attended the garden parties, gaudies or other reunions that the College regularly holds, and even do not plan to visit the celebrations marking 500 years since its foundation. This is partly because I have learned that special experiences are best left as fond memories rather than becoming disappointments due to unsuccessfully trying to repeat them later. There might also be the possibility that the present students would now look upon me as an old

fogey – I do not suppose they change! Nevertheless, the College and University formed a vital part of my education and formative years in general, and I remember them as having provided an alma mater of inestimable worth.

For **Bill Gunn** (1965), 'being a Corpuscle is a source of great pride in my life, and it has provided in fullest measure that sense of loyalty and "belonging" that is such an insistent craving of human nature'. **Nick Witney** (1969) felt 'a sense of intimacy, and of privilege' and recalled 'a couple of almost ecstatic moments, triggered by some literary insight or a dramatic October cloud-shape behind the College roofs, when I hugged myself at my own good fortune'. **Andrew Purkis** (1967) thought 'a very rough scorecard' of his time at Corpus might read:

> Doing well academically: Good
> Great beauty of the environment: Good (made good use of it)
> Making lifelong friends: Good
> New ideas of the 1960s: Fair (imbibed some of them, didn't 'get' many others)
> Emotional and sexual ambitions: Poor.

Mark Atkinson (1971) felt 'the freedom [Corpus] provided me to develop my talents and interests without restriction is a gift that not many are given and has made the rest of my life fuller and more enjoyable than it could possibly have been otherwise'. For **Mel Johnson** (1972) there was ambiguity:

> More than 20 years on, my attitude to Corpus and Oxford is complex and full of contradictions. I report my minor successes to the College, read *Pelican* from cover to cover, and wear my Corpus tie when I want to impress; but, like several contemporaries, my career choice and continued left-wing allegiance reflect a loathing of elitism. Life would be boring if we didn't have to grapple with inconsistencies.[18]

Richard Fitzalan Howard (1974) 'left Oxford having had a rewarding time in terms of making many lifelong friends, having an affection for the City and the College, not least from an architectural point of view, and my interest in history has increased so I read more history now than I ever did then'. **Kenneth Pearson** (1974), a former Ruskin student, recalled 'wonderful days', including

> the Chevrons Club with its garden parties during Trinity Term in the Fellows' Quad overlooking the Meadow, the spirit shown on the sports fields, especially rugby and cricket, in which, as a College, we failed to excel, and the exploits of the Corpus tortoise, who I knew only by reputation, but that reputation labelled him the most fleet-footed tortoise in all Oxford and was always more than a match for the tortoises representing other colleges. I still cannot decide, after several decades, whether the Corpus tortoise was fact or fiction. Unlike the Pelican sundial in the main Quad, the tortoise always seemed somewhat ethereal and perhaps, a part of Corpus mythology as opposed to Corpus history!

For **Richard Abernethy** (1973), 'Corpus was my gateway to Oxford; and Oxford, as well as becoming my new home, was my gateway to the international Left.' The South African **Peter Colenbrander** (1973) 'came away with a deeper, more troubled understanding of the country I had left behind'.

Personal development, friendships – and, increasingly, marriages – continued to stand out in students' reflections. **Brian Swift** (1993) 'definitely matured a lot, having to organize myself academically and socially and so ready myself for life after college'. **Camilla Byk** (1992) recalled 'getting married in my second year at St Aldates, and having the reception in Corpus's relaxed garden and then speeches in the dining room'. **Debbie Welch** (1994) reflected that 'I do still keep up with many people, more actually in the year above. One of my year was our best man.' For **Rachael Wright** (1996),

> My time at Corpus was exciting, challenging and fun, and a place where I made some lifelong good friends. The collegiate nature of Oxford made it easy to have friends with a wide variety of

subjects, especially in a small college. This is something I've really appreciated as medic friends at other universities tended to only socialize with other medics!

Ewen McMillan (1999), a postgraduate mathematician, found his classicist contemporaries 'a fascinating bunch':

Something must have rubbed off since now, 14 years later as a financial mathematician working in one of the big European investment banks, I have developed an insatiable appetite for the works of our classical ancestors and what they have to say about the things that continue to shape our lives today. Corpus will always hold a very special place for myself and my wife (who I married and lived with when studying at Oxford). We made lasting friendships and great memories (from hiking in Wales and the Lake District to the bridge club and martinis with scotch eggs) that will stay with us always.

Carley Chapman (2002) agreed:

I met two of my closest friends while studying at Corpus and I remember fondly our times there together, whether that be in the Library, in the Beer Cellar, at the boathouse or in our flat in Liddell! Two of us are now married and one of us has had their first child and we visit each other regularly. Indeed, we were only last month looking at old JCR photos and wondering what our former colleagues are up to now!

David Upshal (1984) reflected on the afterlife of his Corpus friendships:

Off we all went, our separate ways. Into law, into medicine, into finance, into politics, into the media ... into the Ferris wheel of the real world. Inevitably, no matter how much you try to stay in touch, you're never so close again once you leave. You can't be, because you now have different pursuits, different incomes, different lifestyles, different circles of existence. Despite the best intentions, you end up seeing each other in odd groups at odd times … now and again: every few weeks, every few months, every few … We drift our separate ways. We all graduate into distance. We cherish fond memories, retained as anecdotes.[19]

Sometimes it took a trigger to revive such friendships. In his case, 'it took a death among us to reunite the Corpus Christi College I remember. To bring us all into the same space for the same reason again. As a result, it's only now that I fully understand the value of what I shared there, of just how close and special some of us were to each other and just how lasting that is. Whatever we left behind, we also took with us.' For **David Sooby** (2003) it was a first Gaudy which 'brought home' the importance of the people he had met:

The whole room turned into another night in College, with everyone approaching each other, catching up, and it was as if nothing had ever changed. We may have had some friends who were closer than others, but we were all Corpuscles together and were delighted to be talking to each other after ten years. I am exceptionally proud to have been a part of the College and I wouldn't change any part of it.

Was the Corpus experience different from that of other young people, in different colleges, universities or organizations? **Ben Whitby** (1986) was unsure:

My time at Corpus grew me up. Would I have embarked on a public service career from another college or university? Probably. I've kept in touch with some people from Corpus and Oxford, some of them as real friends (not just social media ones), but have just as many friends from elsewhere. I met my wife through someone from Corpus, though she was not from Oxbridge (and is very objective about it). I'll give Corpus credit for developing and keeping a questioning mind, openness to new ideas and a respect for difference. It also set a high bar for achievement.

All that said, from talking to non-Oxbridge and foreign friends, I'm not sure how it was different to anyone else's university experience. I enjoyed a lot of it at the time, still remember the good bits (living in a city where you could tell the time through church bells ringing) and have forgotten the bad.

Youthful memories are powerful. For Corpuscles, they evoked formative experiences – of personal and intellectual development, and the excitements, humiliations and absurdities of being young. Importantly, they were shared experiences, of people going through a defining period together, often leading to deep friendships. Indeed, the afterglow sometimes burned brighter with time. **Ian McNeill** (1959) was not alone: 'My affection for Corpus just grows and grows. A Gaudy is one of life's happiest occasions.'

New experiences sometimes prompted people to look at their time afresh. In 2011 **Matthew Spencer** (1988) returned to Oxford:

I went, 20 years on from CCC days, to back-to-back lectures on Sanskrit. Alongside me, on their very first day at the University, sat a pair of (clever) 18-year-olds. It struck me then, as first one and then a second world-expert stepped out before them, what I had never thought of before: these people are getting the very best introduction to their subject and they probably don't know it – it all just seems so normal at the time.

For **Catherine Hasler** (1997), it was the birth of a daughter:

There is nothing quite like the arrival of a new generation to make you reflect upon your past. And I found myself thinking at length about my experience of CCC. I had not thought about Corpus for years. I had taken my dreams there and come away confused. My feelings never blossomed into the unbridled nostalgia I had naively expected as a wide-eyed 18-year-old fresher. But I know now that that's OK. I can remember happily the strains of organ music as I worked in the College Library, waiting for the washing machines on a Sunday afternoon, leaving notes in friends' pigeonholes, the tiny garden of Kybald Twitchen where I roomed in the third year, the click of the latch and the weight of the JCR door under your palm, the brie baguette I'd buy from Morton's on Broad Street on the way back from lectures and eat in the warm sun on the Fellows' Building lawn. But more importantly than just memories, as it turned out, I did find myself at Oxford. It did give me a journey of discovery, just as it promises you it will.

The physical settings were particularly evocative. After a decade there, **Gail Trimble** (2000) found Corpus 'overwritten with memory and tradition, both shared and personal'. She recalled the Library, Quad, garden, and the leaves of the copper beech 'which are not copper but a glossy, deep wine colour very faintly overlaid with green and gold'; 'a bench which was, and may be again, the best place in College for a private conversation of emotional significance, since it offered shelter and concealment, but also that same view over the meadow, which gave you a direction in which to look during difficult silences'. She remembered textures and smells – of jasmine near the Fraenkel Room passage, and

the smell of cold concrete and the damp at the edges of windows that fills the landings where pairs of first-year girls talk sadly till four in the morning ... I am not sure how memories of a place like Corpus will work once I leave and am no longer in and out of it all the time, circulating, constantly retracing routes and remembering how I have previously remembered retracing them, over and over again in different combinations and concentrations for ten years.[20]

For **Alexandra Harmer** (2008), Corpus evoked not a single highlight but a rich smorgasbord of experience:

I have so many happy memories of Corpus. Things that immediately spring to mind are (in no particular order): JCR teas; sitting on the steps of the Sundial; revising for Greats in the English Reading Room with piles of classical texts and yellow 'Please Leave' slips everywhere; fun Friday nights – getting all dressed up, going to formal, then down to the Beer Cellar, then out to a club to dance, then back to the JCR to eat chips; the Quad looking beautiful in the sunshine; sitting and chatting on the auditorium roof; living in 4.4 on the Quad in fourth year; nerves before reading out essays in tutes; late-night tea parties in New Building in first year; lots and lots of classicists; everyone taking JCR politics much too seriously; the excitement of the room ballot; brain-aching Thucydides reading groups with John Ma; building snowmen in the Quad; 'borrowing' the MCR Christmas tree; dread of collections at the start of term; cycling down Merton Street; flats in Liddell in second and third years; hours of ping-pong; trying to compose Greek verse; walks round Christ Church Meadow; inspirational Greek literature tutes with Tim Whitmarsh; checking your pidge; going for cocktails round the corner at House; the Library usually being the most sociable place in College; punting; trashing friends after Finals in the garden; late-night games of Articulate in the JCR; the vital importance of Bod. cards and U-keys; fascinating Ovid tutes with Stephen Harrison; the stunning roses; watching Corpus victory on *University Challenge* in first year; chips with every meal in Hall; Latin prose composition with (the famous) Gail Trimble; the biblical-looking gardener; distinguished Classics dons singing *Grease* songs after Greats dinner; making links between Ovid and Brueghel and Auden in the Library; starting Mods on my birthday; playing pool in the Beer Cellar; friends always being around College ... and so many more!

Caroline Knapp (2005) spoke for many: 'Suffice it to say that my time at Corpus played a huge part in shaping the person I am today, and I feel truly fortunate that I was able to spend eight years there.' As **David Mark Jackson** (1959) observed, 'We didn't call it a "Great Little College" for nothing.'

POSTSCRIPT

The generous contributors to this volume, and the skilful editorial weaving of their recollections by Stephen Hickey, can leave no reader in doubt of the hold Corpus has exercised on the affections, memories and loyalties of those who have passed through the College gate since the 1940s. Each Corpuscle's story is unique, yet out of these reminiscences – mostly fond, occasionally critical, commonly self-aware, and frequently hilarious – a remarkably consistent picture emerges, one which casts Corpus as a special place honouring the values of benign care, toleration and liberal scholarship.

My own story is one of special privilege: I experienced College life and the blessings of its friendships not only as an undergraduate and postgraduate student but also – 40 years on – as President. I entered Corpus in 1965, after interviews the previous year with the Modern History Fellows – Trevor Aston and Michael Brock – and the President, Frank Hardie. As others have noted, Hardie was a notoriously shy man, so it was not an interview in any conventional understanding of the term: we sat in silence for long stretches while he appeared to consult his notes, and occasionally asked a question – mostly of the kind inviting only a yes or no answer. My contribution to those silences was evidently convincing, and I was offered a place.

In appearance the College has changed a little, but only a little, since my first encounter. The worn-away step at the main gate and, in the archway, the flapping forest of windblown notices and posters, have given way to a paved ramp and an aesthetic of bare stone. The sand-and-shingle Quad, draughty staircases and rudimentary student accommodation have yielded to flagstones, rich botanic idiosyncrasy, secured entrances, central heating and en-suite facilities. 'Lecture Room 3' has been colonized by the Library's stacks; in generous compensation, the MBI Al Jaber Building, winner of an RIBA award, provides a stunning space for lectures and the performing arts. (What we would have given for that when I was President of the Owlets!)

Far more consequential have been the the broader cultural shifts. In the 1960s, the legacy of Victorian and Edwardian Oxford – intensely male – was still much in evidence. Each evening the Formal Hall of gowns and Latin grace served food from College kitchens where the chief qualification was – as one Old Corpuscle put it – to have had one's taste buds shot away during the war. We experienced the last gasp of what we then called 'College servants'. In the reminiscences of my contemporaries, scouts are ever-present, and none more so than my own, Godfrey Price. Described as 'the genius of the JCR afternoon tea', Godfrey 'managed always to leave you with the impression both that he had forgotten who you were and that he knew something you'd rather he didn't'.[1] Early in my freshman year I caught him sweeping a large pile of dirt under my lino. 'Just poppin' it under there for now, Sir. I'll be back later with my pan.' The debris was still there three terms later (and may still be, for all I know).

As this book makes clear, the watershed into the recognizably modern era came around the early 1980s, with the arrival of women undergraduates and other changes in the College's composition and ways of working. A gradual doubling of the number of students and Fellows, increasingly international in character; ever fiercer competition for places and growing numbers of postgraduates; greater seriousness in the conduct of termly collections; better food and accommodation, prompted by a keen eye on the financial benefits of vacation conferences; better understanding of the value of student counselling and support for mental health: all these changes, and more, have made the Corpus of today very different. Technological changes – computing, mobile phones, social media – have altered the ways in which students communicate with tutors and one another. The place of colleges in the wider University has also changed – evidenced by the growing use of the term 'collegiate University' – both academically and in recognition of the need for consistent standards of student support. Oxford

University Student Union, non-existent in the 1960s, now speaks for JCRs and MCRs across the University (currently two of its six elected sabbatical officers are Corpuscles). This does not diminish each college's distinctive character, or the loyalty it inspires: but it does foster collaboration between colleges and the spread of (both good and less good) ideas.

But that said, Corpus at its Quincentenary is still recognizably the college I joined: a strong and supportive community, self-confident but not showy, committed to nurturing the highest standards of scholarship and teaching, where students are encouraged to develop their talents well beyond the narrow academic curriculum and examinations. We remain amongst the most widely admired of the colleges for our academic quality and ethos, and we continue to produce some outstanding individual sports-folk, even if our teams are not oppressively weighed down with laurels.

The challenges to Corpus and the wider University over the next half-century will surely grow, not diminish. Budgets, fees, redefinitions of educational utility, global complexities: these, inter alia, will be a test of our resolve and resourcefulness. But Corpus will not be found wanting, if it can draw on a spirit similar to that which, on the evidence of this book, has been the genius of the Great Little College for decades past.

Richard Carwardine (1965; President, 2010–16)
October 2016

ENDNOTES

Introduction
1. B. Harrison (ed.), *Corpuscles: A History of Corpus Christi College, Oxford, in the Twentieth Century, Written by Its Members* (Oxford, 1994).

1. 'A Pin in a List': Coming to Corpus
1. *CCC Report* (1951), p. 6.
2. *Pelican* (1988–9), p. 7.
3. L. W. B. Brockliss, *The University of Oxford: A History* (Oxford, 2016), pp. 574–7, 613.
4. *CCC Annual Report* (1986), p. 7.
5. *Pelican* (1987–8), p. 27.
6. *Smallprint* (1985).
7. *Pelican Record* (Dec. 1999), p. 110.
8. *Sundial* (May 2016), pp. 2–5.
9. Ibid., p. 2.
10. *Pelican Record* (1994), p. 56.
11. *Pelican Record* (Dec. 2008), p. 78.
12. Harrison, *Corpuscles*, p. 254.
13. *Smallprint* (Oct. 1988).
14. *Pelican* (1978–9), pp. 28–30; Harrison, *Corpuscles*, p. 403.
15. *Pelican Record* (Dec. 1996), p. 60.
16. *CCC Annual Report* (1985–6), p. 5.
17. *Pelican Record* (Dec. 1993), p. 74.
18. Ibid. (Dec. 2006), pp. 73–4.

2. 'A Sure Cure for Stereotyping': The Corpus Community
1. Harrison, *Corpuscles*, pp. 254–5.
2. Ibid., p. 339.
3. *Pelican Record* (1997), p. 55.
4. A. Alvarez, *Where Did It All Go Right?* (London, 1999), p. 124.

5. Harrison, *Corpuscles*, p. 242.
6. Ibid., p. 308.
7. Ibid., p. 345.
8. Ibid., p. 369.
9. Ibid., pp. 345–6.
10. Ibid., p. 405.
11. Ibid., p. 480.
12. Ibid., p. 482.
13. I am grateful to Julian Reid for this information.
14. T. Charles-Edwards and J. Reid, *Corpus Christi College, Oxford: A History* (Oxford, 2017), table 10.2.
15. E. Jones, *The Freetown Bond: A Life Under Two Flags* (Suffolk, 2012), p. 49.
16. *Smallprint* (1987).
17. Harrison, *Corpuscles*, pp. 446–7.
18. Ibid., p. 458.
19. *Pelican Record* (1997), p. 49.
20. Ibid. (1998), pp. 50–1.
21. Ibid., pp. 56–7.
22. *CCC Annual Report* (1987–8), p. 17.
23. Harrison, *Corpuscles*, p. 447.
24. Ibid., p. 484.
25. *Pelican Record* (1997), pp. 60–2.
26. Ibid., p. 54.
27. Harrison, *Corpuscles*, p. 455.

3. 'Contrarian Irreverence': The Corpus Environment

1. Harrison, *Corpuscles*, p. 429.
2. Alvarez, *Where Did It All Go Right?*, pp. 125–6.
3. *Pelican Record* (1967); (1998), pp. 108–9.
4. *CCC Record* (1971–2), p. 6.
5. *Pelican* (1985–6), p. 47.
6. Alvarez, *Where Did It All Go Right?*, p. 125.
7. Harrison, *Corpuscles*, p. 246.
8. Ibid., p. 456.
9. *Pelican Record* (1997), p. 132.
10. *CCC Annual Report* (1985–6), p. 5.
11. *Pelican Record* (2013), p. 3.
12. Charles-Edwards and Reid, *Corpus Christi College, Oxford*, table 10.4.
13. *Pelican Record* (2015), p. 91.
14. Alvarez, *Where Did It All Go Right?*, p. 124.
15. Harrison, *Corpuscles*, pp. 360, 343.
16. Ibid., p. 276.

17. See B. Harrison, 'College Servants in an Oxford College', *Oral History* (Autumn 2012); T. Judt, *The Memory Chalet* (London, 2010), pp. 101–9.

18. Harrison, *Corpuscles*, p. 339.

19. Ibid., p. 373.

20. Ibid., pp. 420–1.

21. Ibid., p. 424.

22. K. Dover, *Marginal Comment* (London, 1994), p. 192.

23. *Smallprint* (1985).

24. *Pelican* (1985–6), p. 48.

25. *Pelican Record* (Dec. 1994), p. 33.

26. *Oxford Today* (Michaelmas 2014), p. 60.

27. Harrison, *Corpuscles*, p. 408.

28. *Smallprint* (Trinity 1986).

29. *CCC Report* (1953), p. 6.

30. Ibid. (1951), p. 1.

31. Harrison, *Corpuscles*, p. 254.

32. *Pelican Record* (Mar. 1968), p. 21.

33. Harrison, *Corpuscles*, p. 344. See also *Pelican Record* (Dec. 1995), pp. 9–10 where the rules are printed with the comment: 'these make quaint reading, and the practice of sconcing has long since ceased'.

34. Harrison, *Corpuscles*, p. 469.

35. Ibid., p. 480.

36. *Sundial* (Sept. 2013), p. 5.

37. Harrison, *Corpuscles*, p. 251.

38. Ibid., p. 424.

39. Ibid., p. 390.

40. Jones, *Freetown Bond*, p. 50.

41. *CCC Annual Report* (1980–1), p. 2.

42. *Pelican* (1986–7), p. 3; B. Harrison, 'How Computers Came to Corpus', *Pelican Record* (Dec. 1992), pp. 19–34.

43. Harrison, 'How Computers Came to Corpus', pp. 26, 31.

44. *Pelican Record* (1996), p. 143.

45. Ibid. (1997), p. 131.

46. *Freshers' Guide* (1998).

4. 'A Men's College with Women in It'? Going Mixed

1. Alvarez, *Where Did It All Go Right?*, p. 147.

2. Harrison, *Corpuscles*, p. 219.

3. Ibid., p. 251.

4. Ibid., p. 266.

5. Ibid., p. 295.

6. Ibid., p. 274.

7. Ibid., p. 299.
8. Ibid., p. 267.
9. Ibid., p. 318.
10. Ibid., p. 347.
11. Ibid., p. 403.
12. *Pelican Record* (May 1969), pp. 121, 128.
13. *Pelican Record* (2011), p. 62.
14. *CCC Record* (1966), p. 8.
15. *Pelican Record* (May 1968), p. 51.
16. Harrison, *Corpuscles*, p. 337.
17. *Pelican Record* (Mar. 1968), p. 21.
18. Harrison, *Corpuscles*, p. 372.
19. Ibid., p. 393.
20. *Pelican Record* (Dec. 2000), pp. 67–8.
21. Dover, *Marginal Comment*, pp. 186–7.
22. *CCC Record* (1976–7), p. 2.
23. Harrison, *Corpuscles*, p. 391.
24. Ibid., p. 400.
25. Ibid., p. 377.
26. *CCC Annual Report* (1977–8), p. 8.
27. Harrison, *Corpuscles*, p. 409.
28. Ibid., p. 412.
29. Ibid., p. 418.
30. *Pelican* (1980–1), p. 5.
31. Harrison, *Corpuscles*, p. 409.
32. Dover, *Marginal Comment*, p. 187.
33. Harrison, *Corpuscles*, p. 465.
34. *CCC Annual Report* (1985–6), p. 5.
35. *Smallprint* (1987); *Pelican* (1986–7), p. 4.
36. *Smallprint* (Hilary 1990).
37. *Pelican Record* (1993), p. 75.
38. Ibid. (Dec. 1995), pp. 75–6.
39. Ibid. (1993), p. 74.
40. Ibid. (1999), p. 110, and (2001), p. 161.
41. Ibid. (2009), p. 89.
42. Ibid. (2000), pp. 69–70.

5. 'Always Something Unread': Undergraduate Study

1. Alvarez, *Where Did It All Go Right?*, pp. 124–6.
2. Charles-Edwards and Reid, *Corpus Christi College, Oxford*, table 10.3.
3. *Pelican Record* (2012), p. 13.
4. Harrison, *Corpuscles*, p. 240.

5. *Pelican Record* (May 1969), p. 120.
6. Harrison, *Corpuscles*, pp. 326–7.
7. *Smallprint* (1987).
8. Harrison, *Corpuscles*, p. 465.
9. *Smallprint* (Trinity 1986).
10. *Pelican Record* (2006), pp. 72–3.
11. J. Howard-Johnston, 'In Praise of the Tutorial', *Oxford Magazine* (Hilary 2006), p. 5.
12. Dover, *Marginal Comment*, pp. 196–8.
13. *The Guardian*, 1 August 2015.
14. Harrison, *Corpuscles*, p. 338.
15. Ibid., p. 314.
16. Ibid., p. 333.
17. Brockliss, *University of Oxford*, p. 677.
18. Ibid., p. 638.
19. Harrison, *Corpuscles*, p. 264.
20. Ibid., p. 475.
21. Charles-Edwards and Reid, *Corpus Christi College, Oxford*, ch. 10.
22. Alvarez, *Where Did It All Go Right?*, pp. 128–30.
23. *CCC Record* (1966), p. 9; *Pelican Record* (Dec. 1968), p. 79.
24. *Smallprint* (1987).
25. *CCC Annual Report* (1986–7), p. 31.
26. *Pelican Record* (2012), p. 15.
27. Alvarez, *Where Did It All Go Right?*, p. 149.
28. *Smallprint* (Trinity 1985).
29. Harrison, *Corpuscles*, p. 464.
30. Ibid., pp. 476–8.
31. Dover, *Marginal Comment*, p. 198.
32. Alvarez, *Where Did It All Go Right?*, pp. 148–9.
33. Harrison, *Corpuscles*, p. 260.
34. W. Waldegrave, *A Different Kind of Weather* (London, 2015), p. 72.
35. Harrison, *Corpuscles*, p. 316.
36. *Smallprint* (Trinity 1985).
37. *Pelican Record* (2006), p. 75.
38. Ibid. (2008), pp. 7–9.
39. Ibid., p. 1.
40. Ibid. (2009), p. 2.
41. Ibid. (2015), p. 4. In 2016, with 23 firsts, 40 upper seconds, and 5 lower seconds, Corpus ranked 16th.

6. 'Camaraderie': Social Life

1. *Pelican Record* (1992), p. 57.

2. Harrison, *Corpuscles*, p. 264.
3. *Sundial* (Oct. 2015), p. 11.
4. *Pelican Record*, Dec. 2008 p. 80.
5. *CCC Annual Report* (1977–8), p. 12.
6. *Pelican* (1980–1), p. 7.
7. *Sundial* (2013), p. 2.
8. Harrison, *Corpuscles*, p. 350.
9. *Smallprint* (1987).
10. Harrison, *Corpuscles*, pp. 219–20.
11. Ibid., pp. 357, 473.
12. *Pelican Record* (Dec. 1967).
13. Ibid. (2005), p. 108.
14. Ibid. (2009), pp. 2–3.
15. *Pelican Record* (Dec. 1967).
16. *Pelican Record* (2002), p. 137.
17. Ibid. (2006), p. 63.
18. Harrison, *Corpuscles*, p. 400; P. A. Hunt and N. A. Flanagan, *Corpus Christi College Biographical Register 1880–1974* (Oxford, 1988), p. 57.
19. *Pelican Record* (1993), pp. 46–8.
20. *Pelican Record* (1997), p. 120.
21. Harrison, *Corpuscles*, p. 444.
22. *Pelican Record* (2006), p. 58.
23. Ibid. (2012), p. 83; *Sundial* (May 2016), p. 11.
24. Harrison, *Corpuscles*, pp. 159, 181.
25. Ibid., p. 290.
26. Ibid., p. 314.
27. Ibid., pp. 324–5.
28. *Pelican Record* (May 1969), p. 128.
29. *Pelican* (1982–3), p. 14.
30. *Smallprint* (1987).
31. Ibid.
32. *Pelican Record* (1949), p. 65.
33. *CCC Record* (1967), p. 11.
34. Harrison, *Corpuscles*, p. 371.
35. *Pelican Record* (2009), p. 27.
36. *Smallprint* (1985).

7. 'Vive le collège libre': *Politics and Religion*

1. Harrison, *Corpuscles*, p. 203.
2. Ibid., p. 247.
3. Ibid., pp. 270–3.
4. Ibid., p. 298.

5. Ibid., p. 325.
6. Ibid., p. 332.
7. *CCC Annual Report* (1967), p. 12.
8. Harrison, *Corpuscles*, p. 344.
9. Ibid., p. 399.
10. *Pelican Record* (2009), p. 20.
11. Harrison, *Corpuscles*, pp. 393, 396.
12. Dover, *Marginal Comment*, pp. 190–1.
13. Harrison, *Corpuscles*, p. 421.
14. Ibid., pp. 426–7.
15. *Pelican* (1985–6), p. 18.
16. *CCC Annual Report* (1987–8), p. 17.
17. Harrison, *Corpuscles*, p. 466.
18. Ibid., pp. 219, 243.
19. Ibid., pp. 319–20.
20. Ibid., pp. 333–4.
21. Ibid., p. 340.
22. Ibid., pp. 379–80.
23. *CCC Annual Report* (1985–6), p. 18; 'A Tour of CCC at Oxford', YouTube 1 Oct. 2010.
24. Harrison, *Corpuscles*, p. 304.
25. *Pelican Record* (1997), pp. 47–51.
26. Harrison, *Corpuscles*, p. 484.
27. *Pelican Record* (1997), p. 61.
28. Harrison, *Corpuscles*, p. 305.

8. 'Over the Spikes': Junior and Senior Members

1. Harrison, *Corpuscles*, p. 128.
2. Ibid., p. 230.
3. Ibid., pp. 302–3.
4. *Pelican Record* (Mar. 1968), p. 21.
5. Harrison, *Corpuscles*, p. 298.
6. Ibid., pp. 310–11.
7. *Pelican Record* (1998), p. 109; *Oxford Mail* (22, 23 Feb. 1967); *Cherwell* (1 Mar. 1967).
8. Harrison, *Corpuscles*, p. 265.
9. Ibid., p. 290.
10. Ibid., pp. 369–70.
11. Dover, *Marginal Comment*, pp. 190–1.
12. Harrison, *Corpuscles*, p. 407.
13. *Pelican Record* (1991), p. 60.
14. Harrison, *Corpuscles*, p. 478.

15. *Pelican Record* (2004), p. 124.
16. Harrison, *Corpuscles*, p. 434.
17. Ibid., pp. 333, 352, 401.
18. *Smallprint* (Trinity 1986).
19. *Pelican Record* (1994), p. 85.
20. Ibid. (2007), pp. 9–10.
21. Harrison, *Corpuscles*, pp. 159, 252.
22. Ibid., p. 333.
23. Jones, *Freetown Bond*, p. 57.
24. Harrison, *Corpuscles*, p. 260.
25. Ibid., pp. 409, 445.
26. Brockliss, *University of Oxford*, p. 631
27. Harrison, *Corpuscles*, pp. 347–8.
28. Ibid., pp. 393–4.
29. Dover, *Marginal Comment*, p. 228.
30. See Charles-Edwards and Reid, *Corpus Christi College, Oxford*, ch. 10, for a full account.
31. *Smallprint* (Trinity 1986).
32. *Pelican Record* (1996), p. 144.
33. *Sundial* (Apr. 2015), p. 5.
34. Brockliss, *University of Oxford*, pp. 605, 633.
35. Dover, *Marginal Comment*, p. 191.
36. *Pelican Record* (Mar. 1968), pp. 28–9.
37. Ibid., pp. 30–1.
38. Ibid. (Dec. 1968), p. 77.
39. Dover, *Marginal Comment*, p. 192.
40. Ibid.
41. *Pelican Record* (2010), p. 54.
42. *CCC Annual Report* (1982–3), p. 7.
43. Dover, *Marginal Comment*, p. 193.
44. *Smallprint* (1985).
45. *CCC Annual Report* (1987–8), p. 18.
46. Harrison, *Corpuscles*, pp. 468–9.
47. *Pelican Record* (1991), p. 61.
48. Ibid., p. 12.
49. Harrison, *Corpuscles*, p. 479.
50. *Pelican Record* (1991), p. 13.
51. Harrison, *Corpuscles*, p. 479.
52. *Pelican Record* (1992), p. 98.
53. Ibid. (1995), p. 77.
54. Ibid. (2001), p. 161.

55. Ibid. (2002), p. 139.
56. Ibid. (2006), p. 69.
57. Ibid., p. 76.
58. *Sundial* (Sept. 2014), p. 5.

9. 'A Class Apart'? Postgraduates

1. *CCC Annual Report* (1953), pp. 5–6.
2. Charles-Edwards and Reid, *Corpus Christi College, Oxford,* table 10.2.
3. Harrison, *Corpuscles*, p. 173.
4. K. Amis, *Memoirs* (New York, 1991), p. 103.
5. Alvarez, *Where Did It All Go Right?*, p. 152. See also J. Carey, *The Unexpected Professor* (London, 2015), pp. 142–6.
6. Harrison, *Corpuscles*, pp. 275–6.
7. *CCC Annual Report* (1967), p. 4.
8. *Pelican Record* (Oct. 1969), p. 158.
9. J. Lanchester, *Family Romance: A Memoir* (London, 2007), p. 337.
10. Brockliss, *University of Oxford*, p. 617.
11. Harrison, *Corpuscles*, p. 389.
12. *CCC Annual Report* (1977–8), pp. 7–8.
13. Ibid. (1984–5), p. 7.
14. Ibid.
15. *Corpuscles*, pp. 451–2.
16. *CCC Annual Report* (1986–7), p. 14.
17. Harrison, *Corpuscles*, p. 452.
18. *CCC Annual Report* (1986–7), p. 14.
19. Ibid. (1988–9), p. 6.
20. Ibid. (1987–8), p. 15.
21. Brockliss, *University of Oxford*, p. 681.
22. *Pelican Record* (1993), p. 71.
23. Ibid. (2014), p. 123.
24. Howard-Johnston, 'In Praise of the Tutorial', p. 5.
25. *Pelican Record* (2009), p. 2.

10. 'All Corpuscles Together': Leaving and Looking Back

1. Howard-Johnston, 'In Praise of the Tutorial', p. 5.
2. *Smallprint* (Sept. 1987).
3. Open University, *Practitioners' Voices in Classical Reception Studies: Lorna Hardwick interview with Helen Eastman* (Milton Keynes, 18 May 2009).
4. T. Weston, *From Appointments to Careers* (Oxford, 1994), p. 167.
5. *Pelican* (1988–9), pp. 20–1.
6. *Smallprint* (Sept. 1987).
7. *The Guardian* (1 Aug. 2015).

8. Harrison, *Corpuscles*, p. 459.
9. *Smallprint* (Sept. 1987).
10. Alvarez, *Where Did It All Go Right?*, p. 123.
11. Harrison, *Corpuscles*, p. 258.
12. Ibid., p. 411.
13. *Pelican Record* (2008), p. 80.
14. Ibid. (2009), p. 19.
15. Ibid. (2008), pp. 80–1.
16. Harrison, *Corpuscles*, p. 339.
17. Ibid., p. 355.
18. Ibid., p. 369.
19. Ibid., p. 448.
20. *Pelican Record* (2009), pp. 29–33.

Postscript
1. Harrison, *Corpuscles*, pp. 420–1.

BIBLIOGRAPHY

Books and Articles

Alvarez, Al, *Where Did It All Go Right?* (London, 1992).

Amis, Kingsley, *Memoirs* (New York, 1991).

Brockliss, L. W. B., *The University of Oxford: A History* (Oxford, 2016).

Brown, Michael Barratt, *Seekers: A Twentieth Century Life* (Nottingham, 2013).

Carey, John, *The Unexpected Professor: An Oxford Life in Books* (London, 2014).

Charles-Edwards, Thomas, and Reid, Julian, *Corpus Christi College, Oxford: A History* (Oxford, 2017).

Dover, Kenneth, *Marginal Comment* (London, 1994).

Dyer, Geoff, 'Room to Breathe', *The Guardian* (1 April 2015).

Garth, John, 'Oxonian Lives Portrait: David Leake', *Oxford Today*, vol. 27, no. 1 (Michaelmas Term 2014).

Harrison, Brian, 'College Servants in Corpus Forty Years Ago' , *Pelican Record*, vol. 45 (Dec. 2010).

—— 'College Servants in an Oxford College' , *Oral History* (Autumn 2012).

—— 'How Computers Came to Corpus', *Pelican Record*, vol. 38 (Dec. 1992).

—— (ed.) *Corpuscles: A History of Corpus Christi College, Oxford, in the Twentieth Century, Written by Its Members* (Oxford, 1994).

—— (ed.) *The History of the University of Oxford*, vol. viii, *The Twentieth Century* (Oxford, 1994).

Howard-Johnston, James, 'In Praise of the Tutorial', *Oxford Magazine* (Oxford, 2006).

Hunt, P. A., and Flanagan, N. A., *Corpus Christi College, Oxford: Biographical Register 1880–1974* (Oxford, 1988).

Jones, Edward Durosimi, *The Freetown Bond: A Life under Two Flags* (Suffolk, 2012).

Judt, Tony, *'Bedder', The Memory Chalet* (London, 2010).

Lanchester, John, *Family Romance: A Memoir* (London, 2007).

Nockels, A., *Corpus Christi College, Oxford: Supplement to the Biographical Register 1974–1991* (Oxford, 1995).

Open University, *Practitioners' Voices in Classical Reception Studies, ISSN 1756–5049. Interview with Lorna Hardwick* (Milton Keynes, 18 May 2009).

Platt, Christopher, *The Most Obliging Man in Europe: Life and Times of the Oxford Scout* (London, 1986).

Waldegrave, William, *A Different Kind of Weather: A Memoir* (London, 2015).

Weston, Timothy, *From Appointments to Careers: A History of the Oxford University Careers Service 1892–1992* (Oxford, 1994).

Yurdan, Marilyn, *The Oxford Book of Days* (Stroud, 2013).

College Journals
CCC Record
CCC Report
Pelican
Pelican Record
Smallprint
Sundial

APPENDIX: ORIGINAL CONTRIBUTORS

The following individuals generously contributed new and original recollections of their time at Corpus. The full texts are deposited in the College archive. The dates shown are those for matriculation or arrival at Corpus. The *Index of Names* lists all those quoted or mentioned in the book, including those drawn from previously published sources.

Abernethy, Richard	1973	Cane, Peter (*Fellow*)	1978
Afzal, Mueen	1960	Chapman, Carley	2002
Ahmed, Farzana (née Choudhury)	1979	Christophersen, Rolf	1939
Alter, Peter	1969	Clarke, Robin	1955
Aliverti, Ana	2007	Clauson, Oliver	1948
Atkinson, David (*Chaplain*)	1977	Coady, Tony	1963
Atkinson, Jonathan	1984	Cockell, Charles S.	1991
Atkinson, Mark	1971	Colenbrander, Peter	1974
Baker, Michael	1967	Collier (née Tarnoy), Rachel	1987
Barker, Sebastian	1964	Costain, Derek	1948
Barratt Brown, Michael	1937	Curtis, Penelope	1979
Bartol, Krystyna	1988	Dancy, Jonathan	1965
Batho, Rob	1964	Dawson, Peter	1955
Bernard, Sir Dallas	1948	Deahl, Martin	1975
Blackmore, David	1956	Dixon, James	1966
Booth, David	1955	Dolby, Pat	1958
Bridgett, Christopher	1961	Dovey, Matthew	1990
Brock, Michael	1938	Elbourne, Paul	1989
Brown, John W.	1955	Ellory, Clive (*Fellow*)	1985
Buxton, Peter	1978	Fawn, John	1966
Byk, Camilla (née Forestier-Walker)	1992	Feather (née Jarman), Nicola	1981
		Gardner, Charles	1951
Campbell, Martin	1992	Garner, Jonathan	1983
Campbell, Mary (*College Nurse*)	1975	Gold, Dina	1975

Stevenson, Leslie	1962	Waterhouse, Jim	1963
Stogdale, David	1969	Watson, Christopher	1957
Swift, Brian	1993	Weitzenfeld, Julian	1967
Sykes, Louise	1984	Whitby, Ben	1986
Talbot, Marianne	1985	Whitelaw, James H.	1941
Taylor, Christopher (*Fellow*)	1963	Willi, Andreas	1998
Thomas, Rhodri	1961	Williams, Martin	1959
Thornhill, Andrew	1962	Wilson, Hal	1947
Tucker, James Shelby	1955	Wilton, David	1981
Underwood, Malcolm	1966	Witney, Nick	1969
Vaight, Paul	1963	Wright, Rachael	1996
Wagstaffe, Joanna	1980	Wylie, Ian	1958
Walker, Antony	1947	Yeatman, David (*Head Porter*)	2003
Waterfield, Peter	1946		

INDEX OF NAMES

Corpus staff positions are indicated in *italics*